V aa

D0962580

Is It True What They Say About DIXY?

A Biography of DIXY LEE RAY

By LOUIS R. GUZZO

The Writing Works, Inc.

Mercer Island, Washington

Library of Congress Cataloging in Publication Data

Guzzo, Louis R   1919-
  Is it true what they say about Dixy?

  Includes index.
  1. Ray, Dixy Lee.   2. Scientists—United States—
Biography.   3. Statesmen—United States—Biography.
I. Title.
Q143.R345G89   353.0085'6'0924 [B]   80-13319
ISBN 0-916076-26-1

Copyright © 1980 by Louis R. Guzzo
All Rights Reserved
Manufactured in the United States
Published by The Writing Works, Inc.
              7438 S.E. 40th Street
              Mercer Island, Washington 98040
IBSN: 0-916076-26-1
Library of Congress Number: 80-13319

Contents

To Madeleine

ACKNOWLEDGMENTS

Acknowledgments are owed scores of persons for assistance beyond the call of friendship, but space permits listing only those for whom a special thanks must be recorded: Marion Reid, Alvista Steele, David Jenkins, Claire Jones, Jane Orr, Charles Boyle, Dr. Arthur Martin, Dr. Daniel (Bud) Stuntz, Dr. Robert Fernald, Richard G. Hewlett, and Anne Dowd.

An
Uncommon
Woman

When America finally elects its first woman President — a day I believe will come before the 21st Century — she will be someone much like Dixy Lee Ray. In fact, she will have to be.

With a bit more luck of the political draw and one or two coincidences tossed in by fate, Dixy might very well have been presidential timber herself, just as she proved to be of extraordinary gubernatorial quality.

This biography was once titled "Dixy, A Chronicle of Courage," because her most salient, unparalleled virtue has been courage. She has not always been right — and who has? — but from childhood to national and international fame, she has always spoken her mind, without looking about the room to see who was present. At one time, when she was in a specially bitter altercation with the press, I suggested to her that she consider softening her position or offering a couple of alternatives to her stand. She didn't hesitate.

"And compromise my principles? They will either accept me as I am or they can bloody well stuff it!"

It was an answer that needed no explanation. When Dixy speaks her mind on an issue, no one has to guess her philosophy or her intent. Conversely, when others offer suggestions or advice to her, they had better be logical and simple in their presentation, and, perhaps even more important, they had better have their facts in order and well supported, too. That characteristic is one of the reasons I sought her friendship and council 20 years ago and, I trust, explains similarly why she sought mine.

As an editor who crusaded against crime and corruption, I frequently "updated" her on the backgrounds of many of the prominent persons who sought her favor as governor of Washington State. In every case her first question was always the same:

"Can you prove your case, and has he or she ever been proved guilty?"

I should have had more of her stubbornness myself and demanded more definitive facts and statistics when I was a crime-busting editor. Our missions to obtain justice would have been even more successful, and the reporters and sub-editors who answered to me would have been challenged more severely to produce foolproof evidence and pertinent data.

Of all the persons I have known in a 45-year career as a reporter, critic, columnist, and editor, Dixy stands far above all the rest. The warm, witty, generous, human being she is has, unfortunately, often been disguised by her penchant for being painfully honest. It has cost her much more pain than she has delivered, but she wouldn't change a thing.

As I have indicated in this biography, the most amazing fact in the life of Dixy Lee Ray is that someone who has been as devoted to plain speaking and the hard truth as she has could have gone as far as she has. And she did it in what is still a Man's World. If her example could only become the rule in politics, her candor might very well turn out to be the most valuable gift she will have left to the American conscience.

LOUIS R. GUZZO

CHAPTER ONE

The White House Beckons

"Calling Dr. Ray . . . Dr. Dixy Lee Ray. Will you go to a courtesy phone, please?"

The woman in the tan raincoat, long socks, square haircut, and spongy moccasins turned her head abruptly to listen. She wasn't sure the name called was hers. She stopped walking.

"Calling Dr. Dixy Lee Ray. Please go to the nearest white courtesy telephone. There is a message for you."

No doubt this time.

"That sureashell is for me," she muttered to herself. "Now who knows or cares that I'm here right at this minute?"

It was a pleasant spring day outside but there at the Friendship Airport in Baltimore the crowd of people going in every direction didn't seem to be thinking about the weather or anything else, except to get someplace else fast.

That applied to Dixy Lee Ray, too. Never fond of the national capital, she was anxious to get on with it and get back to her island on Puget Sound, her dogs, and a refuge from all the wasted motion Washington, DC, represented to her. She wanted to get back to what she called "the real Washington" and as far away from the Beltway and landlubbers as a marine biologist could. The "other Washington" (which was how she differentiated it for those who didn't accept her "real" label for home) she also frequently referred to as "Washington, D & C."

"Why D & C?" a friend once asked.

1

"Well, it's an abortion, isn't it?"

The answer didn't always draw laughter, but she didn't care who laughed and who didn't when she was talking about the home of the federal government. It wasn't that she actually disliked the capital so much; anything or any place that kept her from her beloved Puget Sound drew a frown.

On that spring day in 1972 Dixy was en route home from an overlong meeting of the National Museum Council, to which she had just been appointed. But she had to stop in New York first. Probably that was the reason for the huff-and-puff. In New York she would be attending a session of the — deep breath, please — Public Understanding of Science Committee of the American Association for the Advancement of Science. Ordinarily, such a meeting would have excited the deep-sea scientist, because she had campaigned long for scientists of every discipline to come out of their cocoons and "level with the public," as she put it. But she missed Jacques, Ghillie, and the other animals on Fox Island, as well as the cool sea. She wasn't in a mood to linger elsewhere.

Plane time was about 25 minutes away, so she had time to find a courtesy phone. Besides, she was curious as the devil. Only her sister Marion and the Museum Council knew she would be at the airport at that moment, and neither had reason to call.

"Hello. Message Center? You paged me? I'm Dr. Ray."

"Oh, yes, thank you, Dr. Ray. Just a moment, please. The White House has been trying to get in touch with you."

"Sure," Dixy said to herself. "The White House, and I'm the Queen of England. Now who could be fooling around?"

"Dr. Ray. . .?" asked a voice on the other end.

"Yes, this is she."

"My name is Barbara Franklin of the White House staff. I run the Women's Office for the President, and you may remember me from our conversation a few years back."

Dixy remembered. About three years earlier Barbara had called her at the Pacific Science Center in Seattle to tell her the President had requested a national canvass of women of skill and distinction who might be considered for important positions in federal government. The idea had been to prepare a list of such women for use by the President in what was obviously a program to win the vote of the fair sex in future elections. Dixy didn't know how her name got on the list in the first place, but she had sent in a biography and a letter of acknowledgment back in 1970 as a routine matter and promptly forgotten the episode as so much political maneuvering.

"Why, yes, Miss Franklin, I do remember. What can I do for you?"

"I know, Dr. Ray, that you said at the time that you wouldn't be interested in any appointment to a federal position, but the President wondered if you might have changed your mind?"

Dixy didn't hesitate.

"Well, no, I haven't. I'm really not interested in a federal government job."

"Oh, I'm not pressing you, at least not at the moment." Miss Franklin had let the cat partly out of the bag. "I don't want to put you in a position of saying yes or no to a job. What I really want to ask is whether you would be willing to have your name considered (and she stressed the word 'considered') as a candidate for a rather important position?"

"What position, Miss Franklin?"

"Well, say, for example, something like membership on the U.S. Atomic Energy Commission. Please, understand that this is not an offer of the position — just a request that you be willing to have your named added to the list of candidates for the job."

What Dixy said to herself was: "Wow! That's something! They must really want me. What for, I wonder. I'm a marine biologist, not a nuclear physicist."

What she actually said was more instinctive: "Well, if it is that important to you, go ahead and put me on the list. Can you tell me more about the job?"

"Certainly. My office is determined to get a woman appointed to the position, which is one of the most important in the federal government. The commission has five members. We also are determined that one of the five be a woman scientist. It's about time. And the President is thinking along those lines, too. The salary is $40,000 a year, and it will be increased soon."

Now, there, at last, was something to appeal to the Scottish soul of a woman who had lived most of her life on a teacher's salary and now, as director of the Pacific Science Center in Seattle, was drawing the extraordinary stipend of $22,000 a year. Good Lord! Forty-thousand a year! She could pay some of those miserable debts with that.

Dixy tried not to be impressed. "Tell me. Is it a full-time job?"

"Yes."

"Would I have to live in Washington the year 'round?"

"Oh, yes."

That did it. Who in his right mind would move from the Pacific Northwest, the Paradise of the Western World, to the hellhole of bureaucracy for a paltry $40,000 a year?

"Oh, Barbara, I'm sorry, but no, thanks, I am not really interested in the position. Just tell the President I'm deeply grateful for his interest, and yours, too, but I love my present work at the Science Center so much that I really have no desire to leave. And it is so pleasant living on Puget Sound. That's where my roots are, and I never like to leave it for long. I am deeply grateful to you and the President for your kindness. I'm flattered."

She was about to hang up, and Miss Franklin obviously realized it.

"Oh, no, please, Dr. Ray. Don't dismiss it too quickly. Don't give me a definite answer now. I just wanted to relay the idea to you. The President wanted just that. Give it some thought. Mull it over at home for a while. Consider the potential. I'll call you again in about a week." She hung up quickly to avoid another "No, thanks."

For the next week Dixy was more puzzled than interested. She kept asking herself why the White House wanted her, and the only answer she could come up with didn't please her. President Nixon had sent out the word that he wanted a woman scientist for the AEC, and he was going to have one in that job, or else. Did he know the difference between a good woman scientist and a bad one? Did he know the difference between a biologist and a physicist — and between a natural scientist and a nuclear physicist? Of course not. If he did, he wouldn't be fooling around with so important a job and insisting only a woman would do.

At first, only the prospect of making the delicious sum of $40,000 a year appealed to her. She needed some advice, and right away. Was it her duty as an American citizen to consider the position? Did she have a right to say no if she were truly qualified? After all, it was immensely flattering to have a President seek you out, no matter what the political reason.

Dixy decided to consult a few friends whose judgment she trusted. One was Edward E. Carlson, then president of Western International Hotels and soon to be president of United Air Lines. Another was the author, then editor of the morning paper in Seattle, the *Post-Intelligencer*. We had been among her confidants for many years and would serve her again in the years to come. Neither of us hesitated. We told her she was ideally suited for the key position and that it was actually a turning point in her life.

We were right about the last point. The airport call would result in making her a national figure — and later a governor.

Friends and colleagues at the University of Washington would agree with us. No one advised her to reject the idea.

A week later, right on time, Barbara Franklin called Dixy at her home on Fox Island, and the marine biologist informed her she would consider the position if it were to be offered. It was soon apparent Dixy was "it." If there had been other candidates for the job, they were never given much consideration. The White House wanted Dr. Dixy Lee Ray on the United States Atomic Energy Commission, and no one else, at that time. She was asked to return to Washington as soon as possible to be interviewed by Dr. James R. Schlesinger, AEC chairman.

Schlesinger was impressed with her, and she with him — in the beginning.

"I wish the respect I had then could have been sustained. Nevertheless, in that first interview and for a time after that I felt that if he were the chairman of the AEC, it would be a fine place for me to carry on the work of promoting an understanding of the relationship energy has with biology and the environment. I told him that if I were to become a commissioner, my primary interests would be communications in science, public under-standing, and better science education. We talked at length about energy and the environment."

In her sheltered academic life, Dixy had never pondered the substance nor magnitude of the nuclear debate nor the Ameri-can involvement in nuclear power. Somehow the entire subject had been remote, of interest only to those specializing in it, not the entire nation or world. Now for the first time she was to come face to face with the immensity of this new science and its impli-cations. As she listened to Schlesinger describe the work of the AEC and its public and private work force of more than 90,000 persons in and outside the United States, she felt she was listen-ing to a fairy tale for the first time. The marine biologist who had been known as an environmentalist most of her scientific career was being ushered into a new dimension in science that was so strange she would be literally a beginner.

In fact, this new "science-fiction," as it seemed to her in the beginning, would soon force her to re-examine her immovable positions in some areas of environmental thinking. The day would come when she would have to make difficult choices between "absolute environmentalism" and a "balance of values and needs of mankind." It was to become for her the most engrossing issue of her life and career — an issue that would demand hard decisions many of her environmental friends would not accept.

The interview with Schlesinger, often strange and sometimes exciting, would never leave her memory.

She remembered she had asked: "What will my duties be as a commissioner. . . ? What does a commissioner do every day?"

The eternal, infernal pipe danced in his hand as he used it for emphasis (how she was to hate that pipe and all others in her one-woman campaign to rid the world of smokers!).

"What would you do every day?" Schlesinger repeated. The pipe went back into the mouth like a sedan to its garage. "Anything you want to."

Those, Dixy swore, were his exact words. She thought he was kidding and looked for the slightest hint of a smile. Nothing there. She didn't know whether to burst out laughing or to ask him why he wasn't. Dixy was to discover the implication of his answer a short time later, to her regret.

"Dr. Schlesinger, do commissioners attend daily sessions?"

"No, Dr. Ray."

"Then why can't I be sort of a part-time commissioner and commute to Washington whenever the commission meets?"

"Because it meets weekly. Once a week, at least."

There went the hope of trying to take advantage of the best of two possible worlds.

Dixy could not shrug off the uneasy feeling that her expertise as a marine biologist was of no consequence and that she was beckoned by the Nixon administration and Dr. Schlesinger for the advantageous "political publicity" she could give them both because she was nationally known as an environmentalist. Whenever she tried to switch the conversation to nuclear physics, weaponry, or the shortage of energy, Dr. Schlesinger deftly brought the subject back to environmental concerns.

When she reconstructed the interview later for a friend, she observed: "The administration and Jim Schlesinger obviously could see what was coming — a growing opposition to nuclear energy, thanks to Ralph Nader and his pals. Schlesinger wanted to be able to say to the Naderites: 'You see, we are deeply concerned about the impact of nuclear-power production on the environment. That's why we've invited one of the nation's leading environmentalists, and a reputable scientist, at that, to sit on the commission.' What a masterpiece of irony lay ahead!"

Although Dixy considered herself an environmentalist and the press and the public did, too, in the Pacific Northwest, she was never a part of the environmental crusade. She carefully avoided identification with any groups, environmental or otherwise.

"I'm not a joiner," she once said. "I want always to reserve the right to change my mind as facts or conditions change. The scientist who is a 'joiner' and sacrifices truth and scientific principle for the sake of a movement isn't much of a scientist. I'm for preservation and conservation, too, but I wouldn't be caught dead with a membership card. I wish more people in the sciences felt that way and stuck by it."

She didn't know how prophetic she was about her own forthcoming dilemma with the environmentalists when she said, long before joining the AEC: "We must conserve, protect, preserve on the basis of reason, fact, knowledge, common sense, not merely because someone or some group has taken an emotional fancy to a part of the landscape or a notion with little basis in research or reality. And I say that with a deeper respect for the land, sea, and air than the pseudo-environmentalists have displayed. God save us from those who would save us!"

Schlesinger's wish to parlay the Dixy Lee Ray name into a buffer against Ralph Nader was shared by others. The marine biologist and the self-styled "savior of mankind" were bound to become the bitterest of enemies. He attacked with epithets (like calling her "Mrs. Plutonium") and emotional outbursts, and she countered by charging him with leading Americans "down the path to ruin like a Pied Piper bent on making the U.S. a third-class power, vulnerable to all our enemies."

In time many of her friends in the energy field tried to arrange a confrontation between Nader and Dr. Ray because they believed she was the only person who could take him on in a public debate and unmask his ignorance about nuclear power. Several attempts were made to schedule the "word battle of the century," but all failed. One that looked most promising was promoted by newspaper editors in the West. It fell through after

Dixy promised to appear, "provided the rules of debate were strictly adhered to and the two contestants observed time limits to the second." Dixy was aware of Nader's penchant for bulldozing other speakers by continued interruptions and heckling. A date had been set for the debate, but after Nader was informed of Dixy's insistence on "fair debate rules," he suddenly developed another conflicting engagement on his calendar.

To her, Nader personified the most dangerous element in American life — the man with a little information but a Napoleonic complex. She once told a reporter:

"What chance do honest, dedicated men and women of science have against this emotional charlatan, who plays upon people's fears for effect? Congress long ago discovered the key to his hit-and-run tactics, and his presence frightens no one in the national capital any more. But television, radio, and the press still treat him like the Prince of Light, despite his half-truths, unsubstantiated charges, and his obvious hatred of the American system of government. He and others like him operate in a devious way. They make a spectacular charge that grabs Page 1 headlines and monopolizes TV screens and radio newscasts across the nation. The rebuttal, if any, that comes from those attacked or from reputable people in the sciences or engineering gets lost in a few paragraphs on Page 43 or the last-minute TV roundup that is tossed in with the weather or the community bulletin board.

"The American people should have their eyes opened to consumer frauds, automobiles and appliances that don't operate as advertised, and foods that short-change or adversely affect the health of the buyer. But these safeguards and investigations must be conducted by adequately trained, honestly motivated, and scientifically based men and women, not publicity-crazed headline hunters like Nader, Barry Commoner & Co. As if that weren't bad enough, we are now being told by the same fringe that we should ignore what the great majority of physicists tell us and follow instead the Gospel according to such great scientific minds as Robert Redford, Marlon Brando, Robert Blake, and Jane Fonda. These flicker idols may be fine actors, but what in hell do they know about nuclear physics? Yet, they are influencing millions of trapped American citizens who also don't know much about nuclear physics but are mesmerized into believing that these overpaid screen heroes are as smart as playwrights and screen writers make them appear."

These thoughts were not yet in the Dixy Lee Ray mind as she listened to Schlesinger in that first conversation, but she would slip into them each time she recalled that meeting.

"If you are in earnest about carrying a message to the public in the energy and environmental fields," he managed to say between puffs on the pipe, "the Atomic Energy Commission would be a helluva platform."

It was one of the few Schlesinger bits of advice Dixy accepted and implemented. But what heartaches would come with it in future years, particularly as governor of Washington State, when her past record as an environmentalist would be ignored or forgotten because of her insistence on reason and balance, plus an almost religious devotion to scientific truth.

Among other conversations she remembered well in those early days of Washington, DC, service was a group session with members of the White House staff. She could not recall who it was who asked the inevitable question, but the question was unforgettable:

"Dr. Ray, would you mind telling us whether you are a Republican or Democrat?"

Perhaps the quickness of her answer was as telling as the answer itself: "Neither."

She could see the malaise in the troops. Eyes darted across the room in telltale directions, which means no direction at all. Eyes have a way of giving up the truth where other parts of the anatomy can retain secrecy.

Later, she was told in a hush that she was the only "top choice" President Nixon permitted who wasn't a Republican or strongly disposed toward Republican philosophy through proven actions or speech. But it was too late now. At least, the White House staffers could say with some relief, she wasn't a Democrat. And they had themselves another important woman in a high and highly visible position in the administration.

Another meeting Dixy would not forget was a brief but significant encounter with an old friend, Senator Warren G. Magnuson, the Democratic powerhouse on the Hill and a longtime backer of Dixy's at the Pacific Science Center and the University of Washington. The senior senator from her home state seemed genuinely excited by the prospect of placing a native daughter on so prestigious a board. In a moment of exuberance he took her from this office to that, introducing her to his colleagues with clout. Among them was Senator John O. Pastore, Rhode Island Democrat, who was a power in nuclear affairs in Congress and who would be a strong voice and stalwart friend in her corner in the energy battles to come.

Maggie, as Dixy and other home-staters called Senator Magnuson, had a storied ability to persuade others to see things his way without making headlines — until he was ready for them, that is. He poked his head through the doorway to Pastore's office, pushed Dixy part way in, and said:

"John, this gal might be nominated to the AEC, and I want you to support her."

In the Senate, Maggie's hint to the wise was frequently sufficient. To an equally headstrong and powerful John Pastore, such an admonition, coming from someone other than Maggie, might have been quickly forgotten. Pastore could trust Magnuson's political intuition.

With support from both sides of the aisle, it was no surprise that confirmation of the first woman to serve on the AEC would be quick and unanimous. Dixy had been informed of the appointment in June, nominated by the President early in July, and confirmed by the Senate in two weeks.

On the July trip to the capital the marine biologist with international credentials found out how little she knew about nuclear science, nuclear physics, and nuclear energy. A series of concentrated briefings at the agency left her overwhelmed and in awe over "this new science, this extraordinary portal to the future." It was one of the most exciting moments of a lifetime for a person in love with science and with a passion for facts. Realizing how little she knew about the new field, she determined that on her return trip to the capital to assume her post on the commission, she would do her damnedest to learn as much as possible about nuclear energy and the AEC complex in the U.S.

As soon as she returned home, she laid plans to tour every AEC installation she could in the month allotted her before beginning duty late in August, 1972. To make it easier for herself and spare the commission the expense of her giant-sized field trip, Dixy invested in a made-to-order motor home she would use not only for her highway odyssey but as a residence once ensconced in the DC area. The specially appointed Dodge she ordered cost $21,000, a sum she could not have afforded without the prospect of a handsome commissioner's wage and discovery of a way to "beat the high cost of living" in the capital.

Although Dixy had owned other motor homes and trailers and resided in a mobile home on her Fox Island farm, she was also taking her first step into the well publicized world of the lady commissioner who lived on wheels "and didn't give a damn who knew it."

The Capital Press Corps was to make much of the eccentric marine biologist turned nuclear savant, and several reporters who should have known better chose to ridicule the outspoken visitor from the Old West who liked to wear comfortable warmup suits or sweaters and skirts and long woolen socks nestled inside thick crepe-soled moccasins. They had been accustomed so long to the tiresome wardrobes of diplomacy and officialdom that they didn't know how to react when someone came along who did as she pleased — or, perhaps more bluntly, did as they would have pleased if they had had the courage.

In Montgomery County, Maryland, Dixy will be remembered a long time by those who admire gutsy people in general and who prefer the low cost and flexibility of mobile-home or motor-home living in particular. When she arrived in the capital in August, Dixy's first order of business was to find a site for her motor home, a permanent residence, in effect. She spent several fruitless and frustrating days looking — and recognizing that most people considered mobile- or motor-home dwellers as untouchables — before finding a pleasant farmer who didn't give a hang for city folks no-how. Landlord and new tenant got along fine until a feature article on Dixy and her unusual life-style appeared in the *Washington Post*. Goaded by a few motor-home-hating residents of the county, the sheriff cited a law that forbade motor homes and mobile homes in all but designated areas and ordered Dixy and her abode to beat it forthwith.

"If I hadn't already raised a helluva fuss in the press because of my dogs, my home on wheels, and my passion for comfortable clothing," Dixy explained, "I would have stayed and fought it out. As it was, I fought, but I didn't stay because I didn't want that nice old farmer to suffer on my behalf. But I fought back."

Determined not "to let 'em get away with it," Dixy pressed her case legally. And won, after several months of prolonged battles in and out of City Hall. As a result, county law and the prohibitions against motor homes and mobile homes were changed drastically. People who now enjoy extended privileges in their movable dwellings in Montgomery County — and probably throughout the rest of the state — owe Dixy Lee Ray at least a tip of the bonnet.

Back at the AEC and in certain quarters on the Hill and at the White House, the most subtle suggestions were made that, ahem, er, gulp, it would be nice if Dixy Lee Ray behaved and got off the capital's Page 1's and evening newscasts. But the hints were like catnip to the neighborhood Toms. They simply egged her on and nurtured her love for a fight. She may have been a relatively new face in Washington, DC, but she wasn't impressed by the pleaders of protocol, least of all when she was convinced she was doing the right thing.

Dixy's decision to zigzag her way from installation-to-installation in the AEC complex before moving to Washington was, she acknowledged, one of the wisest she had ever made. News of her trip preceded her, and she was treated like a conquering heroine. But if they were taken with her candor and tomato-cheek smile, she was even more smitten with the superior brain power and "other world" operations of the plants at Richland, Washington; Idaho Falls, Idaho; Rocky Flats, Colorado; Los Alamos, New Mexico; the Argonne Laboratories in Chicago; and Oak Ridge, Tennessee. What an eye-opener!

Some of the reservations and doubts she had held against nuclear energy as a leading environmentalist were already fading in the light of the fantastic new technology. When she arrived in the capital, she had acquired a little girl's rapture for a most amazing new plaything. It was a reverence that would remain with her forever. She had made many speeches about the astounding things man could accomplish with his brain, but she had never appreciated the extent of that brain power until she saw what could now be done by splitting atoms.

While ruminating in the warmth of friendly company once, she observed: "What wonders must lie ahead! And we will see only a fraction of them. If the statesmen and honest and brilliant men and women among us prevail in this world, we can conquer anything — hunger, hate, pestilence, disease, war, fear. What is it we could not do?"

Those early days at the AEC were wonder days for the new commissioner. On one hand, she was thoroughly confused by the complex budgetary, technical, and political problems thrown her way by the staff and the other commissioners, and she believed it would never be possible to make a nuclear wizard of an ocean scientist. But on the other hand, she was bowled over by the remarkable layers of scientific and technological personnel on the AEC staff. She had been a resident of academe most of her life, but she had never witnessed nor heard of so many brilliant minds in one place pursuing the same objectives.

She must have repeated her words many times: "What is it we could not do?"

In the meantime, neither Schlesinger nor Dixy realized both were racing toward momentous events. Schlesinger couldn't have known his days as chairman of the AEC were short-lived and that Dr. Ray would soon replace him — over his protest — as head of the massive, sensitive agency. When the full, explosive nature of Watergate materialized and shocked the U.S., the cards were reshuffled and previous arrangements voided.

Richard Helms had "screwed up" the Central Intelligence Agency, as Dixy and many others in Washington put it, and President Nixon had to do something quickly to relieve the sticky situation. The Nixon game of checkers with live personalities began again. Why not move Schlesinger into the CIA job to clean things up?

At first, Dixy could not understand how Schlesinger was able to maintain his "good guy" image with the press and public and, as a result, move from job to job under Republicans and Democrats alike and through complete changes of cast in the White House. She eventually discovered he did it simply by accommodating himself and his methods of operation to the persons in charge. Principles? Did he have any? Dixy wanted no part of such tactics, but at least she knew what sacrifices in conscience had to be made to "stay on the team" in politics. She wanted no part of it; Schlesinger's methods were for the birds, she told herself. In fact, she called him "the incorrigible bird watcher," and not without reason.

"I remember a wonderful party out in the Maryland countryside," she recalled. "Schlesinger had been invited. Within minutes after his arrival, he was off into the fields, glasses in hand, to spy on his feathered/friends. Now, I consider bird-watching a rather satisfying pursuit — but in the middle of a house party? I figured that perhaps the only way he could keep that damned pipe lit was to race through the brush after some red-breasted phenomenon or other."

Several years later Schlesinger, newly converted to discipleship in the Jimmy Carter regime, went bird watching on impulse in Washington State, Dixy's home territory. He had been a visitor and a speaker at Washington State University in the eastern part of the state, and he asked permission to take an automobile out onto the sometimes risky mountain roads. Spotting an unusual bird in a field, he stopped the car quickly on the highway shoulder, got out, and raced after the bird. A campus patrolman following behind came over the rise and, not having been warned in time, plowed into the car Schlesinger had been driving. The damage was extensive to both cars. When she heard about the incident, Dixy commented:

"The Nation's No. 1 bird chaser has struck again!"

One notion persists in a magnified look at the Dixy Lee Ray character. The reason she found it hard to get along with persons like James Schlesinger and, later, Henry Kissinger — both of whom she labeled as "supremely arrogant" in their brilliance — was that they could shift political gears on a dime and take an opportunistic detour around personal feelings and beliefs. After all, she would sometimes say unceremoniously when only friendly ears were listening, "One must protect one's ass at all costs in the federal employ." But not Dixy Lee Ray. She had spoken her piece all her life; why start boot-licking now? Had she been willing to "play the game" and subdue that impulse to say or do exactly what compelled her to say or do, she undoubtedly could have stayed on in Washington, DC, for as long as she might have wished — and under Democratic or Republican rule, as Schlesinger and Kissinger had managed.

Dixy would never pay the price of abject obedience, either as a vassal in Kissinger's castle of assistant secretaries of state or as the first woman governor of Washington State. She would pay dearly for honesty and outspokenness, but, as she explained, "I sleep well, thank you."

CHAPTER TWO

The
Little
Dickens

Within two days after her unforgettable first meeting with James Schlesinger, Dixy was on her way back to her home in the Pacific Northwest. She had a couple of Scotch-and-sodas ("with lotsa ice, please!") as she relaxed in the plane, oblivious to all the other passengers and wearing that "gotcha" smile she displayed when things went exceptionally well. If other passengers wondered about the short-haired lady who seemed to be laughing at her highball glass, they said nothing to disturb her.

The alcohol wasn't necessary. Dixy was already pumped up by the adrenalin inspired in the last few days in the capital. Could it be? Was all this happening to the little neighborhood tomboy from Tacoma who would rather have lived barefoot on the sands of Puget Sound than take a condominium in Heaven? Wonder what everybody thought now about "the little Dickens," as her family had once labeled the robust hell-raiser in her youngest years. ("Little Dickens" soon was shortened to Dicks and ultimately to Dixy, which she eventually adopted; in classes and crowds, she never answered to the name of "Margaret," her given name, which she detested. Receiving no help or encouragement from the family to effect a legal name change, she saved her nickels and dollars and, finally, at 16, had enough to remove "Margaret" from her birth records and put "Dixy" in its place.)

Reminiscence was not her "bag," but she was full of it now as the glow heightened. How far back could she remember? Her sisters and friends teased her because she insisted she could remember things they couldn't, and she was often able to prove it. She taunted her sisters with, "Of course, I don't remember being born, but . . ."

Now, 35,000 feet up and tranquilized by alcohol and adrenalin, she played the game alone. How far back could she really remember — without the help of what was told her?

Why did she keep remembering that crib and the lace curtains and the silly sounds adults made and, most of all, the change that came into their voices when they turned from other adults to lean over and goo-goo at her? She was lying down and looking out in her earliest recollection . . . looking out because her vision was fringed by something white she later came to know as lace. From time to time faces came between her and what was obviously a window that let the sunlight in and caused her to squint. The faces kept getting in the way. Again and again the faces would make noises that were meant for her. Why didn't they talk to her the way they talked to others? A strange recollection. . .

Trivial? Of course, Dixy thought. And how she hated trivia all her life! Small talk and cocktail parties and telephone nonsense were among her pet peeves. So much to do and so little time . . . . How could people waste their lives on trivia?

Yet here she was indulging in it — trivia involving herself. Did her brand of trivia have special meaning? Judging from what she later discovered about the crib and the room in which it was kept, she must have been about a year and a half old, certainly less than two, when she looked out into the sunlight permitted by the window and the white lace, broken only by those pesky faces making weird sounds. Funny what the mind chooses to retain.

These memories were like dreams but clearly not dreams. Another recollection she couldn't have drawn from the words of others or a photograph was a scene in a relatively small room in the Ray home. She was not much older than in the crib remembrance. The room was full of people, including her mother, grandmother, and other relatives. It was cluttered with many bits and pieces; it was what Dixy would later recognize as the sewing room. Among the varied cuts of cloth, sewing baskets, an old-fashioned sewing machine with foot pedal, and a stuffed tailor's mannequin were two rocking chairs, one large and one small. The two chairs were indelible in her mind. The large one had rocked a little Ray to sleep hundreds of times. It had no arms, a fact Dixy couldn't forget because she would become arm-weary in those days her turn came to rock her youngest sisters to sleep. If it had not been for the chair's abominable squeak as it rocked, however, she might never have remembered it. How that squeak penetrated and infuriated her! It may have been because the squeak kept the baby she was rocking awake longer. But, of course, she thought, smiling on the flight back to Seattle, the squeak may have been what mesmerized the child and invited sleep. The big chair took on a monstrous personality, mainly because she seemed constantly to be cracking ankle, shin, and knee bones on it. It must have followed her about the room. How else could it have found a vulnerable bone so often?

On the other hand, she loved the little rocker, possibly because it didn't squeak and it didn't come after her leg bones. It was a funny-looking chair that had been painted white over the original red. The white paint apparently had been a very cheap paint, because many bubbles had formed and the paint had chipped off, giving the chair enormous freckles. Ugly to some, but not to Dixy.

In the incident that stayed with her, Dixy was in the nude and was ordered to stand, something she had only recently learned to do. She was very wobbly on her feet and grabbed the arm of the little rocker to avoid falling. It both amused her and made her a bit dizzy. For reasons she couldn't comprehend, she was simultaneously pinching her tummy with her free hand and giggling loudly as she went through her wobbly dance. The performance seemed to send the watching adults into uproarious laughter. Her introduction to show biz . . .

Many years later Dixy recounted the "trivial" incident to her mother and sisters, and all laughed at her. She had to swallow her pride because she had no proof. But several months later her father, who had been "hooked" on photography, brought out a box of early pictures the family had never seen, and there was one of Dixy pinching her tummy alongside the chair and in the supreme State of Giggle. And she was not yet two!

An exceptional memory was to be one of the most important tools in the Ray success formula.

Dixy Lee Ray was the second of five sisters. The oldest was

Marion, and the others, in order, were Jean, Juliana, and Alvista. Their mother and father had eloped while still in high school. Frances Adams was 17 and a sophomore and Alvis, 19, a senior. They had been carrying on a "library romance," leaving notes in books or files that were quickly retrievable. Frances was an only child. Her mother, the Grandma Nellie Dixy loved and the only "Grandma" she would acknowledge, had been deserted by her husband when Frances was a child of five. Because of rough times in the Central States, where the Adamses and their forebears had homesteaded, Nellie once had to send her only offspring to live with relatives in Alberta while she went to work. Frances would grow up under difficult circumstances, made no easier when the family migrated to the Puget Sound region and Tacoma.

Undoubtedly, Frances' unhappiness at home contributed to her decision to flaunt the rules in a rather stern, bible-reading family and elope. It also seemed to account for Frances' collaborating with her husband later in applying rigid discipline to the brood of five girls.

Alvis Ray was a printer, as his father, Edwin Ray, had been. Grandfather Ray was Dixy's favorite. She once described him as "a highly principled man and a very nice man. I liked him. He was a gentle fellow but in a way that the hard-core, hard-shelled Southern Baptist could be. Right was right, and wrong was wrong, and there was no gray between them."

The Rays had come from a long line of preachers — preachers and printers. In the "old" days preaching and printing had gone together like peanut butter and jelly. Grandpa Ray's father had been head of the Southern Baptist Convention, the largest Baptist organization in the South. He was one of 15 children, all of them born in Tennessee. Throughout the Ray clan the church had been the common ingredient. Some of them broke away from the family newspaper or job-printing business, usually to form their own, but they managed to hang on to their religious ties. Even Dixy Lee Ray the scientist once told a reporter she had remained a "devout Baptist" but didn't actively practice her religion.

The comment to a reporter was interesting in view of her sometimes bitter relationship with her overly strict father:

"My family was born and reared in the Baptist Church. One of my sisters, Juliana, became a missionary. For myself, I think that after quite an active childhood in church and church activities, I became more intellectual in my approach to religion, learning about other kinds of things, religions included, and became somewhat more philosophical. I can't see how anybody can fail to have some faith, because there are so many things that cannot be explained otherwise. But I don't find personal satisfaction in the restrictions of most creeds. In other words, I consider myself a Christian, a Protestant, but not an adherent to any particular sect. And I don't like public manifestations of religion. I think it's a very private thing."

And, like most things Dixy has considered private in her life, she avoids discussing religion unless severely pressed.

Grandpa Ray had a serious falling out with his father in Tennessee and traveled west to Tacoma in the 1880's and established the Ray Printing Co. Alvis took over the shop when he died, and Dixy herself took over direction of the business on her father's death in 1947. She had to split her time between teaching chores at the University of Washington and the printing plant for about a year and a half, the time it took to close her father's estate.

One of the most interesting — and most intensely disliked — characters in the family was Grandpa Ray's wife, Marguerite, a strange woman reared in excessive luxury. She had been Marguerite Williamson, a direct descendant of Hugh Williamson, a signer of the Constitution, and a member of the richly endowed Williamson family that owned the controlling stock in the Reynolds Tobacco Co.

"We have many relatives in the Winston-Salem area of North Carolina," Dixy explained, "but I've never contacted any of them. I don't have any desire to. Many of them were a wild bunch, too deeply affected by longtime wealth."

Marguerite's father was probably the wealthiest of the Williamsons. He, too, was named Hugh, like so many others in the family. In addition to controlling the main stock in the tobacco company, Great-Grandpa Williamson was also a judge.

"He was almost as prolific as my maternal grandfather," Dixy explained. "He had half a dozen children by his first wife, and two or three — maybe more — by his second wife. His second wife lived to be 96. I knew her, and I liked her. The family called her Granny, although she was in fact our step-grade grandmother. When Great-Grandpa Williamson died, she divided his lucrative estate among the children but kept a considerable portion for herself so she could assign it all to charities in North Carolina at her death."

No bitterness there, but perhaps Dixy was thinking about some of the poverty days she had endured in fighting her way to her Ph.D. at Stanford and helping others in the family. A Williamson buck now and then in her late teens and twenties would have eased the pain considerably.

The Williamson children who had inherited much of the judge's fortune were never interested in her or any other members of the West Coast family. She acknowledged there were many fine Williamsons among her great-aunts and great-uncles, "but some gambled or drank away their inheritance."

A few of the children of great-aunts and great-uncles eventually made their way to the West Coast, and Dixy found them to be pleasant "and decent."

The oldest of the great-aunts, Estelle, married a shrewd gentleman Dixy remembers only as "Uncle Miller, maybe Joe." As the husband of the oldest surviving daughter of the judge, he had been given duties as executor of part of the estate. He may have been shrewd, but "Uncle Miller," who was provided with authority to invest much of the money of the judge's children, put it into real estate and at one time was the most important landowner in the Palouse country in eastern Washington State. But his shrewdness must have left him, because he went bankrupt. He was simply a little ahead of his time. The land he once owned is immensely valuable today.

It is fascinating to hear Dixy speak of her Grandmother Marguerite:

"Maybe I was too harsh in my judgment, but I was not alone. Grandma Marguerite was accustomed to being waited on and being paid court to. She was, well, terribly spoiled and self-centered. Why my wonderful Grandfather Ray permitted himself to marry her I'll never understand. He was such a fine printer and a preacher. Well, he wasn't exactly a preacher, but he was an elder in the church and deeply religious. And very kind and considerate, so unlike her. Needless to say, it wasn't a very happy marriage, but Grandpa Ray was too honorable to seek a way out. He suffered it through.

"Marguerite claimed to be a child-bride, but I never believed that. Why should I? We could never believe anything else she told us. I have never known a more vain person. She would not let us call her Grandma or Grandmother because that would be an indication of her age. She called her husband Dad for reasons going beyond the fact he was the father of their children. Worst of all, she would pretend she was my father's sister, not his mother! Now, that's a hangup! Even as a child I was mortified and embarrassed by her behavior.

"She did everything possible to give the impression she was considerably younger than she was. For example, Marguerite had a couple of dresses which were 'spotted.' She never had them cleaned, but she would wear them once in a while to make people think she was still menstruating!"

Because Marguerite disliked it, "little Dickens" called her Grandma at every opportunity. It would send Marguerite into a rage.

"She was very irrational and had strong prejudices, likes, and dislikes and made no bones about it. They were often silly or inhuman prejudices which caused me to have no respect for her. When we were very young, Marion and I, she would call us in, look directly at me, and say: 'I don't like you. I like Marion.' She showed her favoritism repeatedly. Little wonder that I grew to hate her. My father was to show the same favoritism, unfortunately. But I think my generous Grandfather Ray went out of his way to be extra kind to me because his wife treated me so badly."

Dixy dwells on the subject of family favoritism because it played so large a role in her growing-up years. Her father was indoctrinated in the family philosophy at an early age. As the elder brother and the firstborn, he was favored at every turn. For example, he was permitted to eat at the table with his parents, while his brother Edwin, two years younger, was fed in the kitchen by the maid. Edwin was told continually that he wasn't the elder son, so he would simply have to take seconds or leftovers or whatever Alvis didn't want. Alvis had all the privileges. Such treatment obviously had a monumental impact on the personalities of both sons. Dixy was to feel the wrath of a father who didn't favor her — a father who also believed in using the rod to enforce discipline, rightly or wrongly.

Uncle Edwin was a broken man, who lived a miserable, lonely life, moving frequently from home to hospital. A victim of schizophrenia, he lived to an advanced age, dying long after his favored but no less miserable brother. Where one son had been put down and disciplined all his life, the other could do no wrong and, as Dixy stated it succinctly, "was spoiled rotten." Alvis Ray was destined to repeat the mistakes handed down through generations of bible-reading, fire-and-brimstone preachers.

Dixy has always parried personal questions as "nobody's damned business," but I have to guess her hatred for her paternal grandmother had most to do with her early decision to replace her given name of Margaret with Dixy. The "little Dickens" theory and her own professed admiration for the great Dixy general and namesake, Robert E. Lee, may have been contributing factors, but they can't match the emotional necessity for obliterating the memory of a family tyrant.

Each of the five Ray girls has a markedly different impression of Father Alvis, with Dixy's view being by far the harshest. Strangely, all five share similar views of their mother as the long-suffering, considerate parent who was the principal victim of Father's rages, excessive drinking, and irreparable passion for playing favorites and physically punishing those who strayed.

Unquestionably, Dixy felt the lash of her father's temper most forcefully and most frequently. Ironically, a strong case can be made for saying he had most to do with her determination to "be somebody, be successful" — if for no other reason than to "show him" and to be rid of his unfair treatment for all time. The love she never drew from him and the pain that she did helped shape her personality and make a tiger of her on one hand and a benevolent, extremely generous pussycat on the other. For that reason she remains an enigma to those who know her only casually.

The tiger and the pussycat are one and the same, the former being a safety mechanism designed to keep intruders out of her personal life and thought and the latter being a surprisingly warm, affectionate, and remarkably kind woman who is extraordinarily gregarious and thrives on having people around her. What created the double image? Her early years at home tell the story.

Marguerite's insensitive and irrational behavior in showering favors upon her son Alvis set the stage. His immaturity and his penchant for taking advantage of parental favors led him to the elopement with Frances Adams. The younger son would not have dared defy parental authority to do such a thing. Alvis, however, not only did so but was welcomed back home to live with his mother and father after the hurried honeymoon trip to

Yakima. Alvis went directly to work in the family printing plant, not bothering to return to high school, where he had been only a few months away from a diploma. Frances never went back to school either.

"That was most unfortunate for both of them," says a more forgiving Dixy today. "Both were very intelligent. Dad had an extremely fine mind. He spoke well. He read well. He read a lot of Shakespeare, Sir Walter Scott, and many others. More than anything else, he enjoyed reading the speeches of Woodrow Wilson. He loved to write, and he wrote well. He was also a fine speaker. Of course, in his day printers had to have a firm grasp of the English language because they composed and edited, as well as set type. My father was self-educated, but I will always wonder what his life might have been had he gone on to school as I did."

And how would a better educated Alvis Ray have treated an education-hungry, inquisitive Dixy Lee Ray?

Without saying it, Dixy hints strongly that another factor played the most decisive role in her father's frustrated existence and his dictatorial attitude toward Dixy and Marion. Despite his talent for writing, editing, and speaking and his love of books, Alvis Ray was a frustrated electrical engineer and inventor.

"That's what he really wanted to do," Dixy insisted. "He was clearly meant to be an engineer. He had developed several devices and had patents for them, but he didn't have the wherewithal to go into production. Of course, he blamed his inability to mass-produce his products on his lack of credentials and the fact that he had not gone on to college for special training. What irony! He invented a method, back in the 1920's, of printing electronically by telegraph, but he couldn't find any financial backing. His trouble was he was way ahead of his time. I know he had taken out several patents, but we've never been able to find them.

"Eventually, the frustration of knowing he couldn't get his dreams made into realities got to him, and he began to drink heavily. The printing business had not provided him with the challenge he needed, and he had blown his chance to pursue an engineering career by eloping into a life of mediocrity and disillusionment. That is no reflection on the romantic life of Mother and Dad. They may have had their spats, but they clearly loved each other deeply and were never ashamed to show it."

Alvis died of alcoholism in 1947, two years after Frances died of cancer.

I once asked Dixy if she would choose marine biology again if she were to have a second chance to pick a career. She said quickly:

"I have always loved my life's work in marine biology, and I have never regretted for an instant that I made the choice. But if I were to start all over again, I think I would undoubtedly be an electrical engineer."

The mystical love-hate relationship in the Ray household would have been worthy of a Eugene O'Neill script. Psychiatrists could have a field day examining every branch in the Ray family tree, and I'll wager that 50 savants would come up with 50 different answers. One of the questions they could never answer satisfactorily is the one that has intrigued me most:

"Did Dixy Lee Ray truly love or hate her father?"

She herself may be the least able to answer it clearly. How does she remember him?

"Dad was one of those men who wanted desperately to have a son, and I was the best he could come up with. For many years he treated me as if I were a son . . . sometimes, not always . . . because I was really a disappointment to him. Not in my whole life can I recall even the faintest stirring of affection for him. Again, I emphasize my memory does go back. My earliest recollections of him are of his speaking to me harshly. He wasn't all that kind to Marion either, but I was the one that usually needed correction, I guess, and I was afraid of him. At times I hated him. Mostly, I didn't respect him."

It was only after his death that Dixy could begin to feel some compassion for him. Those instances in which she felt an active hate for him came when he was administering beatings to her or acting cruelly toward her mother. His cruelty to his wife usually resulted when he had been drinking.

Since Marion, the firstborn, had been assigned the duties of "assistant mother," it was left to Dixy to do the "muscular" or masculine chores of chopping and bringing in firewood, carrying the heavy loads, and doing generally what a Ray would have expected his son to do. Alvis demonstrated little affection for either daughter. Then, six years after Dixy's birth, along came Jean, the No. 3 child. Now the inevitable predilection to exhibit favoritism asserted itself. She became the apple of her father's eye. She could do no wrong — and it didn't take long for her to take advantage of it.

"Partly because of that," Dixy said, "she didn't turn out to be a very nice person."

All the sisters agreed Jean was the prettiest of the five. Unfortunately, Dixy once observed, so did Jean. Only in recent years have the five sisters come together to help heal the wounds they sustained in the embattled early years. The wounds were deep, but Dixy has adopted a philosophical approach to them:

"The passing years and maturity bring one to rationalize the events of friction in early life. In my father's case, for instance, you'd have to have some feeling of sympathy and understanding, granted the kind of background from which he came. Had he been able to go to college, and had he had a different kind of mother.... The game of 'If' is never more devastating than when applied to human beings."

The four other sisters speak sometimes of the happy days in the Ray household. They remember the picnics, the outings, the camping, the parties at home, and the singing and dancing, particularly on holidays. But Dixy, the little workhorse of the troupe and the one who was most often on the wrong end of the whip, spent most of her reminiscent time on her trips alone or with her youngest sister, Alvista.

"In our home the parents believed in corporal punishment. Very much so. And it would be administered mostly for what were relatively minor offenses. It seemed the whippings were given more to remind us about who was boss than for any wrong-doing. Maybe that's why I always spoke up against the idea of corporal punishment through a lifetime of teaching. I got more than my full share of punishment at home. The word 'willow' to me always meant 'switch.' There was a wood lot next to our home in Tacoma. It was almost symbolic to me. That's where the willows came from for the whippings.

"The last time I was switched — and with a pretty good-sized branch of willow — was when I was 17. Imagine that, 17! Dad had been drinking, and I should have been more careful because I wasn't feeling well. I was really hurting, but I didn't know until a few days later that I was coming down with the mumps. My sisters and I had gone somewhere, and I had left without doing my kitchen chores beforehand. I had put on my night clothes with the intention of going to bed. He came into the bathroom, grabbed me by the shoulders, turned me around, and pushed me toward the kitchen. I knew I had goofed on the chores, and I would have gone to the kitchen to do them. But when he grabbed me and brusquely shoved me out of the bathroom, the wrath of a hundred earlier beatings welled up inside me, and I made the mistake of shouting at him to keep his hands off me. He could not tolerate that, so I got the whipping of my life. I was sick, inside and out, and not just from the advent of the mumps.

"From that moment on for about two years I never spoke to him, nor he to me. I was 19 when I left home to go to Mills College in Oakland. In that two-year period we lived in the same house, ate at the same table, saw each other frequently. He didn't try to force me to speak. I simply refused because of the enormous, lingering hurt that was without physical pain. Somehow I managed to communicate with him indirectly but not face to face. A short time before I left home, the word got to him that I had won a scholarship to Mills, and he said he would help me with finances. He never came through with them."

How many tragedies are spawned by an inability or unwillingness to communicate? Dixy's sisters say that in his last years their father proudly referred many times to the honors Dixy had won in high school, Mills, and Stanford. Once he acknowledged she was the "brilliant one," the smartest of all his daughters, then stated she would one day be a famous woman. He was prophetic. But why didn't he try telling it to the one person who wanted most to hear it?

When Dixy left for Mills, she was determined to wind up at the head of her class — which she did. She knew she had to do it to prove to him that she could.

"In a rather strange way, I also wanted him to be proud of me. There was no longer any question about it. I had to make my own way, get my own education, support myself. I refused to be dependent on him. In fact, the last two years of high school I had earned my own money by producing puppet shows in schools, halls, churches, theaters, wherever kids and adults would pay to see the performances."

Spurred on by the determination to take nothing from her Dad, Dixy formed a marionette troupe of five of her friends. She was the producer, script writer, the leading performer, and the designer of the puppets. All members of the family pitched in to help make the puppets, the costumes, and the sets. On "show night" Mother piled the entire brood, plus some of the regular members of the troupe, into the car and off they went to the big event. Sometimes even Dad attended. The fare included fairy tales, for the most part — "Sleeping Beauty," "Jack and the Beanstalk," and "Hansel and Gretel" among them — but Dixy prepared many comic vignettes, too.

"We had a contract — an informal one, of course — with Boy Scout and Girl Scout troops and with school and church groups," Dixy said. "We were guaranteed $8 a show and 10 percent of whatever was made over that. It was good support. I paid off our expenses and gave a modest sum to our various helpers. For two years, my last two years in high school, we had a glorious time. We gave shows several nights a week throughout the Puget Sound region, far beyond Tacoma. As we chalked up the performances, we were becoming quite good at it. In fact, I parlayed my new-found skills into latching onto some good summer jobs, including work as a camp counselor. It was a thrill not to rely on the family for my needs and expense money. Once having tasted that independence, it was forever a part of me."

Dixy tasted more than independence. She had taken her first dip into show business — since her tummy-pinching dance at 1½ — and she liked it. In her first year at Mills she had brought with her some of the marionettes and other paraphernalia she had engineered in Tacoma, and she produced a show every Saturday at the Emporium in San Francisco. It brought in some financial help, "but it was mostly for the fun of it."

But, Dixy said wistfully, there was a time "when I thought I could make a profession out of it." She had the flare, the bold-ness, the literary perception, and, most of all, the phenomenal memory for it. In fact, her love for the stage caused her to minor in drama at Mills.

I remember a plane ride with her when she spoke fondly of the stage, dramatic literature, and poetry in general. She was, as the jargon of the day had it, "turned on." Her reading background was enormous. She may have been one of the world's foremost marine biologists, but she would also have made an extraordinary English scholar, had she chosen. I mentioned that I was especially fond of Shakespeare's sonnets but unfortu-nately could remember only a key phrase here and there. One of my favorites among them was the sonnet that ended ". . . I scorn to change my state with kings."

"Oh, you mean this one," she said, with only a second's hesitation:

When, in disgrace with fortune and men's eyes,
I all alone beweep my outcast state,
And trouble deaf heaven with my bootless cries,
And look upon myself, and curse my fate,
Wishing me like to one more rich in hope,
Featured like him, like him with friends possess'd,
Desiring this man's art and that man's scope,
With what I most enjoy contented least;
Yet in these thoughts myself almost despising,
Haply I think on thee, and then my state,
Like to the lark at break of day arising
From sullen earth, sings hymns at heaven's gate;
    For thy sweet love remember'd such wealth brings
    That then I scorn to change my state with kings.

"Cheez!" was all I could say. She recited four or five more of the sonnets before I could change the subject. I was the English major and the onetime drama critic and sometime actor at college. But an eavesdropper that day on Flight 78 would most certainly have picked the lady . . . .

CHAPTER THREE

An Education
at Any Cost

The plane to Seattle hit a couple of bumps. Dixy, still wearing the far-away smile, looked quickly about her, reached absent-mindedly for her seat belt, cinched it, and quietly lapsed back into reminiscence. She hadn't even noticed that the stewardess had freshened her Scotch-and-soda with lotsa ice, please.

Since printing needs are not high on the list of essentials for everyday living, the Ray family was laid low by the Depression of the early 1930's. Alvis Ray was too proud to go on relief, but he and Frances managed to squeak by without endangering themselves and the children. For Dixy it was simply another instance — in a lifetime of such instances — in which the odds seemed to be stacked against her. Because she had been "the brain" in her class, Mills College had beckoned with a merit scholarship, which she was able to renew each year at the college with grades that won her a Phi Beta Kappa key at graduation. But a scholarship wasn't enough to make ends meet in the high-cost Oakland-San Francisco area.

With nothing coming from home, Dixy had to make every penny count.

"The combination of a milieu from which I wanted to escape and a fist-clenching decision to show 'em I could do something without their help made a person study. Now I had another reason: To get away from the terrible economic stress back home that permeated and controlled every facet of life. When you work at college, not for spending money but because you may not stay in school if you don't, you grit your teeth and do a lot of things and expend plenty of sweat and muscle you might not have to under ordinary circumstances. I missed a lot of sleep in those days, but never a class."

Each of the four years at Mills was a case of "the horse and the carrot stick" for Dixy. She was never in the black at the end of the academic year, but with her tested capability to make her own way, she always managed to pay her debts just in time to start another year. When she returns to Mills on occasion for a graduation ceremony or some other celebration, she goes happily and gratefully. The college gave her all the time she needed to pay up.

Camp counseling didn't pay enough, so Dixy had to seek other jobs. She waited on tables, scrubbed floors, served as a janitor and a switchboard operator, tutored, and in fact, became a house-painter to stay in school. Most of the house-painting chores were found in the Tacoma and Puget Sound area. In the summer of 1935 she painted the family home at her father's request, and he contributed the magnificent sum of $100!

"I threw in the garage gratis."

By that time Father Alvis had already discerned from the scholastic reports he'd received from Mills that No. 2 daughter was something special. It didn't warm up his association with Dixy, however. The strain remained.

Mother Ray was a bit more demonstrative, but she, too, maintained a calculated reserve.

"I was never close to Mother either, perhaps because she, too, subscribed to my father's philosophy on punishment and family austerity, but I didn't have the severe confrontations with her that had marked my life with Dad. Whatever our association, I have always felt sorry for Mother, and deeply sympathetic toward her for her lot in life. She was something of a long-suffering heroine, with her gentle nature and continuing health problems. She was gracious, well-spoken, and well-informed."

In those early years in which a child looks to receiving comfort and direction from a mother, Dixy found hers much too busy with other babies, with household chores, and with her recurring maladies. There were two or three miscarriages.

"Young people these days don't realize how it was before the pill. Mother had a curious anomaly in her left arm. It was a birth defect which involved the circulation. It had been operated on two or three times when she was a youngster, but the surgery never did much good. The blood circulation seemed to pool in her wrist area and the arteries didn't connect properly to the capillary bed, so she had to wear an elastic bandage from her wrist almost up to her elbow. Whenever she went through childbirth, the arm was always very, very seriously affected. When our No. 4 sister, Juliana, was born, I remember, Mother lay in bed for months with her arm suspended upward. Then, probably as a result of so much child-bearing, she developed a uterine tumor that was removed when Sister No. 5, Alvista, was about five. I think the year was 1930, just before the Depression and my departure for college."

Mother gave them all chores to do. Marion and Dixy, of course, drew most of the important ones, since they were the oldest. Care of Juliana was assigned to Marion, and Alvista, called "Wis" because the younger girls couldn't say "Alvista," became Dixy's responsibility. For that reason Alvista was the only sister to draw close to Dixy in friendship and trust through the years Dixy was away from home. From the time Alvista was born until the age of six, when Dixy left for Mills, Wis was Dixy's constant charge. She and Marion were expected to be home from school within an hour. Dixy fed Wis, played with her, took her almost everywhere she went, put her to bed in the evening, and got her up and dressed her in the morning. Wis was actually Dixy's only emotional tie to the family.

"Except for her I wasn't really close to any of the other members of the family in those days. Marion and I have in recent years found a warm, close relationship we never knew before, but I have to confess I felt I was different and that I had a different calling when I was a youngster. Leaving home and going to college was actually a relief, the opening of a door I'd never opened. It was not with any sense of regret that I cut the family ties at all, and once I left, I never returned, except for brief visits at vacation time and for the Christmas holidays."

Although she never returned to live at the family home in Tacoma, Dixy went back to the Puget Sound area often, primarily to visit seaside camping grounds. How she loved the sea and the creatures that lived in it! The family had often visited a campsite it owned on Fox Island about a mile south of the land on which

Dixy and Marion have their homes today and in which all the sisters have a stake. They call it a farm, but Dixy calls it Paradise. The good times Dixy does remember with the family occurred for the most part on the trips to the campsite south of the island farm. It was there, after she left for Mills, that Dixy would spend most summertimes. And it was undoubtedly there that the idea first came to Dixy that she might consider making marine biology her life study. As a child, she had spent many hours, usually alone, on the shores of Puget Sound at Commencement Bay, just a half mile from home. Her favorite spots were down by the docks, where she would toss a homemade fishing pole and gear into the water and bring in flounder and sole. She would explore deep into the sandy beach. It was there she made her first explorations of the thousands of tiny creatures she would later learn to know so well. But in her early years it "was just fun."

However, it remained for a gentle Scot named Alexander Pringle Jameson to coax her into a lifetime career in marine biology. When she entered Mills, Dixy had no fixed notions about a career, although she loved the sea. She might easily have gone into English literature or history, if someone like Dr. Jameson had resided in those departments.

"He was a most remarkable man, not only a gentleman of the highest order but a truly inspired scholar. Dr. Jameson was trained in the classic tradition, as only the Scottish schools can do it. Their educational system is infinitely better than England's, and their universities are better than Oxford and Cambridge together. Dr. Jameson was a product of the universities of Edinburgh and Aberdeen, and he was one of the most ingenious, capable scholars I have ever known. It was he who made a marine biologist out of me. I have absolutely no regrets over my choice; I have enjoyed it thoroughly, and it has opened up for me a world I might never have seen otherwise. It is wonderful to love what you are doing and make a living at it at the same time. On reflection I realize it was something my father was never able to do."

Working with Dr. Jameson proved to be one of "the great joys of my life." With his guidance and firm judgment, it was no surprise that his prize pupil would lead her class in honors at Mills, take a Master's there, then go on to Stanford a few years later, "when I had managed to save enough money to become a student again in search of that elusive doctorate."

After deciding upon a career in the marine sciences, Dixy set her sights on research at or near the sea. Teaching had not entered her mind. In fact, she had shoved such an idea aside.

In a moment of deep reflection and intimate revelation, she said: "When I entered college, I wasn't sure what I would be able to do to earn a living, because I had been work-oriented from the beginning. As a young college student, I was not unaware that Nature had endowed me in a variety of ways. I had a strong constitution and a reasonable amount of muscular strength and endurance. (Dixy had been a long-distance swimmer of championship caliber as a young girl and had been the youngest girl — 12 — to climb the summit of Mount Rainier.)

"I have what I hope is a reasonably decent memory and brain, and I determined to get my brain disciplined. On the other hand, Nature did not endow me with all those things that turn young men's heads. I did not have to worry about brushing off suitors, and, in any event, I think that because of the influence of my father, I was determined I would never become dependent upon anyone at any time."

Dixy's harsh estimate of her physical characteristics, particularly in her high school and college years, has been a surprise to her sisters and to close friends. Sister Jean was the family "dream boat," but Dixy was not unattractive. Her sisters have described her as strong and stocky but never unprepossessing. Marion and Alvista recalled at least two or three budding romances Dixy didn't permit to bloom "because there was still so much to do on the way to a career." Just before any of them became serious, she would turn them off abruptly. Perhaps the most serious chapter came in her early years on the faculty of the University of Washington but that failed to reach fruition, and that time, colleagues related, it was not she who terminated it.

She once said to me in almost embarrassed tones that she never considered marital life because "I'm too ugly." It was the only time I had ever tried scolding her. Of course, it didn't work, but I told her I had seen many photos of her as a child, a teen-ager, a college student, and a teacher, and I thought she was rather good-looking.

In speeches she has sometimes referred to herself as stocky or plump or muscular or short or matronly, but in fact she has been none of these. What some may have regarded as stockiness or plumpness is instead a powerful physique that came from early chores dictated by her father and mother, years of swimming daily in calm and rough waters, hiking over some of the most difficult terrain in America, and mountain climbing in the Cascades, the Olympics, Mount Rainier, and mountain ranges overseas. She has never been afraid of work; it shows in her strong frame. Despite her physique, there is no question that Dixy Lee Ray is feminine. If she had chosen, I'm sure she would have made an exceptional wife and mother. Whatever the reasons, she has never permitted anyone to probe more than surface-deep. And therein may lie another character study worthy of an O'Neill or an Ibsen.

Continuing her explanation of what brought her to a teaching career, Dixy said: "Although I've had many close and very good men friends, the idea of marriage has never been attractive to me. There are too many things to do, places to go. So I've always been career-oriented. In high school for a time I seriously thought about medicine and becoming a doctor. Those were the days when a 'hen' medico was about as scarce as hen's teeth. You have to have a certain pragmatism anyhow. You have to come to terms with what you can do in a real world. It's something I had to face up to, and I had to do it when I was quite young. So, while I didn't know for certain what I might do — and I even thought for a while of exploiting my interest and talent as a puppeteer — I actually did make one vow: *never* teach. I made that vow when I entered college."

As the undergraduate years moved along, Dixy was both a doer and a plodder. She compiled a remarkable grade average on one hand, and she worked every nonschool hour to make sure she would never have to drop out. She was a product of the NYA, the National Youth Authority, which made it possible for her to earn 50 cents an hour doing a variety of jobs, from marking papers and cleaning laboratories to tutoring and preparing experiments. In her junior year she was employed as a laboratory assistant, and in her senior year she was awarded one of two teaching assistantships. It was in her senior year that Dr. Jameson stared at her for a moment, as if he had been pondering a momentous question, then proved it by asking:

"Now, Miss Ray, just what are you going to do when you graduate?"

She was tongue-tied. She hadn't made a decision. He didn't wait.

"Have you thought about teaching?"

She began to say: "Gad, that's the one thing . . ." But she checked it, too late. He understood.

"Tut! Tut!" It was the wickedest expression Dr. Jameson ever used, and he used it often. He proceeded to lecture Dixy on her pluses and minuses. He had watched her as a student, and he had watched her as a teaching assistant and tutor. She was, he said, eminently suited to teach. Yes, that was her special gift. If Dixy had not had so much admiration and respect for Dr. Jameson, she might have waved off his advice. But she didn't. She couldn't. After all, he was the wisest man she had ever known.

The Scottish gentleman was tall and spare. He had a sharply pointed nose — not the Ichabod Crane type of physiognomy, like a New Englander, but the high cheekbones, slimly pointed nose, and rather stern face that is typical of the Northern Scots. Dixy may have been somewhat prejudiced in his favor because she herself could trace much of her ancestry back to Scotland.

"Dr. Jameson was a naturalist of the old school, and while I have had lots of experimental training and have done considerable laboratory and experimental work, my heart is in the broad ecological picture. However, people who now call themselves ecologists would not claim me at all, but I scorn them because most of them can't tell one species from another. They don't know the difference between a moth and a butterfly.

"My old Scottish teacher taught me a lesson I have never forgotten. If I had read it or heard it from someone else, it might not have made any impression at all. But coming from him, it was immediately permanent and meaningful to me. I was dissecting a clam in the laboratory one day. It is not an easy animal to dissect, and I was not doing a very good job. He looked at what I had done for a moment, said 'Tut! Tut!' and frowned. I knew immediately, of course, that he didn't think much of what I was doing. I looked up at him, grimaced, and said weakly:

"'My scalpel is dull.'

"He looked at me, tried an unwilling smile, and answered: 'A poor workman blames his tools.' He turned and walked away. Now, I had heard that old saw many times in my life, but somehow it sounded original coming from him. And it hit its mark. He did it without raising his voice and without a trace of anger. It was one of many lessons I learned from him. In fact, I can trace most of my beliefs in science today — and in many practical, everyday issues — to the influence of Dr. Jameson. He was the gentlest, most understanding, and most humane man I ever met. Yet it was from him that I learned one of the most essential truths on earth: Nature is cruel, not kind. That fact is hard for some people to reconcile. Too many biologists — and other scientists, too — become sloppy sentimentalists because they refuse to accept that truth. They love life, they say, and therefore it cannot be cruel. That's sophomoric. Everything dies. Some things don't have a chance. It is a truth that many persons who call themselves environmentalists or conservationists have refused to recognize. Because of it, they have taken many unrealistic positions in defiance of Nature, and the result has been chaos, billions of valuable dollars wasted, and a serious setback to the American economy. I have been an environmentalist most of my life, but science and my long experience with the sea and the outdoors have taught me that Nature may smile at times but she rules the earth with a terrible fury. They have also taught me that man-kind can make bargains with Nature and use her resources — as it must — provided it uses caution and good sense. The radical environmentalists among us are so afraid of Nature that they would have us surrender to her. That's as ridiculous and unreal as action to plunder the earth with total abandon."

It was Dr. Jameson who was most responsible for Dixy's steadfast philosophy, in the face of the usually cruel and vengeful criticism by Ralph Nader and others, that insisted the 4 billion inhabitants of the earth must balance conservation with intelli-gent use of natural resources — or risk vanishing from the planet.

Dr. Jameson's advice was to use Nature as far as she would permit, "but don't try changing her into a blushing bride or the village idiot."

It was 1937, a year of Recession, that threw a wrench into the national economy just as it seemed the miseries of the worst Depression in history would finally disappear. In the middle of it, Dixy received her Bachelor of Science degree from Mills with top honors — but no promise of a job. Dr. Jameson had taken her aside earlier before the final quarter:

"I've been watching you closely for two years now. May I give you a bit of advice? Get your teaching credentials right away because you will have a much better chance finding work. It will also give you a chance to think about going on with your studies at graduate school."

With Dr. Jameson's help and a few well-chosen words to his colleagues in the Education Department, Dixy was given the one course she needed in order to qualify for the additional year of training required to obtain credentials.

The special course?

"It was the history of public-school education in the U.S. And it was a straight history course. I'll never forget the first lecture. It was about the earliest grammar schools in Boston and the way in which the American pioneers took care of the education of their young. Do you know what the first payment was for a public school teacher? One load of manure! Maybe it was symbolic. Anyway, I enjoyed it. The course, I mean."

"With a line like that, you could make almost any case you chose, regardless of which side of an argument you were on."

With her bachelor's degree in one hand and a paper stating she had completed the education-history course in the other, she gave up her summer to return to Mills. Dixy completed all requirements in a year — and simultaneously fulfilled requirements for a Master's degree in zoology. It was a phenomenal achievement, but Dr. Jameson, who cleared the way for it to happen, never doubted she could do both. The Dixy Lee Ray eyeballs and physique took a beating that year, but her rigorous early life had prepared her for such punishment.

In 1938 the University of California had graduated about 300 students in education and Mills about two dozen. Thanks to her grades, Dixy was one of only nine hired to teach in the Oakland-San Francisco area from the new crop.

Dixy was assigned to Oakland High School, where she taught four years before making enough money to go to Stanford for her Ph.D. in marine biology. Before starting at the high school, however, she promised herself a change of pace and some relaxation. The concentrated final year at Mills had taken much out of her. She was lucky to find a teacher who would let her live in her home for the summer in return for chores. As a result, Dixy found herself taking advantage of her experience: She painted the teacher's wooden fence, gardened, and did other jobs in and around the house. It was a quiet, restful summer, just what she needed.

Late in August Dixy went to her new high school for pre-semester meetings of teachers, new and old. It was there for the first time that she encountered a problem she had been warned about. The Oakland school system seemed to have no young teachers because it insisted on hiring only long-experienced hands. The average age of teachers was somewhere between 50 and 55. When she appeared in the principal's office for assignment, a secretary told her to see her counselor, believing her to be a student. And when Dixy finally made it to her first meeting of teachers, she saw only stony, wrinkled faces. The single exception was the biology teacher under whom she had done her practice teaching the year before. She had given Dixy high marks and had recognized her potential. The new intruder would soon discover the reason for the cold reception. In the faculty cafeteria the first week, she was having lunch with a friend when an elderly teacher one table away stood up and glared at Dixy.

"She was one of those women," Dixy said, "who had a shelf for a chest. She grabbed a tray as she sized me up and down. Then she said: 'In my day no one started teaching in the Oakland school system before she had proved herself by teaching in other districts. All I can say is that when you don't do that, you'll never succeed.'"

Dixy taught biology and a few other courses but the emphasis was on biology. Dr. Jameson had taught her to believe that humans learned biology from life and from living things, not textbooks, but she soon discovered otherwise at Oakland High School. The school's technique was to read ten pages and answer questions at the end of the chapter. It was the crux of a dispute Dixy would be involved in throughout her teaching career at the University of Washington and in the governor's office, as well, when trying to determine educational policy. She has been a lifelong devotee of the "show me" school of teaching, in which the teacher and the student work out problems with hands and heads in the classroom, not through trying to memorize the pages of a textbook. Dixy was not an enemy of textbooks. She simply believed every classroom should be, in effect, a learning laboratory and that textbooks should be supplementary tools.

At Oakland High School Dixy, the raw recruit, took things into her own hands, typical of her in years to come. The biology rooms had laboratory equipment and lab space. A small budget existed for supplies and specimens, but nobody used it. As soon as she found out about it, she began making use of it and scheduling regular lab sessions.

"At college I had been accustomed to collecting my own

specimens, so we did everything. We got ourselves an aquarium, rat colonies, varieties of snakes, many kinds of worms, and all the types of marine animals we could find. We did physiological experiments. I put a lot of time into developing simple equipment the students could make and then use themselves for experiments, instead of looking for the fancy things we couldn't afford to buy anyway. At least the biology rooms had good microscopes, although I was mortified to learn that nobody in the school knew how to use them.

"One day the senior biology teacher came over with a microscope and some specimens she wanted to show her class. Instead of having the students do the preparation, she had decided to put the microscope at her desk and invite the students up one at a time to take a look at what she herself had manipulated. She pointed to the microscope and asked:

"'Which one is the high-powered lens? Is it this little one or is it this big one?'

"That was the Oakland public-school system in 1939, and I'm afraid it was typical, not the exception, in America."

Another teacher across the hall made it a habit to walk to Dixy's room as classes changed and stand at the doorway watching, arms folded. Dixy would be whipping through materials and equipment, getting experiments ready for the next class. She had to hurry because the school had not as yet introduced double periods for laboratory classes and very little time was available for the many tasks she had prepared. As the students walked in, the intruder from across the hall would shake her head and purse her lips:

"You'll never last."

It was typical of the kind of resentment Dixy found in 95 percent of the teachers — all of them so deeply brainwashed by unimaginative administrators and so fearful of losing their jobs that they were locked into mediocrity and doomed to dullness. In no time at all, Dixy became a heroine and an idol to her students, who for the first time were being challenged to think and use their hands and bodies, instead of their posteriors alone. With Miss Ray igniting things, they were off their duffs and doing things themselves. As her popularity with her students grew magically, her stock with other teachers hit bottom. It was inevitable; Dixy was training for bouts like it throughout her life.

"With attitudes like that of the teacher across the hall, I just dug in and stuck my chin out a bit farther. Find another job? Hell, no. I just made up my mind I was going to teach in that goddamn school until I had tenure, and when everybody knew I had tenure, I was going to get the hell out. You had to have three years of teaching there; if you were hired for the fourth year, presto, you had tenure. That's exactly what I did. It worked out just fine. By the time I had four years in, I had enough money to go to graduate school for my Ph.D. in biology anyway."

It might have taken Dixy much less than four years to save the money she needed if it hadn't been for her propensity for helping others. This time the help went to her sister Jean, who had decided to become a nurse. She moved in with Dixy at Dixy's request, and the childhood battles were put aside. Dixy contributed funds, food, and board to her sister's training, but she never complained. And she never got it back. Jean's goal had been medical school, but Dixy didn't have nearly enough to go that far. Jean settled for a nursing career for the time being.

All went well at first. The two sisters buried the hatchet and managed to have some fun together. But the inevitable happened. Dixy won't talk about it, but Marion explained:

"Jean got a little wild. She was very attractive and very much interested in men. While Dixy was hitting the books to gain entry to Stanford and also keep up with her chores at Oakland High School, Jean began collecting boyfriends. By the time Dixy was ready to resign from the Oakland school system and enroll at the Stanford Graduate School and Jean had her nursing certificate, the uneasy peace had dissolved. Dixy didn't mind picking up the tab, but when Jean secretly married a student Dixy had recognized as a 'pain in the butt' who bragged about being things he wasn't, the early bitterness returned. Jean had a part-time job in Berkeley, but it was Dixy who pulled her through. And when Jean turned all her attention and whatever funds she had toward the new bridegroom, Dixy was crushed and angry."

One of the interesting sidelights to Dixy's character is a paradoxical view of human behavior. As a worldly, broadly acclaimed woman of science, she is tolerant of all ideas and practices; with regard to the difference in people's race, color, or creed she is the most unprejudiced person I know. But she is death to "hanky-panky," her single hangup in society.

"When people should be on the job and they are working for

me, I will not put up with any fooling around," she said soon after firing a young man and a young woman on her office staff who had been silly enough to start petting behind an office door.

Frankly, I've always been proud of that one Victorian strand in Dixy. Why shouldn't she be the last frontier against hanky-pankyism? The rest of us seem to have copped out on the subject of old-fashioned morals. It is a mark of the Dixy Lee Ray character that she'll stick to what she thinks, no matter how many friends or votes it costs her. Tell her that Mr. Slick has been accused of robbing the public treasury, and she's likely to say, "Maybe so, but I'll believe it when I see the evidence or a jury says he's guilty." But tell her that Mr. Slick, who has been accused of robbing the public treasury, has been shacking up with his two secretaries while poor Mrs. Slick is at home taking care of the 12 kids, and Dixy might very well say, "Why the dirty bum! He ought to be drawn and quartered. Mrs. Slick would be well rid of him."

Once at Stanford and the pleasant world of Pacific Grove, the world changed for Dixy. She was always happiest when she was researching, testing, experimenting, finding things out for herself, and helping others find things out, too. Dixy had to work to sustain herself, but now it was nearly a lark compared with the four rough years in Oakland.

Nevertheless, the sometimes bitter experiences in Oakland helped shape the character of Dixy Lee Ray. She was destined for a life of controversy, and in fact, she seemed to thrive on it.

Many years later a columnist who knew little about her asked: "Why is it that wherever she goes and whatever she does, tempers get ruffled, people start taking sides, and resignations or firings increase? Frankly, I think she's just a troublemaker."

He was on the mark, but he should have done some research to follow up his hunch. For Dixy, someone with a smirk and arms folded across the chest would always be standing at the door, chiding her for daring to buck the status quo and do things her own way. And, whether it was the college classroom, the Pacific Science Center, the National Science Foundation, the U.S. Atomic Energy Commission, the State Department, or the governor's office, she would do what she thought was right, not what was convenient or profitable.

I doubt whether anyone in American public life has had more personal integrity.

CHAPTER FOUR

The Rediscovery of Marion Ray

And if those of you on the right side of the aircraft would look out," the pilot was droning, "you will see the Mississippi River. Those on the left . . ." Dixy never heard a word. Her mind was on Puget Sound, Tacoma, and Fox Island.

To herself she was saying, "I'll get to spend some time with Marion and Gordy before I go back, and then we'll see about the farm . . ."

No one understands Dixy Lee Ray better nor loves her more than her older sister, Marion Ray Reid, who combines innate kindness and gentleness with a general's firmness and determination and a philosopher's insistence on the truth. When she and Dixy were growing up in Tacoma, they were thrown together often and they got along well, but they were so different in temperament and personality that they were never close. It remained for their gray-haired years to bring them together and to discover each other.

When Gordon Reid, Marion's husband, died just before Christmas, 1974, it was as much a blow to Dixy as it was to Marion. When Gordon retired from the motel industry in California a few years earlier, Dixy asked Marion and Gordy to move to Fox Island to live alongside her in a specially built home. They agreed, and from that time on all three were the closest of friends. Marion and Gordy were good for Dixy; they always leveled with her, even when it hurt. And Dixy reveled in their honesty.

"None of that old nicey-nice bullshit for us," the usually genteel and soft-spoken Marion would say. And Gordy usually went her one better.

Marion and Gordy minced no words with Dixy, and the marine biologist who was headed for important pastures loved it because she desperately needed their friendship and their presence. She may have been a loner at times, but, like her father, she was a gregarious person and thrived on "company." In some ways Marion is the stronger of the two; she has better control of her temper and is somewhat calmer and more patient in a critical situation. Also, she knows how to live alone. Someone knowing the sisters superficially might draw just the reverse impression.

At any rate, no one has a clearer, more discerning, and more honest view of Dixy than big sister Marion, older by two years. Whereas Alvista, the youngest sister, provides the most loving look at her famous onetime baby-sitter, Marion tells it like it is, not only about Dixy but about the family and everyone else. Her impressions of Father and Mother Ray, the sisters, and the early years differ markedly from Dixy's and Alvista's at each end of the family spectrum. And her impressions are the most humorous and salty of all:

"In a family of five girls there was, of course, quite a span in ages. So, the first year I went away to college, my mother had the distinction of having a child in kindergarten, one in grammar school, a third in junior high school, a fourth in high school, and me in college. Just think of all the PTA's she was supposed to join, or Mother's Clubs, or whatever the high school and college equivalents are. The poor woman."

Marion was almost as happy to leave home for college as Dixy was, but she had to bide her time:

"I spent my first year at the University of Puget Sound in Tacoma, and that almost doesn't count because I lived at home. You can imagine trying to study in a two-bedroom house with one bathroom and seven people vying for the utilities. It was a little cramped. Hell, no, it wasn't; it was downright impossible! One closet and a hall. Think of what we had to go through to find anything in a closet holding the belongings of seven people! That's the way it was all through our early lives.

"We had to put pegs up in the hall to take care of clothes, household equipment, and whatever. At one time I remember, we had a baby sleeping in a basket in the living room, another in a crib in the dining room, and a third on a canvas cot in my parents' bedroom. To get more space, Dad built a big front porch and put a big striped canvas awning over half of it. There was an alcove with a small window in it leading out to the porch, and we used that a lot. Just inside was our piano, a victrola, and an early homemade, Marconi-style, battery-operated radio. We helped Dad make the radio. All of this was in the alcove we called our music room.

"One summer we climbed out the window on a little step-stool to makeshift beds on the porch. With conditions what they were inside, Dad decided we ought to try it out in the winter, too. Dixy and I were both deep into Girl Scouting, and we cheered the news. So, when summer ended, Dixy and I continued sleeping on the canvas-covered porch. It was a great big old double bed, and we had plenty of blankets. We woke up several mornings to find snow coming in under the porch railing. It just made us more anxious to spend our evenings out there. Sometimes the little ones would join us, and there was so much heat from the four or five bodies in that big bed that nobody complained of the cold. I think we stayed out there three winters."

Under such crowded conditions it was inevitable that childhood illnesses were many and widespread. When one got the measles, it made the rounds. Ditto with chickenpox, rubella, and mumps. They shared everything.

What was the early life like?

"It was a very normal, middle-class American life," Marion said. "We were above poverty and below affluence. Mother and Dad couldn't afford extra music lessons or dancing lessons or the symphony or the opera. In fact, we didn't get to go to the ballgames until we were juniors and seniors in high school. We didn't have enough money. We did go to Girl Scout meetings. To Sunday school. To young people's meetings. To skating parties, Halloween parties, and birthday parties. We went on hikes and picnics and to the beach, and I think we always had a helluvagood time. It was a good life."

In that day, Marion added, "people had big, round dining-room tables and every time you went to visit them and looked around the table, there was another baby sitting in still another highchair. And the table kept getting bigger and bigger."

Marion was frequently called upon, as the oldest sister, to set an example for the rest of the brood.

"Once a week we'd have a great big thick cut of beef, a pretty deluxe cut that served everybody. We had lots of mashed potatoes and beans and carrots, and I was supposed to eat them because then all my younger sisters would eat them if I would just smile and eat my carrots and beans. Yccccctth! It took me 20 years after I left home to learn to like carrots and beans once again. Dixy's not too hot in the vegetable-eating category either, even today. I'll tell you about another thing that's on both our no-no lists. It's horseradish. I don't even know why we hate it; we never had it at home in all the years we lived together. But when it comes to mashed potatoes and gravy, that's when Dixy and I ask to leave the room. After having them time and again as kids, we never wanted to see potatoes and gravy again.

"Pity my poor sister, please, and tell the reporters out there to go easy on her now that she's governor. Can you imagine how many times she has had to stare at potatoes and gravy — and carrots and beans — on the political lunch and dinner circuit? Her poor old stomach should get a purple star with many oakleaf clusters."

Because of Mother's frequent illnesses, Marion and Dixy shared all the household chores, including ironing Dad's shirts, doing the laundry and the cooking (both are gourmet cooks today) — and fixing the plumbing and doing other fix-it jobs in the house. They shared everything, but there were differences:

"I loved to sew," Marion said, "but Dixy didn't. She hated it. And her hurry-up methods didn't help me at all. She'd shove clothes through the washer and wringer, and buttons and seams would pop all over the place. But she wouldn't repair her damage. That was left to me. We got along, all right, but we had many a knockdown, hair-pulling, punching scrap over whose turn it was to take out the garbage, do the dishes, or scrub the floors. Dixy could be a tiger, and she was strong. She learned to snap a wet dish towel like Frank Beatty whipping his lions and tigers into place. Boy, that could hurt, and she was an expert at it."

Before their teens Marion and Dixy acquired very different likes and dislikes, mostly because Marion had been assigned as "assistant Mother" and Dixy as "assistant Father," with all the chores — and switchings — that went with it. In consequence, Marion liked to play with dolls and help manage the household, while Dixy ran outdoors at every opportunity.

"At first I used to bring Dixy into my house-playing, but pretty soon she got tired of that and went out looking for a baseball or football game with the boys and other girls like her. About the time I was about 11 and she was 9, it suddenly occurred to me that she just wasn't going to be like me. I was hurt, really hurt. It seemed really crazy to me to have this nice, close younger sister and not be able to play house with dolls together and all those other nice things little girls are supposed to do. It was quite a blow to me. After that we seemed to go our own way, even though we still did some things together."

Among the things they did together at high school was participate in the debate club, library activities, speaker's club, and every sport open to girls. Dixy excelled in every sport she tried, while Marion usually made the second team. Dixy also excelled in school, managing A's all the way through, and studying hard. She worked at it, and it came easy to her, Marion observed, while she had to sweat twice as hard for passable-to-good grades. Was there a secret to Dixy's success in school work?

"Sure," said Marion. "Early in life Dixy learned something I wish I had learned. If she encountered something in which she did poorly, she just gave it up and quit doing it. That's how she operated at home, too. She detested sewing, so she gave it up. Her idea of sewing to this day is to use two safety pins and go on to the next job. My idea of doing anything in mathematics, in which she is superior, by the way, is to write a speech in tribute to the computer."

Both sisters have another talent in common. Each is an exceptional speaker (as Dad was before them). Dixy discovered that the ability to speak was a requisite when she arrived to enter Mills. Marion majored in speech and sociology when she attended the University of Redlands after putting in freshman time at the University of Puget Sound in Tacoma.

Marion tends to downgrade her ability. She won a scholarship to Redlands and did well there scholastically. She and Dixy had been exemplary Scout leaders in the Tacoma area, and they continued their work with young people long afterward. Dixy believes Marion is "the best damned organizer of young people — or old people, for that matter — in the world." For that reason Dixy asked her to take on many organizational chores after the election of 1976, including management of the Governor's Mansion and numerous activities involving exchanges with foreign nations. Marion, for many years an administrative hand to doctors, was assigned by her sister to the Washington State Medical

Disciplinary Board as the lay member. At first, a few eyebrows in the press were raised, but when her background was scanned, all traces of doubt vanished.

Some of Marion's recollections of her father differ somewhat from Dixy's.

"Dad did not discourage us from going to college, but he threw it out as a threat and a challenge. 'There's no sense in sending women to college,' he'd say in his most chauvinistic tones. 'The only thing they'll do is get married. Why educate women? They are just going to have babies anyway.' At the same time he would say conflicting things like, 'Well, if you've got grades that are good, you ought to do something with them.'

"He knew I wanted to be a nurse, so he said, 'What do you want to do that for? You may as well be a doctor. Why go around scrubbing floors, cleaning up somebody else's vomit? Be a doctor. Be the best.' He didn't know I lost my interest in nursing when I discovered they spent most of their time changing bedpans, mopping up the rear, so to speak, and taking a lot of guff from doctors and other superior nurses. On the other hand, we didn't have near enough money for me to go to medical school, so that was that.

"Dixy should appreciate the fact that, even though she and Dad didn't get along, he came to recognize her great talent. He used to say to Mother with me listening: 'She doesn't have the brains to go to school. The only reason she wants to go is to study boyology. Now, Dixy, she knows biology, and she should go to school.' So, as you can see, both Dixy and I had to get out and prove something to ourselves and to Dad. I think we both succeeded, but he wasn't around long enough to savor it with us."

Marion, who is the mother of three and has several grandchildren, said she believes Dixy would have been a much happier person if she had known the pleasures, the enrichment, and even the heartaches that can come from having a family. She also recognizes that it never happened because of the bitterness of Dixy's experiences at home and her sharp conflicts with her father. Nevertheless, she had the opportunities.

"In high school," Marion said, "she had a romance going and there was even an engagement — no big engagement party, just the exchange of baby rings and that sort of thing. I remember there was quite a to-do about it at home, a real family blowup, and Dixy wound up crawling out a window to get away — she went off alone at night some place to brood. Then, I got mad at her for some reason and I tattled that she had run away. She hadn't run away; she had just rebelled and disappeared to show her anger and frustration. On another occasion Dad saw Dixy and the same boy on a street corner and he exploded. She tried to tell him they had just been walking home from the library, but he wasn't listening to any explanations. There were other similar episodes at Stanford and the University of Washington, but nothing ever came of them. One was quite serious, and I believe she was burned badly. But none of us ever learned the details, and she certainly won't talk about it. She says 'it's nobody's damned business,' and I think she's right."

No one could draw laughter from Dixy quicker than Gordon Reid. He had had 30 years of administrative experience with a California firm, then 12 more operating a motel and restaurant, but he frequently feigned truck driver's language in discussing the Ray sisters. Before a banquet audience honoring Dixy as the "Man" of the year in Seattle for 1973, Reid brought down the house with his explicit stories about "the five broads" with whom he had become entangled.

A dozen years earlier he had said to Dixy before a group of friends: "You're just another damned egghead. Why don't you get out of that classroom and do something else?"

Not long afterward she did "something else." She left the classroom for the Pacific Science Center directorship in Seattle, the television studios, and eventually national notoriety in the federal government and the top job in her home state. One could say she certainly listened to Gordy.

But it is still Marion who seems to have penetrated the Dixy psyche deepest and read her character best. For example:

"You can't make quick conclusions about Dixy. Just about the time you think she reacts this way, she does something to convince you that, no, by golly, it's that way. By way of explanation, she gives many persons the impression she's a real loner, not interested in being in crowds. But I've known her to jump into her car around holiday time, pick up several friends or Wis and a niece or nephew somewhere, and drive to the home of a relative for a few days. I know. That home was very frequently ours. This so-called loner, I think, is more in need of friends than most people I know.

"Similarly, she sometimes shows impatience with children,

particularly in recent years. Well, that's true; she has often shown impatience with children — but the reverse is true, too. You should have seen her with the large brood of children that often descends upon her at the Mansion. If she has affairs of state off her mind, she can be a most compassionate grandma-type. Also, no one can ding her over her relationships through the years with young people of high-school and college age. She has knocked herself out for them — and she has never asked recognition for it. That's the wonderful thing about her.

"Dixy has not only helped her sisters and nieces and nephews with jobs and even money. She has also parted with her own scarce cash to get bright, needy young people through school. I wish somebody would collect notes about her many philanthropic actions. Her colleagues on the faculty of the University of Washington know about them. I know she won't ever mention them."

Obviously, Marion is as proud as she can be critical of her younger sister. With exceptional frankness she said:

"She has come full circle in many ways. I know she may not realize it, but she sounds more like Dad every day. It's not a new development. When I was married many years ago, I'll never forget what she told me: 'Well, your college experience was wasted, wasn't it? What are you going to do with your training now? I've come to recognize that marriage is the right way for those who want it because it's a necessity to sustain the American home and family. So, I guess marriage can be fine, especially for you.' At that moment I could have wrung her neck. Today Dixy believes the family unit is the most important factor in our society, but I'll bet she also still believes nobody should waste college training. Some of her conservatism and strait-laced beliefs come from Dad, too. And I think that's fine. It does make you wonder, though, doesn't it?"

CHAPTER FIVE

Life
With the
Young Turks

W e have begun our descent into the Seattle area," the muffled voice was saying, "and we should be on the ground at the Seattle-Tacoma Airport in about 20 minutes."

Dixy awoke from her reverie with a jolt at the sound of "Seattle-Tacoma Airport." Home, almost home, she was thinking . . . but she wouldn't be here too long this time. How long would she have to stay away?

For the first time she had a clammy feeling, and it had nothing to do with the three Scotch-and-sodas or the bumpy air over the Cascades. Had she done the right thing? She would miss Puget Sound and the Fox Island farm so much, so very much. And what would happen to the Pacific Science Center, which she had virtually created with her own hands — and sometimes her own pocketbook — and kept alive at great sacrifice? Then there were the incomparable friends at Friday Harbor in the San Juan Islands and the University of Washington and Fox Island — and particularly the "young Turks" at the university. Well, they weren't so young any more, but they were still full of vinegar and imagination, and she loved them all.

The early years came back to her. At Stanford and the nearby Hopkins Marine Station she had done the research and writing and reading necessary for her doctorate in biology. They had been two of the most pleasant and hard-working years of her

50

life. She taught on the side to help her get through and she met many of the greatest minds in the world in zoology and biology. Tragedy forced a change in target when she was halfway through; her principal mentor had been Tage Skogsberg, internationally distinguished invertebrate zoologist, and the "drawing card" that had attracted her to Stanford. His death while on a special mission for the military in the Second World War forced her to shift from her first choice of invertebrate zoology to fish morphology, primarily because Skogsberg was the only invertebrate zoologist on the graduate-school faculty. It is also possible that continued work with Skogsberg would have resulted in a teaching assignment in California or a marine-science installation far away from the Pacific Northwest. As it was, Dixy let it be known quickly upon adding the prefix "Dr." to her name that she wanted to return to Puget Sound to teach or conduct research.

The call was not long in coming. Among the institutions to which she had sent an application was the University of Washington in Seattle — and Seattle was just 30 miles north of her home town of Tacoma and, of course, also on her "mare nostrum," Puget Sound. The opening was for a teacher in invertebrate biology, her first choice, but her switch to morphology had muddied up the waters of employment.

It was advice to the faculty committee by Dr. Arthur Martin, who was to become a lifelong friend, that eventually swung the necessary votes to Dixy. He acknowledged Dixy had steered far "off course" from invertebrate zoology in getting her doctorate, but he pointed to her exceptional work earlier in her studies with the illustrious Skogsberg and finally cinched his argument with a reference to C. B. van Niel. Dr. van Niel, one of Stanford's most celebrated faculty members, was frequently listed among Nobel candidates. The widely acclaimed microbiologist had written to his friend, Martin, to tell him about the young Puget Sounder, Dixy Lee Ray, who was one of the most impressive graduate students Stanford marine scientists had seen in a long time. He added he thought Dixy was certain to be one of the finest teachers on the Washington roster. What a prophet he was!

When she arrived in the fall of 1945 for her first classes, some of her enthusiasm fell through the cracks of the old floors of the building that housed Zoology on the first two floors and Botany on the third and fourth. Although it was one of those rare cases in which Zoology and Botany were reasonably compatible on a university campus, Dixy soon realized she may have walked into a petrified forest. Both Zoology and Botany were relatively small departments for a major university, but the problem lay in their state of antiquity, not their size. The two department chairmen, who had held the positions for so many years no one could remember when they didn't, seemed to be interested primarily in holding down the budgets for equipment and materials for research to a ridiculous sum. Their reason may have been to impress the many university presidents they had outlived with their frugality, but the result was inadequately prepared students and graduate students.

Both retired about the time Dixy joined the faculty, but unfortunately in the case of Zoology, the new chairman was unequal to the challenge. Soon after Dixy's arrival another newcomer, Dr. Robert Fernald of the University of California at Berkeley, was hired to teach embryology. Their vigorous, fresh outlooks inspired other young members of the faculty to compare notes and meet frequently to seek solutions to Zoology's ailments. And Botany's, too. Now the young Turks included Dixy and Fernald, Martin, and Arthur Whitely, as well as Dr. Daniel "Bud" Stuntz from Botany.

Not long thereafter, Botany was given a new chairman, an imaginative and sensible scholar who began throwing tantrums in the university president's office until he received enough money to buy long-needed microscopes, research equipment, and other materials. But Zoology was not so fortunate. Its new chairman, "a likeable fellow," was content to continue his predecessor's hoary methods and unwillingness to spend money. Before the young Turks made their voices heard, Botany and Zoology each had a budget of $2,000 for the entire year for equipment and materials! What students couldn't find in textbooks they were unable to find anywhere else because of "the mummified condition" of the two departments.

In speaking of the two earlier department chairmen, Bud Stuntz complained: "Those fellows never threw anything away. Little wonder they never bought anything new; there would have been no place to put it. The labs were like junkyards. Disorganized and old. We needed space for teaching. After all, that's the reason we were there. As the revolt began, guarded at first, we began tossing out a lot of junk to make room for the students and the new experiments that were required."

The war ended, and university enrollment boomed. Now, the swing was to the new: "Get with it or get out."

Nevertheless, Zoology hung back. The new chairman refused to make changes in what Stuntz called "the old fossilized zoology, which was the zoology roughly of 1910 and which had persisted until 1940." Other universities had long since made changes, but not Washington. Not yet. How long could it go on this way without losing total credibility in zoology among the universities and colleges of America and the world?

The action that precipitated the urgently needed change of command and a breath of fresh air was initiated by Dixy and Bob Fernald, almost unwittingly. At the end of their first year of teaching, both had expected promotions, which were understood when they were hired because they had come on at low salary levels "for a look." When promotions and salary increases were denied once more by the department chairman after they had completed their second year of teaching, the two put their heads together and submitted their resignations.

Ordinarily, faculty resignations are accepted without fanfare. But this was no ordinary circumstance. Dr. Edwin Guthrie, then acting president and one of the heroes of University of Washington history, noticed a report of the two resignations. He also noticed that within two years Dixy Lee Ray and Robert Fernald had risen to "the top five" in the listing of "best teachers on campus" by the student survey. Guthrie had been the originator and early champion of the student survey of teachers, although he understood it could never be accepted as the lone factor in a judgment of teaching ability. He made inquiries among students and faculty members himself and discovered Dixy and Bob were, indeed, extraordinarily gifted teachers who worked their students hard but had their respect and admiration.

When he investigated the administrative and operational record of the Zoology chairman, Guthrie acted immediately. The chairman was fired and a search for a new chairman ordered. At first the search extended to universities everywhere in the United States and abroad, without success. The years of museum-like operations and unimaginative administration and teaching methods had given the university a zoological wart on its academic spine. Nobody on the outside wanted the job; those on the inside knew the potential, but that didn't help.

Fortunately, the university eventually settled on Martin, and what a shot in the arm he provided! Ironically, an allergy had forced Martin to leave his basic discipline, physiology, and move into a related area. He could no longer conduct the "cat labs" required in physiology because of the allergy, so he had sent out feelers.

On the verge of accepting a position with the University of Iowa, he was called into Guthrie's office and offered the chairmanship of Zoology, where his physiology division once had been before reassignment to the new School of Medicine. And it also meant returning to membership with the "young Turks." He accepted with a wide smile.

Martin never hesitated to gavel the faculty to order and to be firm when he had to be, but he opened every phase of the Zoology Department's existence to scrutiny by the entire faculty.

Dixy and the rest of the Turks were rapturous, and, in consequence, they worked twice as hard. It was both a collective and highly individualistic effort that brought Washington's zoological reputation to the exceptionally high level it now enjoys — a level it should have attained much earlier because of the school's environment and its proximity to Puget Sound, the Pacific Ocean, and the lakes and rivers of the Northwest.

Dixy was one of those rare teachers who was extremely tough on her students in most courses — particularly graduate students — but simultaneously popular because she was gifted in the art of making the difficult sound simple. She wasn't popular with all her students, but her ranking among the top five in the student surveys spoke for itself. Those who disliked her usually did so because she was uncompromising in expecting every student to burn midnight oil and "work his butt off." With her, the opportunity for a college education was so great a gift that she would put up with no backsliding or fooling around. "We're not here for fun and games," she would caution someone who failed to turn in a paper or refused to cooperate in research or a class project.

Dixy and Bob Fernald, the most energetic of the young Turks, were rebels in another respect. They detested and actively opposed the university's "publish or perish" policy, under which promotions, salary increases, and even new appointments were based primarily on the faculty member's ability to publish the results of his research. It was a policy that drew newspapers, public officials, and educators of Washington State into a boiling dispute after the war years. Nobody won the argument, but the university softened its policy and acknowledged it was possible to advance as a savant without publishing a word.

The irony in Dixy's case is that she conducted one of the most successful marine-science symposiums on record at the university and published a book as a result that included her work and reports by many of the internationally acclaimed scientists she drew to the event. She served as editor, as well, for the collection, titled "Marine Boring and Fouling Organisms." Dixy had written other reports on the subject, too, but her interest remained in teaching, not publication for personal aggrandizement. Fernald had similar feelings and had the courage to state them to anyone who would listen. His work at the university's laboratories at Friday Harbor would bring him acclaim, too, but he wasn't interested in compiling library credits.

Dixy's indefatigable work with the tiny invertebrates that destroy piers, docks, seaside buildings, rafts, ships, and anything else that comes into contact with the sea was to contribute to her growing reputation in the national capital and abroad. The Navy became particularly interested in her "unpublished" research. So did the National Science Foundation, which invited her three times to join its staff in Washington, DC, for special research.

"She began to make a name for herself in invertebrate zoology," Martin related. "When he had recommended her several years earlier, van Niel had said she had a green thumb in the laboratory and could raise anything. She had once done an amazing job at Stanford's Hopkins Station with a soil amoeba. In the experiment she had shown with amazing ease how the amoeba ingests the bacteria it feeds upon. Dixy would raise plates of bacteria and grow the cysts of the amoeba, which she had learned to bring out of the dry stages and start cultivating at any time. As the amoebas crawled across the plate, they'd leave a nice, clear area as they ingested all the bacteria in their path. It was an important technique and discovery, and Dixy later wrote a paper on it that most people don't know about — and, proud as she is, she's not going to tell them about it. She has been criticized by some who haven't taken the trouble to find out what her accomplishments are. If they knew her bibliography, they'd understand what she's done."

It was her subsequent interest in "wood digestion" by invertebrates that attracted naval and foundation brass. Once again her success with the experiment stemmed from her talented green thumb. This time she grew the small sea creatures called gribbles — small to the marine biologist but monsters to naval and pier communities. She placed the newborn gribbles in a dish of sea water and added a small block of wood, nothing else. And they lived! They would burrow into the wood and digest it as they went, and Dixy was able to show that these small sea animals actually have the capacity to digest the wood themselves. It was quite a breakthrough for Dixy and the Navy. In addition, Dixy obtained a patent on a substance she developed to treat pilings, docks, all other wood exposed to sea water, and handed over all her findings to the Navy.

It was her gribble study that prompted the Office of Naval Research to ask Dixy to plan the symposium that resulted in the publication of "Marine Boring and Fouling Organisms."

"There is no question," Fernald said, "that Dixy's experiment with gribbles and her technique for treating pilings and other wood saved the Navy millions." Martin and Stuntz agreed. They also believe the research has saved millions more for cities and towns repairing or installing new docks and piers since then on both American coasts.

It was no solace to Dixy to be acclaimed in Naval and marine circles everywhere but at home, where her successful experiments meant nothing to many members of the Zoology faculty. All the opponents would say was that she can't be "very productive if she's not publishing."

Dixy had known male chauvinism before in her life, but for the first time it was sneering at her openly. Martin, Fernald, and Stuntz tried to convince her she should ignore it because it was juvenile jealousy, but she has acknowledged it hurt deeply. Upon her arrival at the University of Washington and for many years thereafter, she was the only female faculty member in Zoology or Botany, and those who could not abide having a mere woman show them what success in teaching and research really is demonstrated their resentment openly. As a result, she accepted eagerly all the invitations that came her way to visit marine-science laboratories in all parts of the world and to take leaves of absence for U.S. Navy and Coast Guard work and National Science Foundation special projects.

Without realizing it, she was playing into the hands of the

chauvinist fringe at the university. Now her detractors could say — and they did, "You see, she isn't really interested in publishing research papers and her students. She wants to be famous."

"I wish all the graduate students she helped could have had a chance to talk to the chauvinists among us," Martin said. "Many of them are successful scientists and teachers today because of Dixy. We had a working arrangement between us, which we kept secret until I could stand the criticism of her no longer just a few years ago. If she had any graduate students who were pressed for money to continue their studies and were in danger of being forced to drop out, she was to talk it over with me, and we would together split the bill and bring the student through. It was to be applied only to those students of merit who had a good chance of making the grade if they could get the necessary funds. I can't tell you how many students Dixy brought to a graduate degree in her work at the school. It was a great many. But generosity was nothing new with her. All her life she was known to put her own cash on the line to help others, even when she didn't have it. I know for a fact that she helped keep the Pacific Science Center alive that way. The agony of all this is that she has never received credit for her kindness, most of all because she refuses to talk about it herself. She'll be angry with me when she reads this."

But that wasn't the only way she helped undergraduate and graduate students. Bud Stuntz amplified:

"I have no doubt that Dixy Lee Ray is one of the very best teachers this or any other university ever had. Her enthusiasm was one of the reasons. She simply couldn't understand how it was possible for a student to show no interest in invertebrates. That feeling communicated itself to her students, perhaps even more than she realized. So the students who attended her classes on invertebrates were captivated by her sometimes humorous lectures — except for those few who were completely insensitive to anything outside their own personal interests or, more to the point, who resented being there because she made them work hard. She has always done that, and it's been an important part of her success as a teacher.

"Sometimes Dixy threw erasers or chalk at someone who was sleeping in class or carrying on a private discussion. And she had remarkable accuracy. Her athletic training was not wasted. But I'll tell you one thing. Nobody fell asleep or yawned on field trips. Dixy Lee Ray's field trips were famous on campus. She not only brought the lessons down to earth — or sea in this case — but she made it a lot of fun. And, best of all, she joined in. Sometimes she cooked. Sometimes she would supply the refreshments, which often included beer. Best of all, the former Girl Scout leader and mountain climber and hiker taught a great number of young people how to get along in the outdoors. She was witty, and she had a sense of humor the kids could understand. One of her favorite admonitions to students on field trips was:

"'Just don't pay any attention to getting wet. The human body has never been known to dissolve in water.'"

Martin and Fernald agreed with Stuntz that Dixy demonstrated special talents in bringing graduate students through. When she gave a graduate a difficult assignment, she didn't hand him a terse charge and leave him to his own devices. She stayed with him until she was sure he understood the task thoroughly and knew precisely how he would proceed with his study and research. And she was available to him whenever he needed her thereafter. She refused to wait until the deadline approached to find out how the student was progressing; by that time it would be too late.

Another Ray success her opponents were determined to ignore was her work in elevating the Friday Harbor laboratories to international significance. Fernald, who was director of the labs from 1958 to 1972, said:

"She played a very important part in getting things back on the road after the Second World War. It was she who drew world attention to studies at Friday Harbor very soon after the war and helped insure its position as a center of marine research. In the war years the university was forced to close the installation, and faculty assigned there retired or went to work at other schools. When Dixy joined the Zoology faculty, she was a most eager addition to the Friday Harbor roster when the labs reopened in 1947. That kind of work was right down her alley."

Fernald gives her the major share of the credit for her fund-raising efforts in Washington, DC, and elsewhere. Because she knew so many persons in key administrative roles at federal and private science-oriented agencies, she was able to swing the help the Friday Harbor labs needed. Her efforts paid off principally in a $1 million grant from the National Science Foundation and the gift of 400 additional acres of land by the federal government for laboratories and housing. Fernald added:

"She loved doing it. Friday Harbor is a marine biologist's dream, with its cold, clear, deep waters, abundance of marine life, and remoteness. No bridges connect the San Juans. The only way to get there is by ferryboat or amphibious plane.

"She has always been an outdoor biologist. It was no surprise that Dixy spent almost every summer for the next 25 years at the Friday Harbor labs. I think she would have done it without pay."

Why, then, did Dixy invite criticism from some students, faculty members, and others at the university and wherever she went thereafter? It isn't necessary to get the reasons from her enemies, because her closest friends know and don't hesitate to say why.

"She couldn't stand small talk," Bud Stuntz volunteered. "When a meeting or party or field trip became a bore and the talk trivial, she could be brusque and turn on her heel. Dixy has never had time to 'waste,' as she put it. Some people didn't like that. They thought her impolite or crude in her disinterest or her sudden disappearance, and I guess you might agree with them. But, you see, she has never liked to pretend to be amused or interested when she's not. Isn't that the height of integrity?"

Martin agreed with Stuntz and added: "Dixy is the most outspoken person I know. If she doesn't like something or somebody, she doesn't wait for a 'safe' place to blow off steam. She doesn't look around a room to see who's there before making a statement. She says what she thinks right now, and let those who are faint of heart watch for the shrapnel. Now, I don't do that and most other people I know don't either, but by God that takes courage. And she has plenty of that."

I can recount numerous instances to illustrate Martin's point, but the classic, perhaps, came when, as governor of Washington State, she invited legislators, press, and others into her office for the signing of a rather routine bill. Among the bill's sponsors was a legislator who had knifed her constantly in the press. Standing alongside as she was signing, he changed the subject to volunteer information on how she might solve a serious problem then before the Legislature and the public. Dixy finished signing, turned slowly, then up at him, nailed him with a stare, and said so the large group in the room could hear every syllable:

"I don't really give a goddamn what in hell you think!"

He needed no interpreter.

Fernald observed: "Some students raved about what an inspiration she was to them in their studies, while others disliked her because they said she was much too impatient and far too demanding."

As a longtime associate of Dixy's, I can understand and agree with those who accuse her of impatience and being demanding. Where her detractors see those traits as odious, however, I interpret them as a precise reflection of her character. She is impatient and demanding because her mind grasps issues so quickly she cannot see why others don't also. When she recognizes she has been brusque or impatient, she makes amends whenever she can. I don't know a kinder or more considerate person, nor one who feels stronger remorse when she realizes she has hurt the feelings of someone she cares about.

Although I made the political voyage with her to the governorship, I remain astounded that a person who is so truthful with everyone at all times could have succeeded in politics. It has cost her many heartaches since she walked into the Mansion, but she has set a standard for moral courage few politicians have ever matched. Or ever will match — and win.

Fernald, one of her greatest admirers and friends, also acknowledged she is not always so patient as she might be with people who don't grasp things as fast as she does. He also said she would sometimes throw out an opinion just to see the reaction or to get a discussion going. Those who understood what she was doing, he added, fell right in with the game or satire. Those who took her seriously didn't like her.

"She has strong opinions, and she bears grudges," said another colleague. "She doesn't easily forget those who have crossed her or have been cruel or unkind to her. Dixy was fiery and unpleasant in my relationship with her. She was not the great teacher she's made out to be. She was an intemperate, feeble-minded old bitch. I'd just as soon forget she ever lived."

It was no surprise that the colleague demanded assurance that he would not be identified in any article or book.

Feeble-minded? One of the finest minds in science feeble-minded?

The turning point in Dixy's career may very well have come in the late 1950's, when Seattle's educational-television station, based at the university, suggested she do a series of half-hour programs on marine science. The station's executives had heard about her teaching prowess, her unusual field trips, and her gift of gab, as well as her eccentricities, and they guessed accurately that she had the makings of an attractive TV personality. Not one to take things lightly, Dixy created a remarkable seagoing set, complete with large glass tank and other equipment straight out of the laboratories. She collected all the sea life and other materials herself and took no notes with her on the set, to the astonishment of the program director and crew. She needed none.

Dixy, the easygoing, informal "character" who had come out of the land of the Ivory Tower, was an instant hit. She produced a program a week for nine months, and then she was through. But her image went on and on. The station kept repeating the series some eight or nine years and also put together an abbreviated version for other public-service stations throughout the country.

What few persons realized at the time was that this was the public's first concentrated look at the little round character from the scientific world, and it liked what it saw. Unlike many other public-service talk shows, Dixy was easy to understand, humorous, and able to simplify the most difficult scientific information.

Nearly 20 years later, when she announced she was thinking seriously of making the race for governor, the public knew the face that went with the name of Dr. Dixy Lee Ray. The first newspaper poll asking the public to indicate which of the dozen or so potential candidates it favored for the governorship showed Dixy way out in front. Unquestionably, Miss Television, as some of her university foes had dubbed her, had hit paydirt through science, of all things.

Dixy ultimately paid a price for her courage and behavior at the university, with the help of the underlying chauvinism the chauvinists would never acknowledge. When the time came for Zoology faculty consideration of her candidacy for a full professorship, something she wanted very much, the onetime young Turks found they were outnumbered. An expanded faculty and several departures had severely eroded the pro-Dixy sentiment.

"The painful part of it all," Martin said, "was that they were too shortsighted to recognize what Dixy had done for the university. They continued their prejudice through the years she became chairman of the Atomic Energy Commission and finally governor of Washington State. The university has for many years recognized the value of public service provided by faculty members and alumni. Here was a case of a faculty member who had brought unparalleled distinction to the university, first as the savior of the Pacific Science Center, then as a member and chairman of the U.S. Atomic Energy Commission, the highest post to which any woman has climbed in the federal government, and finally as the chief executive of her home state. She should publish first before being eligible for a full professorship? Why? So she may be eligible a quarter century after her death to have a university building named after her? Rubbish!"

Life wasn't all test tubes and microscopes for the young Turks, however. Dixy's arrival signaled more than the beginning of the five-star field trips that became her trademark. With her penchant for gourmet cooking, seafood, and good conversation, the young Turks' "dining club" came into being. In the beginning it included Dixy, Fernald, Stuntz and Mrs. Stuntz, Whiteley, and, for a time, Martin. They collected $10 a week from each person to pay for dinner five nights a week, plus a drink or two to loosen tongues. They would shop together each day after classes, and the cooking chores, cleanup, and dishwashing would be rotated. Each had a flair for cooking, but Dixy's bouillabaisse and other fish dishes brought the raves. Dinner would usually wind up at 8:30 and the cleanup by 9; then all would return to their labs or offices at the university for another hour or two of work.

The conversation was reportedly as interesting as the food. Within a short time the science grapevine carried news of the young Turks' "fantastic" dinner evenings, and visitors from other colleges, universities, or laboratories in the U.S. and abroad would "suddenly find themselves available" for dinner and a chat with the "dinner club." Mr. and Mrs. Stuntz were hosts through-out the 15 or 16 years the group met at table.

Card-playing, games, or entertainment were not needed and wouldn't have been countenanced. Conversation was the pièce de résistance, after the food and drink ran out, of course.

Dixy continued with her old friends and the dinner group until she took a year's leave of absence in 1960 to join the National Science Foundation for a deep-sea research project. Only a short time before, her first bid for a full professorship had been turned down by the Zoology faculty, an action that must have helped her make her decision to accept the NSF request.

She returned to the university to teach at Friday Harbor in the summer of 1961, but she was back with the Science Foundation to take care of unfinished business in the fall. She had cooked her last bouillabaisse for her old friends at the university.

CHAPTER SIX

Museology
and a
Mutiny

It was inevitable that Dixy and I should become friends. As managing editor of the morning newspaper in Seattle, I preached the notion that people in communications had an obligation to learn more about the sciences. She, on the other hand, spoke constantly of the pressing need for scientists to learn more about communications. In no time we were plotting how to accomplish both ends; we did it over clam chowder and tuna fish sandwiches at noon in her new abode, the Pacific Science Center.

One of her comments was indicative of how strongly she felt on the subject: "If a scientist cannot relate what he is doing or what he believes to the layman in simple, understandable language, then I must seriously suspect he doesn't really know what he is doing himself."

The noontime meetings began a short time after Dixy was appointed director of the Science Center. It was autumn of 1963 and she had just spent a summer teaching at the University of Washington's Friday Harbor laboratories. She had been offered the position in the spring, after returning from service with the National Science Foundation, an absence that had infuriated her opponents at the university's Zoology Department more than ever. When she accepted the Science Center position, jealousy and chauvinism broke out in a rash in some campus quarters.

Dixy didn't care any more. She had set her targets, and she

had much to prove, primarily in communicating the sciences to the lay public. The Science Center would be her laboratory for one of the most significant research projects of her life.

The setting of the Science Center itself was important and closely related with what she was trying to prove. For the six months of the Seattle World's Fair of 1962, the Science Center, then a federal exhibit, was immensely popular and undoubtedly one of the principal reasons for the fair's success. One of the most compelling aspects was the neo-classic Japanese design created in the five-building complex and the outdoor campus by Minoru Yamasaki, a Seattle native who has become one of the nation's foremost architects. Graced by five tall arches of varying sizes and a pool that flows underneath walks connecting the buildings, the Center gave Seattle one of its most attractive man-made spots.

But all that was not enough. Not for Dixy.

"The exhibits inside drew long lines daily, and they quickly became the chief drawing card for visitors from distant states and foreign countries, as well as the home folks. But it seemed to me that public reaction in 1962 could be summed up this way: 'This is all-powerful. It's all-good. Scientists can solve all our problems and all these things are meaningful. But I can't really understand them. Must I become a scientist to appreciate what they know?'"

Because it was Uncle Sam's exhibit at the fair, funds for the displays within were almost unlimited.

"All the exhibits were designed by scientists," said Dixy, "and they pleased scientists. The scientists thought them great, and they said so in the press, on television and radio, in magazines, wherever they had an opportunity. For a time the public thought the exhibits were great, too. Well, they must have been; after all, didn't Dr. What's-His-Name say so the other day to Walter Cronkite? The public believed because the public had a mystic reverence for the species and wouldn't dare challenge the bigdomes."

Dixy liked to point to one conspicuous example. It was a 15-foot-high, completely accurate model of the GMA molecule, with every hydrogen atom in place and every facet clearly and properly indicated. It stood in the spotlighted area of one of the big halls, and it turned on a pedestal.

"The scientists, particularly the biochemists, labeled it one of the most remarkable exhibits they had seen. But for 99.999999 percent of the general population, it was — well, just a great big thing turning around under a spotlight. Big deal. It meant absolutely nothing to the guy who pays the bills for science and everything else. The explanations on all the exhibits were similarly poor, and, like the GMA monster, didn't tell a story. Graphics were limp or nonexistent everywhere."

Despite the shortcomings, Dixy added, the devoted public, "smitten perhaps by the exterior Yamasaki beauties into believing that what was inside was equally auspicious, said emphatically that the Science Center was a good thing and that it had to continue as a community asset. And, of course, the public was right. It always is."

In the preceding three years Dixy had spent all but two summers with the National Science Foundation in Washington, DC. Her principal role was to participate in a foundation study of the proper function it should serve in the field of biological oceanography. The work took Dixy to Capitol Hill several times a week as liaison between the foundation and congressional committees. At the same time, she was serving on the Academy of Science's committee on oceanography. The combined functions helped her play a strategic role in the establishment of NOAA, the National Oceanographic and Atmospheric Administration. Her ally at the time and for many years thereafter was Senator Warren G. Magnuson, or Maggie, as voters had been encouraged to call him, at least every six years. Maggie was the central figure, not only in the creation of NOAA but in development of the Seattle World's Fair and the Pacific Science Center.

Another project in which Dixy participated is significant because it nurtured in her a tough policy she never abandoned with regard to the disturbing avalanche of "free money" available to universities willing to undertake any kind of research.

"We conducted a very analytical and sensitive investigation," she explained, "of the influence on universities and colleges of funds and grants to individual faculty members and researchers. How effective was the grading system under which funds were provided by the foundation or outside agencies or firms? It was an internal study into which we poured a great deal of time, sweat, and dedication. And our recommendation was damned bold. It called for a complete change in the system because of the bias that was being introduced into schools. It not only changed the loyalties to the institution involved, but, as the foundation moved more and more toward matching grants, it forced the institutions to put more of their funds into science than they would have done otherwise — or, worse still, forced them to take funds from other, perhaps more worthy, needs to avoid losing the scientific grants."

Was it more than coincidence that the University of Washington itself at that time and to the present day has been a leading contender in the annual Grantsmanship Derby? More than once, it has led the pack in grants.

Never one to pull punches, Dixy said to anyone who would listen:

"The system of grants was a bad thing, on the whole. It did more harm than good, but I'm certain relatively few scientists will agree with me. But, then, most scientists haven't been in a position to see both sides of the argument, to gain an adequate perspective of the issue. They have not investigated beyond the fact that each scientist or science program received some seed money to carry out an assignment and was permitted to do so with complete freedom and without any restrictions or controls. Sounds fine, and I'm equally certain many good things resulted, but I also believe it was vastly wasteful of public funds in many respects. Most of all, I am concerned because it helped create some of the deep troubles we're experiencing in higher education throughout America today.

"The tail is wagging the dog in university and college research. Public and private grants to departments for research have made the faculty members receiving them so independent they don't have to abide by university and college rules, for the most part. They are calling the tune because they have drawn the cash. As a result, they answer to the agency or contributor, not the college dean. In some cases they have even built new buildings almost completely with grant money and have gone their own way in curriculum and research.

"Now what college president without a courageous bone in his body would look that kind of a gift horse in the mouth? I suppose we really should be grateful there are those who have told the public and private Santa Clauses to shove it, but they are not in the majority. I think it's unfair pressure to put on a college president who has integrity and an earnest desire to keep his school in the black without selling out to research he can't control."

It was inevitable that Dixy would keep saying those things whenever the opportunity presented itself. She would forever be a "teacher" in principle; she loved research, particularly research she could conduct outdoors, but it had to have a higher purpose than keeping the researchers in the chips or maintaining the "prestige" of an institution. "Research," she said, "was the blood-line of learning, not the mother lode for the aristocrats of higher education."

Fifteen years later Dixy would be saying the same things, but this time as a governor with the statutory right to probe or instigate probes. However, her critical report with the Science Foundation has never been published.

"Why was there so much emphasis on the foundation study? To this day it has not been released to the press and I wonder why?"

In her NSF stint in the early 1960's, she discovered another group of Americans that had an even greater need to know more about the sciences than the public in general. The group was the politicians, the members of Congress — and, by inference, all other lawmakers across the land at every level of government. For the first time Dixy realized that congressmen — as well as bureaucrats, appointed officials, and the vast army of staff members — didn't seem to understand the basic, underlying needs of science and technology. She was horrified by the realization.

"In effect, they had the same attitudes I found later in the blindly devoted and trusting public. 'This is all-powerful, it's all good, and scientists can do anything and solve everything,' is the way the hypnotizing tune goes."

Dixy heard scores of professional witnesses from the sciences and technology speak from the congressional witness chair in dispassionate tones and a strange language.

"Official Washington simply wasn't talking the same language as the professionals," Dixy continued. "And the scientists and engineers may as well have been talking to themselves. I am not referring to scientific jargon; their attitudes with respect to what they knew and understood were so completely different and so much from another world that they didn't know or seem to care about what the other guy was saying. As I have seen happen in so many cases, the busy officials and bureaucrats accepted science and the need to support it on faith alone. Of course, there were exceptions, but you could number the lot on your fingers and have a few fingers left over."

Anyone who heard Dixy declaim in fearless tones in the

early 1960's must have recognized that the woman was unquestionably headed for a position of leadership. Anyone could understand her language and her attitude:

"Because of the 'faith in science' syndrome, no one in official Washington was inclined to challenge science or scientists, and that's a mighty weak foundation for progress. Perhaps I need not add that I am totally and completely convinced that science, by and large, is a good thing and that the acquisition of knowledge is fundamental and crucial to human existence and progress. Nothing shocking there, I suppose.

"But I insist also that the acquisition of knowledge is the most human thing people do, and the more we know, the more responsible we're likely to behave. Ignorance has no value; we can never know too much. Which brings me to the point:

"The root of the hostility toward science will be found in the failure of science itself and those who teach it to make a strong effort toward getting information and understanding about the sciences to all those people out there who never have and never will become scientists. As I have said so many times, the public is always right, not because it is actually right but because it is the public. The continued health of a free society depends upon the electorate's right to make critical decisions affecting its health and safety. How can it do so — make the best decisions, that is — if scientists and technicians make no attempt to speak the common language?"

It was in that spirit, she said, that she determined in the early 1960's to teach science differently.

"I didn't give a damn what my colleagues thought. I was going to do some 'popular science' teaching. Now there's a phrase I'll bet turns a few stomachs and minds belonging to the untouchables on science faculties."

When she arrived at the Science Center with the keys to the door, then, she determined this was the opportunity she had been waiting for. She recognized her appointment as a summons to practice what she had been preaching. As if she were seeking additional heresies, Dixy also determined, by God, that it was not only right but highly practical to concentrate the Science Center's effort on the adult population! Children wouldn't be excluded, of course, but they were finally getting better science instruction in the schools and didn't require the attention Dixy had in mind. Although many programs for children were mounted and offered to school children in western Washington, she drew a bead on the general public without regard to age.

In the ten or eleven months immediately after the Seattle World's Fair ended, the Science Center had foundered under an interim director who had no scientific background. Chaos and budgetary disaster threatened, and the public stayed home, indifferent to the dilemma. The interim director and his staff had changed virtually nothing; the exhibits that drew thousands during the fair now attracted no one. Dixy had been right. Without the drama of the fair itself, the public yawned over the Science Center exhibits that explained nothing to anyone.

Within her first year Dixy had thrown out virtually every exhibit from the fair year. Everything was new, and the new motif, by order of the new boss, was that the Science Center was to become a "living" room that would house only those exhibits and experiments that "moved."

"I'll be damned," Dixy said, "if I'm going to become landlady to a hoary museum. I like museums — but only those that don't mummify. Walt Disney may be a nasty word to the elitists in science, but if his techniques permit me to explain the sciences to anyone who passes by, bring on Mickey Mouse and Co.!"

Before Dixy had completed her first year as director, the Science Center became once more a very popular place, not only for the school children who were bused there or had classes there but for thousands of adults who were getting a "simple" look at science for the first time.

It wasn't easy to sustain. The Pacific Science Center Foundation provided barely enough funds to keep the doors open. It was Dixy who had to scratch for support wherever she could find it — from foundations; local, county, and federal governments; the estates of science-loving people; and private individuals Dixy had charmed out of their wallets. She never revealed it herself, but foundation members discovered she frequently purchased equipment and materials — and even helped buy a truck for the Center — out of her own relatively small pay. She was at it again. Money never meant anything to the defiant zoologist from the sands of Tacoma's Commencement Bay. With feathers and string and that tomato-like infectious smile, plus a lot of her own money, she not only kept the Science Center from extinction; she gave it life. Staffers estimated she contributed at least $5,000 of her own earnings "and probably a lot more" to keeping the Science Center alive.

Dixy was a package of paradoxes. She could mount pressure on a prospective contributor with the pizzazz of a Los Angeles car salesman to get funds to support the Science Center. But more than a decade later, when it came time for her to raise funds for her own gubernatorial campaign, she was as bashful as a chubby kid at her first ballet recital. She's embarrassed to plead for herself but a tiger when begging for others.

Under Dixy's magic wand, the Science Center became an adjunct of public and private schools. The buses pulled up to the buildings daily throughout the school term, and youngsters not only saw some of the most ingenious experiments offered any- where — from gravity-defying, perpetual-motion demonstra- tions to white mice with extraordinarily high IQ's — but also attended special classes in mathematics, physics, and general science. She coaxed NASA into sending her several Space Age exhibits before they went on the road to other museums. She smooth-talked other scientists, industrial and fine-art photog- raphers, engineering firms, and educational institutions into lending materials and devices they weren't touring, even for money. The short-haired schoolmarm with the gift of gab hyp- notized people across the land into helping her keep the Science Center alive. And it worked.

The interior of the five buildings changed dramatically. A gigantic moon, painstakingly contoured to replicate the real thing, hung over one of the largest exhibition areas and over- whelmed persons seeing it for the first time. It was as close to a show-stopper as a science museum could get. With the help of a local benefactor, Dixy, a lifetime devotee of Indian history and art, moved an entire Indian longhouse into the Science Center.

In the midst of the hectic early years at the center, Dixy found time to work on what would have been the coup of the century for Washington State if it had succeeded — which it very nearly did. Utilizing the prestige of the state's two powerful senators, Warren G. Magnuson and Henry M. Jackson, and the many important friendships she had made on Capitol Hill in her stints with the National Science Foundation, she went after one of the most important goals of her life: converting the Pacific Science Center into the Smithsonian Institution West. She knew the Smithsonian had been contemplating decentralizing into several regional facilities as soon as Congress was ready to appropriate the necessary funds. Why not now? And why not start with a branch in Seattle?

Hearings on the issue seemed to be producing the desired result until an educator cast considerable doubt on the advisability of the entire venture. It was enough to inspire a move to delay a decision, and the proposal was shelved. Dixy could never rally the same forces again, and a golden opportunity was lost. The educator who had supplied the coup de grace to the near-coup was from the same university that had refused Dixy her full professorship!

In the meantime, Dixy was pulling strings nationally and internationally, and the Science Center drew notice in a variety of periodicals at home and abroad. She instigated the prestigious Arches of Science Award, an annual $25,000 prize to a person who had contributed outstanding service to science. Among early winners were René Dubos and Margaret Mead. The award, named for the five arches symbolizing the Science Center, had to be discontinued for lack of cash support when Dixy departed.

Only one major interruption marked Dixy's ten-year directorship. Before accepting the Science Center job, she informed the center's board of governors she had already agreed to head a scientific expedition to the Indian Ocean in a sailing ship. The board approved without a murmur.

On the face of it a scientific ship on a mission to the Indian Ocean sounds like a routine exercise. Nothing Dixy touched remained routine. All that happened was: (a) defiance by an incompetent captain and engineer that forced her to take over the ship in a legitimate mutiny, (b) a fire that nearly destroyed the ship at sea, (c) continuing breakdowns in the ship's machinery that almost caused cancellation of the voyage, (d) a variety of illnesses of tropical nature, and (e) a different kind of mutiny, in which some graduate students turned on Dixy because she tried to force them out of their lethargy and go to work. Otherwise it was a rather uneventful trip.

The marine biologist with the proclivity for making things happen first became affiliated with events that led to the expedition while serving with the National Science Foundation and its special committee on oceanography. Established in 1957, the committee was one of many created to examine the international status of certain fields of science. In addition to initiating the studies that eventually brought NOAA into existence, the committee laid the groundwork for international studies of the vast ocean floor and sea life.

After several years of study, Dixy acknowledged, most of the committees spawned by the foundation deteriorated into "nothing more than justifications for putting more and more money into this field, and that field, and the next field. Hell, anybody can do that! Who needs scientists to tell us that all any project needs is more cash?"

But in the first half-dozen years, before the dollar syndrome struck, the scientific members of the oceanographic committee, at least, were earnestly interested in more discovery above all other considerations. How did Dixy get involved in the first place?

"The committee came up with recommendations on what it proposed to do and what budget it would need to do it. When I first heard about it, I was encouraged by proposals to spend at least one third of the funds in the biological sciences. Then I got boiling mad when I discovered not a single biologist had been named to the committee that would direct the spending and the research! The membership was dominated by the big oceanographic institutions — geophysicists, physical scientists, meteorologists, and so on — and, of course, they are strongly oriented toward physical oceanography."

Knowing that the committee had been created primarily by her old friend Maggie, Dixy sent a letter off to the senator, asking him to look into the imbalance on the committee and the absence of marine biologists to talk about issues that were the province of biologists. Maggie circulated the letter to the "right" people, and the director of the academy soon called a special meeting of the committee.

"Anybody can guess what happened then," Dixy said. "You open your mouth and you get appointed to fix the problem. I was on the spot. Now I had to put up or shut up."

Dixy "put up" as marine consultant to the committee. She began an odyssey to marine and oceanographic institutions in every region of the nation, as well as every scientific-administration office in Washington, DC. When she was ready to make her own recommendations, she had a ready audience, within the committee and outside it. She pointed out that ships operated by the oceanographic institutions were designed to do physical studies or take boring samples from the bottom. They are built and equipped to do high-speed chemical sampling of ocean waters and record temperature and other attributes that required constant movement of the vessel.

"To do biological work at sea," she told the committee, "you have to take a vessel that stands still or moves very slowly. You can't do both kinds of work on the same kind of ship with good results for either."

Dixy and those who joined her position urged the committee to acquire at least two ships, one for biological research in the Pacific and the other for the Atlantic. She also recommended that the ships be operated by private institutions, not the government, because they would then be more flexible and freer to operate on the high seas without the regulations that constrict vessels under state and federal rules. It was also recommended that the private institutions be Duke University for the Atlantic expeditions and Stanford for the Pacific.

Dixy's persuasiveness brought all recommendations home. Duke and Stanford were chosen, and the committee decided to contract for ships that would devote their work exclusively to biological considerations. Twenty-five nations were cooperating in the long-term venture, and the U.S. government, with the State Department doing the negotiating, agreed to participate for at least five years. Eventually, Dixy and her biological cohorts managed to get two ships for the Pacific alone, one for work on the high seas and the other for shallow waters and inshore research.

"For the high-seas expedition," she said, "we were able to get the famous old ship, the *Williamsburg*, which had been Franklin Roosevelt's yacht and Truman's. We got her out of mothballs, recommissioned her, rebuilt her, equipped her, and renamed her the *Anton Bruun* after one of the most remarkable oceanographers and biological oceanographers of modern times. It was Bruun, The Great Dane, who singlehandedly organized the finest of deep-sea expeditions. It was his ship, the *Galatea*, that discovered and investigated the Philippine Trench and the great depths of the Pacific. I have great admiration for him. He was a fine man, a marvelous field man who somehow became a seafaring biologist. And he did it all despite being crippled by polio. Bruun had to use crutches to get around. What a man!"

How she admired "gutty" people! Roosevelt and Truman, for example . . . She didn't care for their ultraliberalism, but she thought both men were "terrific" because they had the courage to say and do what they thought. They were men of action.

Dixy never flinched herself when action was needed. The State Department objected to naming the recommissioned ship the *Anton Bruun* and ordered another name. It was tangling with the wrong li'l ole marine biologist. By-passing the State Department, she wrote directly to the King of Denmark, asking him to intercede on behalf of Bruun and to use whatever diplomatic clout he could muster. The King did, and the State Department saw the light. The *Anton Bruun*, which had been named for the Danish hero of the high seas at the request of the King of Denmark, no less, was assigned to high-seas work in the Pacific, which had been Bruun's principal playground. Duke would not get its ship immediately; it would wait for one under construction at an East Coast yard. So the Pacific segment of the expedition now had two biological ships.

For the inshore ship to be operated by Stanford in the Indian Ocean, a 135-foot sailing vessel, the *Te Vega*, was obtained. A ship powered by sails was better suited to inshore work and particularly the dangerous research in shallow waters.

Although Dixy had been the "mover" in the preparation of the expedition and the acquisition of the ships — including authorizing, funding, and research planning — she had no intention of joining the expedition herself. It was inevitable, however, that Stanford would ask her to take one of the "legs" of the *Te Vega's* excursions to the Indian Ocean. She gave her approval several months before the directorship of the Pacific Science Center was offered her, so she asked for "about a three-month leave of absence early in 1964." The three-month leave became a six-month nightmare through no fault of her own.

Dixy had been getting reports of trouble aboard the *Te Vega* long before she flew to meet her at Colombo, Ceylon (now Sri Lanka), the last week of January to take over as chief scientist and "expedition boss." But trouble up to that time was principally mechanical. Her predecessor, Dr. Rolf L. Bolin, was chief of the entire Pacific expedition; he had also been her mentor at Stanford's Hopkins Marine Station and supervised her work for a doctorate many years earlier. It was also Dr. Bolin who coaxed her to sign up for the second leg of the Indian Ocean research to give him a breather and a chance to catch up on his work at Stanford. Dr. Bolin's cruise was productive but not nearly so much as it could have been. In the ship's outings since June, 1963, much of the time was lost in port awaiting repairs. Her cruise was cut short more than two months by a broken propeller shaft.

When Dixy boarded the ship for the first time, she said the *Te Vega* looked like a fine vessel — and then she stepped down to the deck for a close look. She was shocked. She had never seen anything so filthy on the sea before, and she didn't waste time raising hell. Summoning the captain, she pointed here and there and everywhere and said firmly:

"Now, I want this ship cleaned up immediately! Everybody is going to pitch in. The crew, the staff scientists, the graduates, and me, too."

She learned something about conditions and morale in quick time. The captain complained:

"We can't do that, Dr. Ray. We don't have any fresh water."

She fumed. "Well, use sea water, damn it! Look out there. There's miles of it. And that's only the surface!"

Nobody laughed. Her colleagues aboard joined in to help without grumbling. In fact, the scientists told Dixy they were relieved that somebody finally showed up to bring some order. The graduate students, however, were another matter. Some of the holdovers from Bolin's class and several hands Dixy had recruited rebelled and "got lost" conveniently to avoid the cleanup work. That wasn't why they had signed on. After all, they were graduates and researchers and professionals. They hadn't reckoned with Dixy Lee Ray. She'd see to them later.

A crew member wrote in a letter: "Looks like we're going to be here forever waiting for a new propeller shaft. These people move so slowly. Wow! I wish I had a photo of Dr. Ray when she came aboard. She couldn't believe what she saw. The air was filthy with soot residue from large ships, our own coal-burning boilers, and the land itself. Worst of all, there's no wind to cool things. The water is the worst. Indian ports don't seem to have any restrictions on what is dumped into the harbor. Maybe that's why the captain told Dr. Ray he couldn't get the ship swabbed down until he got fresh water."

The propeller-shaft repairs had been promised since Dr.

Bolin had ordered the damaged *Te Vega* into Colombo two months earlier. Dixy was told the work would be done by February 15 and she could take off then; the original sailing date had been February 1. *Te Vega* didn't leave Colombo until March 15!

In the meantime, problems multiplied for the crew and the staff. Before the March 15 sailing everyone except Dr. Ray had suffered from dysentery. An eye infection was causing her trouble. Dixy took stock of the medical supplies and saw the ship was short of many necessary items, particularly a drug to relieve dysentery and quinine and other medications that would be needed in future weeks in the malaria region. When she went to work on a project in earnest, she got results, or else. The medical supplies arrived pronto. She did the same with food stocks and clothing.

"This ship," she told the captain when it seemed the cleanup had bogged down, "will not put out to sea unless she is painted, varnished, and washed and scrubbed down to my satisfaction."

One of the problems with the *Te Vega's* helm was that the captain was an expert elbow-bender and the first engineer was inept and fond of persuading some of the graduate students to do only the work "scientists were supposed to do." He fancied himself as a spy sent out to arouse the grumbling students to rebellion.

From Dixy's own record of the voyage comes a revealing look at her feelings: "I worked hard, very hard, as an undergraduate and a graduate to get the education I wanted. It wasn't easy trying to get a degree on one hand and working to support myself as a janitor, dish-washer, waitress, and house-painter on the other. But if you want the degrees enough, you do these things without complaint. Most of my associates who joined me at the university's Zoology Department after the Second World War had worked hard, too. We had had such a rough time, however, that we wanted our graduate students to spend all their time on their studies and not have to give their valuable time to after-school drudgery. What a terrible mistake we made! We didn't realize until well through the end of the 1950's that we had spoiled them rotten and made prima donnas of them. It was beneath their dignity to clean and wash lab tables and floors; we discovered we had unwittingly taken over the work of cleaning up the crud while they waltzed in and out at their pleasure to get assistance in teaching! So, by the time I was on my way to

Colombo to join the *Te Vega*, I was damned concerned about whether the pendulum had swung too far.

"We had ten graduate students and five certified scientists aboard, plus a crew of 15 more, including the captain. I had been given the final say on selection of the scientists and graduate students, but I actually knew only two of the students beforehand. Ironically, they turned out to be the most spoiled of all and the gravest morale problems. Half the graduate students responded superbly and did marvelous work under the most miserable conditions imaginable. But the other half . . . .

"Those who caused the trouble and wouldn't stoop to doing the cleaning and other housekeeping chores necessary to keep the expedition in order had been recommended as 'the cream of the crop' and 'outstanding scholars.' After living with them in close quarters several months, I came to the conclusion that what we had been doing with graduate students was totally wrong. They had no concept of responsibility. They had been told again and again how bright they were, how much smarter they were than any other generation, and how much society needed them and owed them. Whatinhell for? The clean-fingernail bunch had been handed its education on a silver platter and hadn't even bothered to say thank you.

"They were excused from common tasks because they were obviously superior to others, but when the chips were down and things got tough — as I saw on that voyage in hurricanes, typhoons, mechanical breakdowns, and even a serious ship fire — their reaction was to turn against any person in authority. In periods of stress some of the darlings blamed me openly for putting their precious lives in jeopardy! As I say, I'm grateful the criticism applied only to half the graduates. If it hadn't been for the other, more stable and mature students, we might never have made it."

Dixy said she really felt sorry for the spoiled graduates, "because they believed they were the elite and should have everything made special for them — but they weren't all that good." She was critical of their poor study habits.

"They were much more interested in their physical comfort than their mental diet. On one occasion I bawled out the whole bunch, including the good ones. We had been ashore on a small island and had been doing a lot of snorkeling to bring many species aboard ship. Some of them had to be pickled right away and sent back for permanent collections, while others had to be returned to the sea or placed in the ship's tanks for future study. We had been diving all morning. It was noon, and I was the last one back on board. When I got there, I saw no one. All the diving gear was lying in a heap and alongside in numerous buckets were loads of sea animals dying in the bright sunlight. All the students were down in the galley. By God, they weren't going to miss a minute of lunch.

"I dashed below, and quicker than you could say, 'Pass the butter, please,' I had them back up on deck. They knew I wasn't very happy. Where in hell, I wanted to know, had they learned the rudiments of marine biology! I wanted the lesson to stick, no matter what they thought of me, so I minced no words. They took their medicine, most of them, in good fashion, because they knew I was right. Two of the most rebellious students had not come topside. They just sat at the lunch table and glared at me defiantly, daring me to do something. I wouldn't give them the satisfaction. Besides, I could see that most of the graduate students and the crew sided with me."

Now Dixy realized there were two major mistakes that had been made with the new generations of students. The first was that they were relieved of the drudgery of working to support themselves through school, and now the second was that they wouldn't or didn't know how to take an order from a superior. Dixy knew the meaning of rebellion; she'd been a rebel herself most of her life. But she also knew the importance of following orders to maintain order.

"There was absolutely no discipline in any fiber of those kids. They had never been put in a position in which they had to do something simply because someone told them to do it. On board a ship, for example, there are times when the skipper tells his hands to do this or that and he can't stop to explain why. Those kids wanted to be consulted about everything."

Perhaps most surprising of all to Dixy was that "those kids" couldn't stand physical discomfort of any kind. Each one had learned there was a pill or salve or medicine for anything that ailed them.

"We ran out of aspirin once," Dixy said, "and you'd have thought we'd encountered the black plague. I told those with headaches to go and lie down and put a wet cloth over their foreheads. The only thing we had was morphine, and I wasn't about to give them that. A wet cloth! Why, you'd have thought I had prescribed the guillotine.

"They thought I was insensitive, callous. I know some of them began calling me Captain Bligh!"

When she returned from the voyage of the *Te Vega*, Dixy was convinced it was no kindness to be lenient with students. Her colleagues at the university were puzzled over "the new, tougher Dixy," but she made students toe the mark after that. She no longer wanted the responsibility of having contributed to "ruining a generation of people through pampering."

When Dixy inherited the *Te Vega*, the sailing ship came with a series of faults that had not been attended by her predecessor nor by Stanford University, to which she ascribed most of the blame. The choice of a drunk for a captain was bad enough; selection of an engineer who apparently knew little or nothing about sailing ships and engines was the coup d'état. The break in the propeller shaft was not the fault of the manufacturer; the engineer had simply forgotten to grease it — or didn't know in the first place that it had to be done! For similar reasons there were breakdowns in valve operation, holding tanks, and other strategic machinery and equipment. Much could be blamed on the engineer, but Dixy's predecessor had to share the blame, too, for not insisting on thorough checks of the vessel before the *Te Vega* was accepted for the Pacific runs.

"I had to spend valuable research time to get parts and repairs," Dixy explained, "and in the course of the expedition, I think I must have leaned on every friend I had in the world at one time or another to get the communications and help we had to have. And they all came through."

An example of what she had to contend with came early. The *Te Vega* appeared to be ready at last to leave Colombo. The shaft had been replaced, and everything else that had shattered or come apart had been repaired. Still, no movement.

"One of the first things a person learns on a ship if he's part of the crew is that you must keep the scuppers clean," Dixy said. "That was so elemental that we all assumed it had been done by the Stanford people before the first voyage the year before. When all other inspections turned up nothing, I asked for a check of the scuppers on a hunch. You know, those are the openings that permit water aboard to find its way out to the sea. Sure enough, the scuppers wouldn't drain. Carpenter's clips, caulking, gunk from a hundred sources, and God knows what had accumulated and apparently hadn't been cleaned out for perhaps half a dozen years or more. Through cable, mail, phone calls, and even prayer, I combed the Far East for divers. And we finally found a pair. They went down and opened up the scupper valves after removing loads of debris."

The captain was Stanford's responsibility. It was clear no one had checked his record before hiring him. Once in the middle of the night, after the ship had been buffeted by a hurricane, all hands were bending to the task of putting things right and cleaning up. Even Dixy was involved in the emergency operation. In the midst of the cleanup, the skipper, obviously inspired by his best alcohol, went to sleep, leaving everyone else to do the big job. When Dixy discovered it, she vowed to take no more. She relieved him of command, ordered him confined to his cabin, and put the first mate in charge. She took immediate action through Stanford authorities and the National Science Foundation to find a replacement not only for the captain but for the first engineer, as well. As chief scientist, she had been given authority to take over the ship if she deemed it necessary.

Dixy's bold move did not please the student dissidents and some of the deck hands, all of whom had been brainwashed from the beginning by the engineer and the captain and were spoiling for a fight. The anti-Dixy group threatened action, but it never materialized. Dixy held them off with a jutting chin and a stare that dared anyone to move against her. The authorities were on her side without a dissenting vote. They had heard more than they needed to know about the captain's habits and the engineer's incompetence. When the new captain arrived, along with a new engineer, operation of the ship began improving overnight. Unfortunately, they had not arrived until after the engine-room fire incident. Within a week the comparison between the new and the old removed the last mutinous thoughts from the dissidents.

From the starting point at Colombo in March, the *Te Vega* had moved to the Maldive Islands, including Dunidu and Imma. Stopping for two or three days at a time to bring up fish, plants, and invertebrates, the ship proceeded to the Male Atoll and Fadiffolu Atoll, Mafilefuri and Maro Islands, Miladummadulu and Teladummati Atolls, before leaving for the Indian mainland. Desperate for a multitude of repairs, the *Te Vega* barely made it to

Cochin, where she was paralyzed nearly a month. After visiting Ongu Island, Wala Island, and Addu Atoll, the worst happened.

As a culmination of the neglect and mismanagement of the engine room by the engineer and a captain who didn't care or didn't know, the worst accident of the voyage occurred, one that could have been disastrous if the *Te Vega* had been far out in the open sea, far away from any port. A heavy sea washed over her bow. Water rushing aft entered the engine room, which should have had better protection, and shorted the main switchboard. A serious electrical fire was touched off, and all hands were summoned to fight it. Fortunately, the ship was able to put into Gan for help, but the damage was severe and the entire contingent of scientists and crew was seriously shaken. In that remote part of the world it would be impossible to get the needed repairs and replacement parts. Dixy sought and won the help of the commander of the British Air Force Base at Gan. With his help and her new captain and engineer, she stuck it out with the ship and the crew until the *Te Vega* could be made ready at least to negotiate the trip to the port at Mauritius, where major repairs could be provided.

The National Science Foundation and the 24 other nations involved in the worldwide research credited Dixy with saving the ship and keeping her in the oceanographic fleet. Dixy had managed to obtain so many new parts and get so many old ones repaired that the *Te Vega* was virtually a new vessel. Although her mission and the first one were severely hampered in productivity, subsequent expeditions succeeded admirably — free of serious mechanical troubles. If Dixy had not played "Captain Bligh," perhaps the *Te Vega's* trip in the first half of 1964 could well have been her last. *Te Vega's*, not Dixy's.

In the space of a couple of years, the marine biologist's stock at her home university may have fallen because of shortsightedness and professional jealousy, but in the world of science she was something of a heroine. Who else had saved a potentially magnificent Science Center and a seagoing scientific vessel from extinction through sheer courage and a stiff upper lip?

CHAPTER SEVEN

The Nuclear Adventure Begins

The judge's voice intoned her name and ended her daydreaming . . . .

"Dr. Ray, will you please place your hand on the Bible and repeat your oath after me . . . ?"

Dr. James R. Schlesinger was holding the Bible. President Richard M. Nixon looked on much too seriously as the routine ceremony ran its course in the President's office at the White House. It was at that moment that cameras clicked for the TV clips and news photos that would be sent across the nation. The date was August 8, 1972.

It was a pleasant event, with smiles all around and an unlimited supply of niceties. Watergate was barely a whisper and the polls showed Nixon would win in a landslide against George McGovern in the fall. Dixy, unaware of the implications of the recent break-in at Democratic headquarters, as were most Americans, was deeply impressed by the ceremony and the presence of a President. At that moment, she was grateful to be there, a very small part of history. She would do her thing as best she could, then return to her life's work on Puget Sound and enjoy the memories of a brief though perhaps uneventful sojourn with newsmakers. She had no inkling of the political explosion immediately ahead and the path the Watergate eruption would open for her.

Schlesinger asked her to be on duty by September 1 for a week of concentrated briefings, so she had three weeks for another fly-back to Seattle and a return across country in her new motor home to visit the nuclear installations. Dixy acknowledged she had much to learn, but she didn't realize how valuable that trip would be until much later.

The specially built Dodge home on wheels was ready for her when she returned, and the dealer had done a good job. It had to be good. First, it was to make at least four crossings of the United States in the next three years, and second, it was to be her home throughout her stay in the capital. The motor home suited her perfectly. It had ample work space, cleverly designed storage and dressing-room areas, all the bed she would ever want (and a firm, if expensive, mattress — which was fine, because she believed her capability was closely linked to a good night's sleep), compact and remarkably efficient cooking and shower facilities, and room enough to entertain more than a dozen guests — which she did often the next three years. Big Ghillie, the massive Scottish Deerhound, and little Jacques, the sassy, proud, four-legged Gaul, would be welcome boarders. Ghillie stood as tall as a small horse, while Jacques was a couple barks above a Chihuahua in stature and a thousand in IQ.

Persons who might have come upon the Dixy Lee Ray motor home just off the rural road might have been startled to see four-star generals and admirals and some of the most important personages in and out of government at a cocktail party, of all things, at the four-wheeled Dodge motor home out in the country. Dixy frequently had VIP's attend her most unusual parties. They didn't mind; why should she?

Of all the expenditures Dixy would make in her life, the $21,000-plus she paid for the motor home would be one of her most satisfying. To help her pilot it across the country, she recruited Jane Orr of Annapolis, who had worked for her at the National Science Foundation and whom she quickly hired as her personal secretary for her years in the capital. Jane would become one of her valued confidantes.

Dixy was to become one of the most popular commissioners the AEC had in its three-decade history — popular with the workers and scientists and engineers in the field, that is. The principal reason was the "shakedown" land cruise she undertook before moving to her desk at the capital and her many visits thereafter. She was the first and only commissioner to do it.

David Lilienthal, the first AEC chairman, had visited many of the installations, but he did it as chairman, and he did not call on all those Dixy saw. The net result was an educational and morale-building experience on both sides; at last, the work forces recognized they had a sympathizer and a friend at court, and she discovered thousands of new Dixy converts who would rally to her cause when she made many controversial decisions on AEC policy later.

It was a lesson she would never forget, and it was a lesson that was to help make her the first woman governor of Washington State in 1977. Dr. Ray, the marine biologist and television personality, found out that you win elections through the rather ordinary and traditional practices of "showing up" and shaking hands.

At the nuclear installations, she was frequently greeted with such comments as "You're the first commissioner who has ever bothered to come and see us and listen to our gripes." Translated to a later time, it was going to come out this way in the large and small cities and towns of Washington State: "You're the first candidate for governor who ever bothered to come this way, and we're going to vote for you." It was as simple as that. Dixy never paid much attention to the shelves full of books on political strategy and the erudite treatises on how to win elections by mail, newspaper, radio, or television.

"I think much of the loyalty I was to receive from the AEC crews later," Dixy said, "derived from that first trip and the many visits I made in the next three years. Why other commissioners didn't do it I'll never know, but I can make a strong assumption that things would have gone much better for them, the workers in the field, and this nation's nuclear-energy program if they had."

She didn't visit every installation in the U.S., but she did get to most of them that first time around. The trip was important because it gave her a total concept of what the AEC was all about, an understanding of the nature of the vast new empire, but most of all, a realization of the astounding collection of scientific and engineering talent assembled by the federal government and the private companies contracting with it to produce nuclear power. No other government in the world had ever put together a larger, more impressive roster of brain power.

The trip also introduced her to names and problems she

would soon know firsthand. Later, she would remember well what "the guy in the field" told her about those who made policy in Washington and the policies they made. One of the names she heard most was Milt Shaw; her curiosity was aroused early because mention of his name was usually made in irritation or resignation. She didn't have to jot it down.

On her arrival at the AEC's headquarters building in Germantown, Maryland, Dixy once again asked the question she had put to Schlesinger three weeks before. This time she directed it to a commission staff member:

"What does a commissioner do?"

"Well, Dr. Ray . . . ," the response began from a suddenly uncomfortable young man, "just about . . . just about anything you care to . . . I think . . . ."

She asked twice more and the answer was substantially the same, except that one bright young woman with imagination added:

"Your responsibility as a commissioner, Dr. Ray, is to look over the policy papers and reports that come to you and check the information papers and consent-calendar items — whatever crosses your desk. You'll get them here, in your 'In' basket, and just initial them and then put them here in your 'Out' basket. We'll do the rest."

Mmmmm, thought Dixy. A bright one. I'll have to remember her; she deserves a raise. At least she seemed to know where the wastebaskets were.

So this was what she was expected to do for $40,000 a year! Her heart went out once more to the American taxpayer, as it would many more times in the next half dozen years.

She saw Schlesinger briefly that first week.

"Jim, I've been wanting to ask you. Is there some distinct duty, some special field I might be assigned to for research or investigation. I want to jump right in and get started. Never could stand being idle or useless."

"Sure, Dr. Ray. Let's see now . . . ." The pipe Dixy would grow to hate as something of a hypnotic barrier between Schlesinger and anybody he faced now was eased back into his mouth and clenched firmly. He grabbed on with one hand as if he were preparing to pole-vault out of the room with it, and looked over her head and at the ceiling, where, as everyone knows, the words of the Oracle are always written.

"Sure . . . . Sure . . . . Why don't you look into plutonium?"

He said it around the pipe stem, never unclenching his teeth. It had the sound of Mama asking Mabel why she didn't go out and play hopscotch with Tessie.

"Fine," Dixy replied, not knowing why really. She said it as if she didn't mind playing with Tessie at all. Been doing it all the time, right?

It was obvious Schlesinger had very little interest in what Dixy would or wouldn't do. He would soon learn . . . .

Dixy began asking questions everywhere and, because she was a commissioner, got answers. She didn't quite understand all the answers yet, but she was getting an education fast. Without realizing it at first, she had barged into a most sensitive area — a major flap in the Defense Department over naval vessels that were carrying nuclear weapons. They were not being properly protected and were getting an unnecessarily high neutron dose. When her questions forged into the forbidden zone and began reverberating in high places, a message relayed through Schlesinger asked her, in effect, to "lay off." She was causing needless embarrassment, and besides, the AEC was already taking care of the flap, as she would discover in her first meeting with the rest of the commissioners.

Now, another flap emerged. How in hell did the brash newcomer, and a woman, at that, find out about the neutron scare in the face of strong security measures and a "Top Secret" lid? She was never questioned directly nor lectured nor even cajoled. But she knew from all the quick exits and entrances and the diplomatically phrased memos on the subject that she had put her finger in a 220-volt socket — and everybody else got the shock instead.

While playing sleuth her first two weeks in Germantown, she was also getting the most intense briefing she had ever received. She was staggered by the weight of the information, the technical difficulty inherent in it, and the sincerity and competence of the scientists who made the presentations. How, she wondered, would a nonscientist get through even a quarter of this material with no knowledge or acquaintance with the scientific jargon? She vowed that if she ever got the opportunity, she would simplify the material and spread it out over a much longer period.

In the meantime, Dixy thought she'd badger Schlesinger

once more with her question: "Jim, tell me, what does a commissioner really do?"

Pipe up. Jaw squared. Eyes to ceiling. Long pause. Same answer.

Now Dixy was smiling. "Jim, do you ever feel like a bird in a gilded cage?"

Pipe out. Jaw relaxed. Mouth agape. Eyes straight ahead. "No, Dixy, but I can see how you would." That was all he said.

Touché, at last. He was right. Dixy had always detested any semblance of a cage, while he could never live outside one, bird-watcher or no.

Under Schlesinger, commissioners were left strictly alone, as advertised. There was one exception: James Ramey. It became clear very quickly that Ramey ran his own show, while Schlesinger was boss in other areas. Ramey had chosen certain fields in which to roam and make decisions. In those areas he actually ran the AEC, and Schlesinger avoided them as if he were obeying a "Keep Off the Grass" sign; no tippy-toeing on Ramey lawns. But in all other things, Schlesinger not only ran the commission; he tolerated absolutely no interference and would not respond satisfactorily to inquiries for information. It was a strange, suspicious way to run one of the world's largest agencies, and a public agency, at that.

Everything was settled before any commission meeting was held. After a few exposures to such outlandish sessions, Dixy decided to go her own way and see if she couldn't be of some service until she could come to grips with "this anachronistic existence of mine." For example, she actually persuaded Schlesinger to adopt a Publications Review Board to bring some order to the vast number of pamphlets, reports, books, bibliographies, and other printed matter created by the AEC for the scientists, engineers, and general public, as well. It worked.

She also made suggestions concerning improvement of the public information system, and they were accepted, too. It seemed, however, that whatever small successes she had were tolerated because they didn't tamper with the meaty provinces in the Schlesinger and Ramey domains.

Dixy was disturbed by the evidences of empire-building inside the AEC — and outside, as well. She had made courtesy calls before confirmation on all members of Congress' Joint

Committee on Atomic Energy, and had made some discoveries about the "channels of power" that were to become painfully clear in later months. Her calls were of some surprise to the congressmen involved; no one had ever made the effort. They were very pleasant, and most of them were helpful and seemed to be pleased that a prospective federal commissioner would take the time to visit.

"I learned for the first time, through that exercise, that the JCAE didn't mean the membership of the committee; it meant Representative Chet Holifield of California. And it meant Senator John Pastore of Rhode Island while he was chairman. I learned to have no respect for the first, but a great deal for the second. Nevertheless, I was bothered then — and still am — by the extraordinary and unfair power Congress and the American people are willing to bestow on a few individuals. It is not only extraordinary and unfair. It's damned dangerous, particularly if the subject is nuclear power."

With the Holifield, Schlesinger, and Ramey kingdoms staring her in the face, she could see trouble ahead. But it was still rather hazy in outline.

At the AEC Dixy plodded along, reading everything she could get her hands on concerning the agency and the relatively new field of nuclear physics. It wasn't her chosen discipline, but she was engrossed with the subject and could not resist its fascination. Although she had virtually no decision-making authority, she could get an education in nuclear energy and federal administration and operation. It was to prove invaluable in the turbulent days ahead.

She had been told that Schlesinger had made more changes in the few months he had been chairman than anyone had effected in the preceding 20 years. The staff, it was said, was in turmoil over the changes, which most said were not made to improve things so much as to make certain the Schlesinger imprint would be clear for all to see. Changes merely for the sake of changes . . . He had ordered revisions in the entire paper-shuffling system, as well as all other methods of procedure, and, staffers complained, no one knew what was going to happen next. Dixy was told there had been "normal times" in the past, but the period of her arrival was certainly not one of them.

None of those things was evident to her. She saw no evidence of staff turmoil. Nor — and this is more important — did she see any signs of significant and productive changes in the system of operation.

If any area of operation needed change, it was in the meetings of the five-member commission. The sessions were dismal. Two impressions were distinct: First, they were an extraordinary waste of time because the real decisions had already been made beforehand and the meetings deteriorated into gabfests without purpose. And second, they proceeded aimlessly because Schlesinger simply didn't know how to conduct a meeting properly, for all his vaunted experience and expertise.

"I must temper that," Dixy said. "I was comparing the AEC sessions to some of the board of directors' meetings and committees on which I had served — never an agency with so many earth-shaking decisions to ponder. Now, there's a laugh. Earth-shaking decisions! The way Schlesinger — and Ramey — ran the AEC, no decisions of any magnitude were ever risked in the scrutiny of the three other commissioners. If anybody wanted to say anything at a meeting, that was fine. 'Bring it out on the table and we'll have at it.' The meetings went on, as a result, and on and on and on, dully and to no discernible purpose. If the paper system or the procedural system had been altered by Schlesinger in any way, it wasn't evident to me in the slightest."

That invited a most ironic recollection in Dixy. "Although they didn't offer me a chance to get a word in and play the sleuth, the briefings I'd had from the highly skilled and competent AEC technical staff were excellently prepared and staged. One at least could discover what was expected from each installation and each executive and employee in the field. The job descriptions were detailed and exact.

"Every man and woman working for the AEC or for private firms contracting work with the AEC knew what he or she was required to do and what was similarly required of superiors and subordinates. That is, and here's the irony, everyone from the AEC in Washington, DC, down to the smallest entity — *except* the five commissioners, who, by law, were responsible for running the entire national complex! Nobody could tell anybody how a commissioner could or should operate.

"Manuals on job responsibilities throughout the massive AEC structure were available at each installation, but not a word could be found anywhere on what was expected of the quintet that was required to create policy and coordinate one of the most complicated operational agencies of government with the White House and Congress. I find that extraordinary and baffling. Little wonder that Schlesinger ducked my questions on what a commissioner was supposed to do!"

That serious omission may have contributed to Schlesinger's decision to run things his way and shut out the rest of the commission, but it didn't explain his willingness to permit Ramey to set up and rule his own kingdom within a kingdom. When Dixy said she noticed no significant changes whatever that could be credited to Schlesinger, she acknowledged a strong bias — a bias based on the direct knowledge and observation that he recognized several extremely serious and dangerous problems and did nothing to correct them, although it was in his power to do so.

Dixy believed he failed to act because he had rationalized them for fear of jeopardizing his own political future. She drew a bead on the overriding, insufferable problems of the perilous tie between the Joint Committee on Atomic Energy and the AEC, as well as the separate and unregulated behavior of Jim Ramey in dictating policy and decisions within his own domain, without reference to Chairman Schlesinger and the three other commissioners.

The nation could not sustain a system in which a committee in Congress operated an agency! Worse still, it could not have a single congressional overlord control that agency and make it toe the line according to his whimsy or indigestion. The umbilical cord between the Joint Committee and the AEC was strangling one of the most important functions of government and an agency staffed with many of the brightest minds in or out of government.

How could Schlesinger permit the continuation of a modus operandum whose password was "Clear it with Ramey"? If Ramey approved a working paper, a policy position, or whatever, everyone seemed to accept the fact that there wouldn't be a problem ensuing and it was "safe" to let it take its quick course to approval and execution. Schlesinger certainly must have recognized how detrimental such a scheme was to an organization like the AEC. Yet he did nothing to counter or at least audit Ramey's operations. Nothing. Never.

CHAPTER EIGHT

The Gavel Changes Hands

T hroughout most of December, 1972, rumors wafted through the corridors of the sprawling Germantown headquarters building that James R. Schlesinger, chairman and father-figure of the AEC, was leaving. According to "sources," President Nixon had tapped him to take over as director of the Central Intelligence Agency to extract it, presumably, from its post-Watergate dilemma.

Few seemed to approve of the idea that Schlesinger might leave the AEC. Almost from the first moment he had become chairman after the 11-year reign of Dr. Glenn Seaborg, the headquarters staff felt Big Jim had rescued the AEC from stagnation and slow decline. He was just what the agency needed at the time. Jim thought so, too. Being chairman suited him just fine. Clearly, he did not want to leave, but he parried direct questions, and the rumors persisted.

Commissioners Clarence Larson, William Doub, and Dixy discussed the possibility that Schlesinger might leave. They agreed a change in the chairmanship would not be good for the AEC just then. Nevertheless, all three were more than a little annoyed at Schlesinger's refusal to discuss the subject with the commission. That is, it was clear each felt that way, despite the fact nobody spelled it out directly.

Meanwhile, it was a joyful White House that Christmas

season. The President's re-election triumph was still relatively untarnished; inauguration and a new four-year term awaited at the turn of the new year. A series of Christmas parties — relaxed, happy, informal receptions — rewarded the party faithful, the election workers, members of the official family, and presidential appointees. Dixy was invited to the last of these, on the evening of December 18.

No thrill can match that of being driven through the White House grounds, along that magnificent sweeping stretch to the south entrance, there to be greeted by the Marine Guard and escorted inside.

There is a curious blend of history, pride, and respect that seems to make a person a bit taller and to persuade him to step more softly whenever he crosses the threshold of the White House. Dixy was not immune to the emotion, and it was with a sense of elation that she made her way upstairs, past the stately pillars wrapped with wide, red ribbon, like peppermint candy, and hung with holly wreaths. A crowd of about 200 was gathered in the East Room. She wandered around, greeted the few people she knew, and made her way to a fairly uncrowded corner.

She had barely reached the open spot when the loudspeaker boomed:

"Ladies and gentlemen, the President of the United States!"

So, she wound up right in front. The Marine Band played "Hail to the Chief!" President Nixon walked in buoyantly, and all in attendance cheered mightily. Nixon spoke briefly and to the point. He thanked everyone for helping in the campaign and declared his high hopes for achievement at home and abroad in his second term. She had the strange but persistent feeling that every so often he directed his remarks especially to her, but she had to put it down to the fact that she was right there, only a few feet from the podium, and that she probably stood out like a sore thumb in her white jacket and red shirt, while nearly everyone else in the room was dressed in black or some dark color. 'Anyhow,' she said to herself, 'this is your first White House party; don't be stupid.'

Later, as they shook hands in the reception line, the President asked Dixy how she was enjoying her work on the commission. "Very much, Mr. President. It's a remarkable agency. Please don't take any action that might weaken it."

She was referring to newspaper reports that the Department of Interior would take over some of AEC's functions and that there might possibly be a change in the chairmanship.

The President laughed and said, "Don't worry. Now, I think we have something in mind for you . . . yes, yes, indeed we do." He smiled again and turned to greet the next guest. The line marched on, and so did Dixy, deeply wondering what he meant . . . .

The next day her Christmas holiday started, and for a while she forgot the President's remark. It was late when she finally arrived home, because she had been forced to wait at the Seattle-Tacoma Airport for the little single-engine commuter plane that set her down at last at the Tacoma Industrial Airport, only 10 minutes away from her private Paradise, Fox Island.

There was a message waiting for her. Call Dr. Schlesinger immediately. She looked at her watch — 11 p.m. (2300). It was 2 o'clock in the morning in Washington, DC, so she decided to wait, rather than phone at such an unreasonable hour. She knew Schlesinger himself never hesitated to call in the middle of the night, but only the gravest emergency could compel her to do so.

It was mid-morning of December 20 when the following conversation — as close as she could recall it — took place:

JIM: Well, it is certain that I'll be leaving the AEC and going over to the CIA. I wanted you to hear it from me.

DIXY: I'm very sorry about that. I think you're needed at the AEC. But if it's inevitable, I guess the question now is who will be the next chairman?

JIM: Well, the signal from the White House is that it will be you.

DIXY: Me!?!? But . . .

JIM: Yes, and I also want you to know that I don't support you for the job! I don't think it's a good idea.

DIXY: Well . . . I appreciate your frankness. Mind telling me why?

JIM: No, I don't mind. You haven't been on the commission long enough. You don't have any experience running a federal agency. I doubt whether you can control either the commissioners or the staff.

DIXY: Well . . . in general . . . I guess I'd have to agree with you. Obviously, I still have lots to learn about nuclear science and about the federal government . . . . May I ask who you think should be chairman?

JIM: Obviously, no one else on the present commission is possible. We had anticipated that you would eventually become chairman, but only after having had at least a year as a commissioner. No, I think it would be a mistake for you to be moved now. I am supporting Ed David (President Nixon's science adviser) for the job.

DIXY: I know Ed, of course, and I think he would be fine. I'd be glad to work with him. Does Ed have any special knowledge about AEC and its functions?

JIM: No, but he understands the administration. I don't know whether the White House will support him or not. (David resigned shortly afterward as a result of one of those soon-to-become-familiar White House power plays.)

DIXY: Oh, yes, I see.

JIM: The White House has suggested I could give you some coaching and a "crash course" on being chairman.

DIXY: That would be very helpful.

JIM: Well, we'll talk about it when you get back.

DIXY: Fine. Merry Christmas, and thanks for the information.

Thus it was that Dixy first learned she might be chosen the AEC's next chairman. The conversation with Schlesinger also clarified what President Nixon had meant when he said he had "something in mind for you."

Why was she selected? Were there reasons other than merit? Was she to be the administration's token woman agency head? She still does not know but suspects John Ehrlichman, whose roots were in Seattle, was involved in the selection. Schlesinger had a very healthy respect for John, Nixon's No. 2 aide, even though he did not know him well and seldom had direct contact with him.

When Dixy returned to Washington early in January, the word was out that Schlesinger would be leaving the AEC. Now speculation turned to the question of his successor. Various names — not including hers — were bandied about and widely discussed, and everyone seemed to have a favorite candidate. She enjoyed it all.

As soon as she returned, she went in to see Schlesinger.

"Well, it was kind of interesting . . . what you said on the phone. What's the situation now?"

"There's not much support for Ed David," Schlesinger replied, "and that kind of bothers me. They're still talking about you. I guess we could give you a crash course."

There was his "crash course" talk again. And just talk.

That's the way it went. Schlesinger was noncommittal. He refused to talk about the subject of his successor. No word came from the White House, and she continued to keep her own counsel. Only Doub started a campaign — for Doub. But he was never seriously considered.

Twice in the early weeks of January Dixy sought to discuss the issue with Schlesinger and, if she were really being considered for the post, to get his thoughts and advice on some of the commission's outstanding problems. But he was reluctant to talk, saying only that no decision had been reached. He was also too busy getting ready for his next assignment. He spent considerable time at the CIA and in the H Street office of the AEC, and he was seldom seen at the commission's Germantown, Maryland, headquarters.

Nevertheless, Dixy recalls vividly one memorable occasion, a farewell party for Schlesinger, staged in his fourth-floor office by the staff of the Division of Military Applications. Several dozen employees, all in costume and carrying signs, crowded the big office to sing a specially written version of "On Top of Old Smokey."

A retired Air Force general had donned ridiculously funny 1920's aviation attire and stalked around with his shirt tail hanging out. It had been a source of considerable staff merriment that Schlesinger, no matter how neatly attired, could never keep his shirt tail tucked in. Another general wore a blond wig and shorts and, like the others, sang lustily. There were presents and mementoes and silly jokes. It was a happy, sad, nostalgic party, and Schlesinger must have left the AEC with a good feeling. He also left behind those unresolved problems — problems that he recognized full well but did nothing to correct.

Jim Schlesinger bequeathed to those who followed "closets"

full of skeletons, many, of course, inherited from the past. He left a number of trusted staff in key positions; they were persons he would depend upon to keep him informed of commission business — and particularly what the new chairman did or didn't do. Schlesinger tried to take the AEC with him to the CIA, or, rather, to continue to have an influence on commission policy after he left. He had grown to respect the competence and responsiveness of the AEC staff and to enjoy the perquisites of the chairmanship.

Although he was in the process of moving to the CIA, Schlesinger continued to work on the AEC budget and to prepare for the hearings scheduled in January on authorizations for the 1974 fiscal year. He suggested that Dixy attend the hearing, but he offered no comment on his planned testimony. Nor was she given any special briefings on budget strategy or planning. She was left to her own devices.

His words came back to her more than once. "The White House has suggested I could give you some coaching and a 'crash course' on being chairman . . ."

Later that January, Dixy was interviewed by John Walsh of *Science* magazine. He turned out to be knowledgeable, well prepared, and intelligent. It was a refreshing contrast to some of the reporters she had met so far in the nation's capital. He actually refrained from asking her the inevitable, frustrating question that was to her the ultimate in asininity: "What does it feel like to be a woman on the commission?"

In a short time it was to be: "What does it feel like to be a woman chairman? . . . chairwoman?? . . . chairperson????"

Her stock answer was: "How would I know? I've never been a man. Why don't you reporters ask men the same kind of questions you ask women? For example, 'Tell me, Dr. Kissinger, what does it feel like to be a man?'"

Dixy actually got along well with most reporters in the capital. One of the peskiest fancied himself as more knowledgeable about science and energy than most others, including Dixy. He baited her constantly. One day, after a barrage of loaded questions, he asked her:

"By the way, what do I call you — Miss Ray, Ms. Ray, Dr. Ray, or Chairman Ray?"

Fixing him with a stare, Dixy said: "Oh, you can call me Your Highness!" And she stalked off, grinning with satisfaction.

Walsh didn't even comment or ask for comment about her

dogs, motor home, or casual dress. What a refreshing experience! Here was a dedicated reporter who actually thought the nation's nuclear policy and operation to be of greater importance than her pets, residence, or wardrobe.

They were conversing in the otherwise empty H Street office of the AEC in downtown Washington. Although it was midwinter, the day was sunny and clear, and the combination of the usual overheated federal building and afternoon sun streaming through the windows made the office hot. But temperature alone was not the principal cause of her sudden sweat. In strode Schlesinger, unannounced, at the height of the interview. One look at his face and she knew . . . The decision had been made. She was the next chairman. And she was totally untutored.

Schlesinger asked her to go to his office, so she quickly concluded the interview with apologies to Walsh.

"Well," Schlesinger began as she approached his desk, "the signal is loud and clear. The White House wants you to be chairman. They (whoever the 'they' are when the mind is pointed to the White House would make a book of its own) insist on it. You know how I feel about . . ."

"Yes, I do. I'll do my best."

"Do you think you can handle it?"

"Yes." I knew he expected me to say that.

"Do you think you can control the commission?"

"Well, I can try."

After a brief but awkward pause, she asked: "Do you think you can give me some answers? I have a lot of questions?"

"Oh, we'll have plenty of time for that."

Another awkward pause. Finally:

"They (there it was again) have given me the task of selling the idea of having you as chairman to the Joint Committee."

That did surprise her. She knew the Atomic Energy Act called for the President to select one of the commissioners to serve as chairman "at his pleasure" and that the Joint Committee had to be consulted. But she thought that had already been done and that it was only a matter of courtesy anyway. Why the histrionics now — and by a man who had already informed her she was not his choice to succeed him?

Schlesinger told her later that all members of the Joint Committee had indicated no opposition, except for Congressman Chet Holifield, who growled his reluctance to see a woman occupy the chairman's post. Schlesinger said it was only after considerable discussion and some arm-twisting from the White House that Holifield agreed not to make an issue of her appointment. It was only the beginning of a relationship with the eternal chauvinist that would lead Holifield to label her as "that evil woman." He went further. Despite his formidable reputation as the prime mover in America's nuclear program, he seemed to be willing to stand aside and watch the scuttling of the Atomic Energy Commission, rather than let her remain in power.

In the weeks Schlesinger remained at the AEC before moving on to his new job with the CIA, Dixy saw him many times but only once when she was able to ask him a few questions. She had boiled them down to the few essentials because it was obvious he had little time for her. Nevertheless, he always seemed to have time and an inclination to give her advice when they were in a group or crowd.

On the single occasion she was able to ask a few questions, she received few answers. He seemed particularly concerned about her lack of interest in the weapons program. More correctly, it was what he *considered* her lack of interest. She had had no chance to learn much about the weapons program before joining the agency and very little after joining because of the press of other issues — plus the fact she had already indicated her major concern would be in the areas of communications with the public and nuclear safety. Also, she was to discover how little the commissioners had been permitted to know about nuclear weapons because of the "closed club" status imposed by Schlesinger and Ramey.

When she asked Schlesinger for a brief rundown on the weapons program so she wouldn't take over as chairman in a sea of ignorance, he grabbed his pipe, waved a hand with some impatience, and said:

"Oh, it will run itself. You don't have to bother about it."

He obviously didn't know her well. That's the kind of advice she could never take, particularly when it was she who had been given the ultimate responsibility. Although her principal attention for several months when she became chairman was to reorganize the general manager's office at the AEC and civilian nuclear-energy matters, she found enough time to learn a great deal about weapons and intelligence.

Dixy's reference to finding Schlesinger "alone" for questions has to be modified. He was alone only in the sense she could address questions to him without interruption. Someone else was there in the H Street meeting, and it was the ubiquitous Marty (Martin R.) Hoffman, Schlesinger's shadow. He was seldom far from Schlesinger. Thanks to the close association, Hoffman eventually was rewarded with an appointment as Secretary of the Army, a choice Dixy characterized as incredible in light of her experience with him. She was surprised by the fact that President Ford appointed Hoffman and even more surprised by the rapidity with which the Senate confirmed him.

Had Dixy not been in the process at the time of moving from the capital back to her home on Fox Island, she would have protested the appointment to the senators she knew best. She said Hoffman performed so poorly as counsel to the AEC while she was chairman that she had to ask him to resign. Only his willingness to find other employment — a chore he took his sweet time doing — caused her to withhold his firing.

Schlesinger lectured Dixy once more about "controlling the commissioners." Again he made it clear he believed the chairman's job was beyond her capability. Now he went a bit further. He impressed upon Dixy the need to keep his "team" in place. She had no intention of doing so, but she wondered why he had insisted "the White House" wanted it that way. As it turned out, the White House couldn't have cared less!

Sure, she told Schlesinger. She'd keep his team intact . . . "for the time being." She tried to get some expression of opinion from him about uranium-fuel enrichment, radioactive-waste management, safety problems, regulatory programs, private-industry relations, and the controversial breeder-reactor program that was so important to America's future as a nuclear power — or any kind of power. But he wasn't interested in talking about such things. About the breeder program he simply waved his hand and said, airily:

"It's no big deal. They haven't built anything for so long that they've forgotten how. And anyway, the breeder's not important."

Astounding! Coming from him, it was also alarming. Because of his remark, she had to ask him a question about Milt Shaw, who had been in charge of the breeder program — the botched up breeder program, that is — and who was to be one of her biggest problems as chairman.

"Jim, is Milt Shaw indispensable?"

His answer was "Hell, no!"

When Schlesinger appeared a short time later before the

Joint Committee, actually his last performance on behalf of the AEC, she could not believe what she heard and saw. "Performance" is the right word because it was contrived melodrama. Schlesinger switched character and went into an emotional outburst on behalf of Shaw that was awkward and macabre. He must have known Shaw's days were numbered with the AEC because of his problems as a manager and administrator and his friction in the field. Yet, Schlesinger delivered a florid oration concerning Shaw's virtues. Dixy was convinced it was done to thwart her in her determination to clean house in the AEC.

She had to carry the burden of Schlesinger with her to the chairman's seat. She also had to fend for herself because the man who had promised a "crash course" and who said there "was plenty of time" for questions, never delivered. Because he couldn't or wouldn't?

CHAPTER NINE

Running
the Nuclear
Show

For all his opposition to Dixy as chairman, James Schlesinger did his job well in carrying out a White House mandate to "get her accepted" by the Joint Committee. He also helped write the official announcement that would launch her with as much apparent administration support as "they" felt would be needed to "do the trick."

She bit her tongue several times during that period, however, as Schlesinger kept reminding her:

"Don't worry. Nobody expects much from you, and that could be an advantage, probably your only advantage." What arrogance!

He also revealed that one key White House staffer, Peter Flanigan, had been vigorous and unrelenting in his opposition to her. On the other hand, Bob Hollingsworth, general manager of the AEC ten years, had strongly supported her from the beginning. Together they were to bring fundamental, urgently needed changes to the agency — changes others had been afraid to make for fear of damaging the old political image.

Dixy had been like a puppet waiting for her strings to be manipulated. No fanfare accompanied her assumption of the chairmanship. She was never called to the White House to discuss the chairmanship. A simple announcement came from the President's office on February 6, 1973. "Dr. Dixy Lee Ray was named chairman of the AEC today by . . ." She wasn't even invited to attend the press conference at which the announcement was made! Ronald Ziegler read the statement, which had some nice words in it that had been worked out at the AEC. Because no groundwork had been laid, the announcement was greeted by a combination of incredulity and amusement from certain segments of the press and the nuclear industry. But she had expected it.

She was more determined than ever to do the job right and do it well. She wasn't interested in a political future in Washington, DC. She knew it was corny, but she was earnestly interested in doing her best for her country — and what an opportunity lay before her to do just that! But what heartaches were to go with it, as well.

It didn't take long for her to sound her own horn in what may have been the first shot for Dixy's independence heard at 1700 Pennsylvania Avenue. Ten days after taking over the chairmanship, she was called down — perhaps "summoned" is the more accurate word — to the lordly Office of Management and Budget and given the word. And what a word it was!

"The entire civilian reactor program is going to be moved over to the Interior Department, as well as the production program, and the AEC is going to be cut up, carved up, and redistributed. Only the regulatory function will be left. The other divisions will go to Interior, the National Science Foundation, Commerce, or whatever. Or there will be created a new Department of Energy and Natural Resources."

What a bomb that was! She had fought total dismantling of the AEC, and everybody in the capital knew it. But now she was being informed by the OMB that the decision had already been made, not only by the White House but by the AEC itself.

"The AEC," OMB staffers told her, "was on record just last year in support of the breakup in either direction."

She stood her ground.

"So sorry. Too bad. That was last year. This year we have a new chairman."

It was time to make some noise. She went to John Ehrlichman. Neither option pleased her nor did it please most AEC technical and administrative staffers. But of the two courses, the move of the civilian program, the production program, and the assignment program into Interior, giving the research responsibility to the NSF, was much the better of the two options, in her opinion.

"If you take the entire works into a Department of Energy and Natural Resources," she said, "all you will have is another blown up Interior. What I really prefer is that both options be junked in the nation's best interest."

John listened intently, scratching his chin, those massive eyebrows in a state of "ponder." She hadn't "rung his bell" yet, so she continued, obviously nettled:

"Look, if you want the AEC to be receptive and helpful to the administration and to carry out the big job it has at this time, this is a helluva lousy time to start carving it up. I'm going to resist this sort of thing."

The bell rang. He looked at her in a "kind of funny way," and said:

"You're right. We won't do it that way."

From that moment on, the signal went out: The AEC was not going to be carved up and portions delivered to Interior and the NSF. From that time forward the administration and many segments of the AEC itself, including Dixy, began thinking about another alternative. That was the origin of ERDA (Energy Research and Development Administration), which eventually replaced all but the regulatory function of the AEC. If only the measure that eventually came out of Congress could have been as well conceived as the ideas that went in . . .

She gave Ehrlichman an "A" for effort, at least. He had heard her loud and clear. There was a way the AEC could work with the administration, and there was a way in which it wouldn't, she had informed him. She didn't think they wanted to appoint a chairman one day and have her leave within a month. Her threat had been quite a gamble, but it worked.

Some of the White House cohorts didn't quite believe the word handed down by Ehrlichman, and they carried on a word battle with her over her stand and her protest to John. She resolved to take further action. The agency's position had to be committed to paper, so she spent an entire Sunday putting it together. It went in the form of a memorandum to Ehrlichman and to Roy Ash at the budget office. The memo pulled no punches. Nor did it endear her to the pussyfooters at the OMB and elsewhere in the administration, "but I didn't give a damn. I wasn't running for King of the Hill. Or Queen."

The executives and staffers at the AEC couldn't believe what she'd done, but they were happy and a bit proud of the fact that somebody had had enough lip to face down the pugnacious budget crowd on behalf of saving the AEC, as well as going to bat for it. The news spread quickly throughout the international AEC complex. A star was born.

Dixy saw John Ehrlichman three more times before he left the White House at the "request" of President Nixon. One of the pesky problems was Marty Hoffman, who had to be removed as the AEC's general counsel because he wouldn't cooperate and do his job. She wanted to compare notes with John because she didn't want to work crosswise with the White House if she gave Hoffman his marching orders. The oddity was that the general counsel in all other agencies was a presidential appointee, but not in the AEC. Nevertheless, she believed it was the proper, courteous thing to consult with the White House.

She also wanted to discuss with John the need to do something about Milt Shaw and the snafued breeder-reactor budget and program. Finally, she needed his ear and that of the President over the sticky situation with regard to Commissioner Jim Ramey, whose "one-man show" within the AEC had to be terminated for the sake of the agency and the nation's nuclear program. Ehrlichman became a valuable pipeline in that brief period, and he helped her on all three issues — as long as he was able. After he was gone, the AEC became virtually an orphan agency as far as the White House was concerned. From that time forward Dixy operated without any direct signals from the White House on what the administration expected of the AEC; nor did she have the support of the White House, despite the fact she could have used it often in doing battle with the budget office.

In the meantime, Dixy was doing her homework for the battles she knew were ahead. She never received the "crash course" Schlesinger had advertised, but she was in a constant crash course of her own making from the day she was appointed to the day she left. She determined, almost in self-defense, to become knowledgeable in every phase of AEC operations, a determination that was accelerated on becoming chairman.

The AEC became a passion of study. Seven days and seven nights every week of the year she pored over reports, pamphlets, books, records, charts, maps, everything available to her to learn more about what she called "this most amazing development of man in the 20th Century." When she left the AEC, she could not profess to be a nuclear physicist, an engineer, a chemist, or any other type of scientist other than what she already was — a biologist. But she honestly felt she knew the ropes as chairman of the AEC and that she could hold her own with any delegation from Congress or any public or private entity involved with the nuclear process.

What an education it was! Although she had been a student all her life, she had never put in a more intensive stretch of study. It was to bolster her immensely in the many bitter confrontations she had to face in one of the most sensitive areas of government involvement. Dixy often had to go it alone in the face of severe criticism from the press, Congress, and even, at times, the private sector, but the hundreds of hours of homework gave her the confidence she needed to hold her ground and dare be the maverick she had to be to oppose greed, political gain, chicanery, and even corruption.

CHAPTER TEN

The Housecleaning Begins

When Dixy took the commissioner reins February 6, she moved down the hall to the big suite of rooms first occupied by Dr. Glenn Seaborg, the California scientist, when the Germantown headquarters was constructed, then by James Schlesinger for 18 months. The first time she saw the placard, "Dixy Lee Ray, Chairman," it gave her a start. The new life had begun. Welcome, Madame Chairman, to the Nuclear Age.

As she had expected, the Atomic Energy Act of 1954 notwithstanding, the chairman was de facto head of the agency and universally treated as such. A series of special briefings — for the AEC chairman only — gave her a clear look at some of the government's most secret security arrangements. She received her special code and instruction book and ID card that would admit her to the underground command post in the event of a military emergency.

In the first few weeks Dixy received the cooperation and help of the other commissioners, but the camaraderie didn't last long. Once more male chauvinism asserted itself. A woman had taken over through "political luck," and the male members of the commission didn't hide their antagonism. William Kriegsman was to be Dixy's major problem. She couldn't understand why he seemed to invent ways to oppose or rile her. She found out in time; he had a "connection" at the White House. William Doub was frequently amenable, but he wanted the No. 1 job himself, and he never forgave Dixy for climbing over him. When he didn't get his way, Doub pouted — and displayed his temper at times to gain attention. On a couple of occasions Dixy had to summon help because of his sudden displays of emotional fireworks. Clarence Larson, a "yes" man who enjoyed the perquisites of being a commissioner, was in far over his head as a policymaker for the most sensitive operational agency in the federal government.

None of the three, in Dixy's view, had the qualifications necessary for so important a position; even she did not have the background she would have thought necessary for a seat on the commission and most certainly for the chairman's job, but she had at least made a gigantic effort to learn. The others had been satisfied to let staffers do the thinking while they concentrated on the dinner circuit.

A neutral observer might have found credit and blame on both sides. Dixy, always the workaholic and perpetual seven-day-and-night student, found supreme joy in driving herself through layers of knowledge and absorbing every morsel. She had the brain and capacity for it, and she thrived on burning midnight oil, as she had from childhood. The three other commissioners wanted to be comfortable in their lofty positions. They were more politically minded and had neither her drive nor thirst for information.

Nevertheless, right was not always on her side. One of Dixy's closest friends acknowledged: "With a little bit of finesse, Dixy could have had the three other commissioners eating out of her hand. But, as was the case many times in her life, she disliked any suggestion that she compromise her principles for the sake of momentary gain.

"Kriegsman, for example, did much to earn her displeasure. but she did much to earn his, too. I think he started it all, but she could have called a halt to the childish displays with a dash of diplomacy. Once he had assumed a frown, there was no retreating for her. As one simple illustration, I remember that each time she was required to absent herself from a commission meeting, she had to designate an acting chairman. It had been custom to tap the next in line in seniority. Well, Kriegsman was next in line, but Dixy always passed him by, anointing one of the other commissioners instead. She kept Kriegsman at arm's length from the first sign of his disdain; she never considered extending him an olive branch. Too bad. She might have disarmed him if she had and embarrassed him out of tattling to his White House sources whenever he had a run-in with her."

In the summer of 1973, William Anders, the astronaut, was appointed to the commission vacancy left by Schlesinger — and Dixy at last had a genuine, intelligent, and cooperative friend on the commission, and someone who wanted to work. She didn't always get a majority for the decisions she wanted, but with Anders' help and the power given the chairman by past performance and the Atomic Energy Act, she was able to run one of the biggest agencies in government smoothly and efficiently. It was her experience with the three other commissioners and the frustration of trying to do things by committee that soured Dixy permanently on the commission system of running governmental affairs. When she became governor of Washington State four years later, she drew a bead on all commissions and boards and committees that seemed to have been created primarily for political officials to find places for men and women who had helped them get elected.

Once again Dixy felt threatened by the same emerging chauvinism that had caused her so much grief as a faculty zoologist. But now, at least, she was in the driver's seat and had scores of supersensitive nuclear issues to keep her busy. Of the many programs she now began delving into in earnest, one that intrigued her most, perhaps because it combined work at sea with nuclear functions, was Project Jennifer.

Dixy first learned about the project in the summer of 1974. As chairman of the AEC, she had been invited to attend a top-secret meeting of the gold-braid military and intelligence officials. When she left, she was exhilarated by what she had seen and heard. Although she was sworn to secrecy — a condition which prevails to this day, she could talk in general terms about what she had seen and what the Central Intelligence Agency, which was running the show, had revealed. Ten months later, while ensconced in the new position of Assistant Secretary of State for Oceans, International Environmental and Scientific Affairs in Dr. Henry Kissinger's tepee at Foggy Bottom, she was both amused and infuriated when Columnist Jack Anderson led a newspaper barrage that sank Project Jennifer.

As assistant secretary, she was to wonder whether the Nuclear Age had been supplanted by the Age of Burglary. Like the Ellsberg-Pentagon Papers brouhaha and Watergate, a burglary touched off an international incident over Project Jennifer. In June, 1974, burglars broke into Howard Hughes' Summa Corp. headquarters in Los Angeles and absconded with secret papers that included a supersensitive memo detailing plans to recover a Soviet submarine that had exploded and sunk to a depth of 16,000 feet in the Pacific Ocean 750 miles northwest of Oahu, Hawaiian Islands. Los Angeles policemen, entrusted with the job of finding the burglars, let the cat out of the bag. Word of the seriousness of the situation made its way to the *Los Angeles Times*, the *Washington Post*, and the *New York Times*.

An anonymous figure threw the peanut brittle into the fan when he sent feelers to the federal government indicating the papers could be "bought back" for $1 million. The FBI arranged for an intermediary but the mysterious figure, whoever he was, never showed up and made no more contacts. The mystery remained unsolved.

When the *Los Angeles Times*, hot on the scent, published a teaser piece about the project, William E. Colby, then director of the CIA, jumped into action, He asked that the story and the subsequent detailed series promised by the Los Angeles paper be shelved. Similar reports had been prepared by the *Post* and the *New York Times*. Colby was successful with all three. They were impressed by his account of the seriousness of the project and held up their series, provided "no one else broke the news ahead of time."

Now the project could start up again. The *Glomar Explorer*, built by the Hughes complex as a ship designed to seek mineral deposits at the bottom of oceans, had brought up parts of the Soviet submarine in the summer of 1974, when Dixy and others had been briefed. However, a misfunction in the lifting gear had caused parts of the sub to fall back to the bottom after it had come up 8,000 of the 16,000 feet to the surface. In the summer of 1975, the *Explorer* would return when the weather improved to finish the job.

Still at the bottom were at least three newly designed Russian missiles with nuclear warheads and a code machine! They were the prize — and the reason for the super-secrecy. If the Russians became aware of the undersea expedition, one of the greatest intelligence schemes in American history probably would have been thwarted.

"Well," Dixy commented a short time later, "what the Russians couldn't find out for themselves, the columnist, Jack Anderson, was able to find out for them and tell the rest of the world, too."

When Anderson heard about Project Jennifer, he made arrangements to go on the air with the story, despite the fact the nation's three most prestigious newspapers had agreed to hold up the report in the national interest. Attempts to persuade Anderson to hold the story until the *Explorer* could go back out to bring up the Soviet missiles and code machine were waved off. The public, Anderson said, has a right to know what's going on, and that was that. Realizing Anderson intended to break the story on his radio program and in his column, the newspapers did so, as well.

Colby, Dixy, and the entire American military and intelligence network were never to know what secrets the missiles and the code machine would have unveiled. The CIA, already under severe attack on charges of perpetrating assassinations and terrorism in many nations, was forced to retreat. A direct confrontation now over the potentially embarrassing predicament of one nation recovering another's secrets in the open sea was a battle the CIA could not afford.

If Dixy had been in command, the order would most certainly have been: "To hell with the Russians! Anything that finds its way to the bottom of the ocean belongs to anybody that has the savvy to go down and get it! As far as we know, they probably have recovered some of the things we have lost at sea or out of the air in the past 50 years without telling us about it."

But Dixy was not the commander, and the *Glomar Explorer* was returned to drydock and eventually, a year later, to mothballs. Fortunately, she was recalled to duty in 1978 and leased by the Navy to a private company for undersea explorations.

"I can't talk about the nuclear aspect of the sunken sub," Dixy said, "but I wish all the American people and the press could have seen and heard what we did at the 1974 briefing. They would have a new respect for American ingenuity and extraordinary engineering skill. Mr. Colby and the CIA told us they got

Howard Hughes in on it because they wanted to disguise the vessel's purpose. They advertised it as an experimental ship designed to mine strategic manganese nodules and other minerals at sea bottom, but their real purpose was to go after the submarine.

"You know something . . .? I think they inadvertently got their values twisted. They would have learned relatively little, I think, from the Soviet missiles, and with the frequent leaks we've seen in American government, I have no doubt the Russians would have discovered their problem and scrapped the old code anyway. On the other hand, a magnificent ship like the *Glomar Explorer*, which can reach down 16,000 feet or more to the depth of the ocean and bring back whatever is down there is something no other nation in the world has come close to building."

In the State Department she came face to face with the demands of the Third World for an equal share of the First World's riches. While she acknowledged some compensations may be in order to help those undeveloped nations of the world, it "would be madness" to give in to their demands.

"When someone tells me that the United States must turn over most of the resources it finds in the oceans to many other countries because those countries are inland and have no access to the sea, I say he must be a damn fool. If we use our ingenuity, our talent, our financial resources, and our time and effort to find new supplies of food, energy, and minerals, I don't see why we must then turn it all over to another country, big or little, that has expended not a muscle nor a brain cell in its own interest. What would happen to incentive if that should become the law of the world?"

Dixy's on-the-job training as AEC chairman continued at an intense clip. Every morning a special classified information book landed on her desk. It was picked up by special courier about 6 a.m. at the CIA and brought over for her perusal before going on its way through other top-echelon government posts. For a while she read it religiously, but it was dull, dull, dull, and terribly repetitious. It contained all the gleanings from the "community," as the intelligence groups in different agencies were called collectively. Occasionally, however, significant items appeared in the classified book, so she remained steadfast in her early-morning reading. More and more she relied on the staffs of the ISA and DMA (International Security Affairs and Division of Military

Applications) to bring the important items to her attention as internal and domestic problems loomed larger and larger.

Undoubtedly the greatest crisis Dixy faced as chairman of the AEC, next to the final days in which Congress finally split the agency, came with the inevitable clash between the new chairman and Milton Shaw, director of the nuclear-reactor program. He was a longtime employee of the AEC, and he had drawn many protectors over the years, particularly among the commissioners who preceded Dixy and certain elements within the commercial nuclear industry. With ties inside the AEC, in the industry, and in powerful congressional circles, Shaw turned out to be an extremely formidable adversary, even for tough Dixy Lee Ray.

The naval program has always been an integral part of the nation's nuclear complex, which means it was part of the AEC. And yet, because of the prima donna status accorded Admiral Hyman Rickover by congressmen who worshipped at his feet, it has always been an entity unto itself. Dixy frequently praised Rickover's role as the "Father of the Nuclear Navy," but his inflexibility and insistence on having his own way, risky as it often was, disturbed her deeply. Perhaps she has never realized she was much like him; had she been a man, I am positive Congress would have sainted her, too, just as it had Rickover.

Shaw was one of the admiral's protégés. Rickover had trained him and given him considerable responsibility in the naval-reactor program. The principal reason the U.S. today has embraced the light-water technology and that the light-water reactor is the nation's primary nuclear reactor was the influence of Admiral Rickover and his early direction of the Navy's reactor program. In the very beginning, two types of reactors were being tested in submarines. One was the light-water reactor and the other the liquid-metal reactor. The first used water to cool the process, and the second, sodium, which is alternately metal or liquid, depending upon temperatures.

All nuclear reactors in the U.S. today, except for certain test or experimental reactors, are light-water reactors using ordinary water, or H_2O. Canada and most other foreign nations use heavy-water reactors; the heavy-water, or D_2O, has much more than the usual heavy hydrogen (deuterium) atoms, and it is used as a moderator or coolant because it slows down the neutrons in the fission process. The slowing down permits use of considerably cheaper natural grades of uranium for fuel.

The use of sodium permits an even slower process. Its great advantage in the highly controversial liquid metal fast-breeder reactor, for example, is that it permits creation of more fuel than it uses.

When the Navy first experimented with nuclear submarines, a light-water reactor was utilized in the *Nautilus* and a liquid-metal, or sodium, reactor in the *Sea Wolf*.

"The *Sea Wolf* had the only liquid-metal reactor ever built and operated," Dixy said. "It was very successful, but after it was installed and operated for a considerable length of time, Admiral Rickover decided the possibility of reaction with water was too great, and he ordered discontinuance of the liquid-metal technology. Now, I don't want to blame Rick for this, but if we had continued our work with the liquid-metal reactor we would have had a successful breeder program many years ago — and the paranoia over breeders fostered by the Nader clan never would have taken root. As it is, the decision to shelve the breeder program by Presidents, as well as by admirals and others, was a disastrous blow to America's energy future. The Russians and French have had successful breeder programs many years, but we — who created the technology and engineering for it — have yet to build and operate our first breeder."

Shaw was the manager of the *Sea Wolf* reactor for Rickover, and Dixy long suspected his attachment to the *Sea Wolf* experiment and his intense determination to prove to the admiral that the liquid-metal reactor was a good one heavily influenced his later actions. Despite that difference of opinion in the two men, Dixy believed Shaw was actually trying to be another Rickover. However, it was evident he left the Navy program to join the AEC and take charge of the Division of Reactor Technology Development because of the Navy's decision to table the liquid-metal reactor.

"He went into the AEC program in the mid-1960's," Dixy said, "and he became the fair-haired boy of Chet Holifield and Jim Ramey almost from the beginning. Milt Shaw was an engineer, and a good engineer. But he was not a successful manager because he insisted upon imposing not only his decisions but his methods of work on everybody under him or around him, He had a manner I can describe only as Prussian. Shaw was a very complex man, and I really felt sorry for him and those who worked for him. He had very strong opinions, and he was sure that if he were simply stubborn enough and refused to compromise long enough, he could have his way on any issue.

"One of the notions he held that I had to fight was his stated desire to destroy the Oak Ridge National Laboratory. I never really knew exactly why, but I was equally determined that that fine American institution should live forever. At one time he could have accomplished his goal, because he had Congressman Holifield on his side and both of them detested my old friend, Dr. Alvin Weinberg, who ran the Oak Ridge lab. To this day I don't understand the Holifield-Shaw dislike of Oak Ridge, but I have to believe it had no place in the Holifield nuclear empire."

In addition to Shaw's close allegiance to Holifield and Ramey, he created two major problems for Chairman Ray, and they represented two of the most significant problems in the days to come for the American people.

First, Dixy demanded a breakup of the nuclear-reactor division and a separation of safety engineering from reactor development. Her contention from the beginning was that the people who create and develop reactors should not also decide how safe they were. Safety measures, she said, should be virtually in opposition to the development wing. How else could the nation be confident that safety factors would not be swept under the rug? She had the same philosophy in championing the division of the AEC into a regulatory component and a development department.

Second, Shaw loved the breeder program to death. Dixy agreed that it was necessary to pursue fast breeders to insure a continued supply of nuclear fuel and expand the nation's energy supply. But Shaw ran the reactor division as if breeders were the only program on the AEC agenda. Other programs were neglected. The irony was that Shaw invited continued severe criticism of the AEC because it was devoting time and money that should have been going to other programs. Shaw's "breeder blinders" also contributed to a serious lag in the AEC's program of nuclear-fusion research.

In all his excesses Shaw had the support of Congressman Holifield, who had fought long and hard against the "strong chairman" philosophy because it cramped his style, and Commissioner Ramey, who derived his power from Holifield because he had been chief of staff of the Joint Committee and had been ushered into the AEC as a commissioner with Holifield as his protector and patron.

"It's nice work if you can get it," Dixy quipped sardonically.

When events began leading to a certain showdown in the spring of 1973, a short time after Dixy had taken over the chairmanship, a new element inserted itself into the already ugly situation. Dixy was getting vibrations — very subtle but quickly discernible — from the private nuclear industry that certain sectors that had already fared handsomely at the contractual hand of the AEC were "disturbed" at the prospect of a disruption in the status quo. Now, she feared with good reason, she had run smack into an undeclared "troika" establishment that ran from Congress to the AEC and to industry. She really had her work cut out for her. It would probably cost her her job to break up the alliance, but she had no choice. She did — and it did.

The sad footnote is that the "line of communication" she destroyed was never investigated by Congress or any other agency of federal government. It was far more subtle and much better disguised than the often-assailed military-industrial complex, although it had much in common.

The road to a showdown began with the notice to Dixy that it would be her responsibility to defend the AEC budget before Congress. It was her predecessor's budget, not hers, and she was anything but happy with it, to say the least. The two sore spots were the reactor-development program in general and the breeder section in particular.

"Not all was being told," Dixy related, "and I was damned if I was going to lie to Congress or to anybody else."

She rebelled. To the staff and other commissioners she announced it might not have been her budget, but she was "the pigeon" who would have to defend it in the spring of 1973 and thereafter.

It was time for some integrity and the Ray upper lip to reassert themselves.

CHAPTER ELEVEN

A Declaration of Independence

Holifield, Ramey, and Shaw had plenty of troops for the forthcoming battle, but Dixy had a pair of aces and a few wild cards of her own. The aces were her general manager, Bob Hollingsworth, and John Abbadessa, her brilliant comptroller, and the wild cards were several influential senators who would hear her out and who owed no allegiance to Holifield & Co.

She knew that Hollingsworth and Abbadessa had been required to swallow numerous practices in the past without being able to take action against them. Explaining to them that she recognized their past transgressions — because they would most certainly have been fired if they had blown a whistle — she asked for some positive action. Daredevil Ray ordered them to undertake a review audit of the entire reactor-development program. It was a wise decision.

"Shaw had never been required to report on his budget!" Dixy explained. "Never! Can you believe that? He knew his division could not stand an audit. When he realized nobody could stop it from the outside or the inside and that I was insistent on it, he resigned. Hollingsworth and Abbadessa, who had their fingers in their ears waiting for an explosion, were relieved. It had been so easy! Why wasn't it done before?"

The demand for an audit review shook up the old palace guard. More than one voice on the Hill and elsewhere wanted to know what "that bitch in Germantown" was up to. What disturbed Dixy most of all, she said, was the fact that the "practices hinted at were encouraged, hidden, and even initiated in some instances by persons in high position of public trust."

Why were Shaw and the reactor division permitted to get away without an audit year after year? A "historic" explanation offered to Dixy was that the Joint Committee wanted it that way because that was how Admiral Rickover desired it in the interest of security, secrecy, or whatever. It was a limp argument, but after having witnessed the manner in which some congressmen worshipped at the feet of the admiral, Dixy believed there might have been something to it. Other more valid explanations lay deep in the AEC woodwork.

Hollingsworth and the chairman began the job of reorganizing the division immediately. Some safety work had to be retained in the engineering and operational area, but they established a clear division between the confirmatory and developmental research in the safety area. When the plan was ready, Dixy drew the support of Commissioners Larson and Doub. Ramey was a different matter. He didn't seem to be aware of the depth of Dixy's proposal at first because he apparently didn't think she would dare try so extensive a reorganization — nor one that would touch so many sensitive nerves. When she put it on the table at the next commission session, Ramey wasn't prepared.

"We had done our work carefully and with the assistance of our counsel," Dixy said. "I introduced the general idea first, then distributed a broadly worded paper the second time, asking for comment. Still Ramey didn't take us seriously. Thus, when I called for a vote the third time around, Ramey was taken by surprise and finally was jolted into realization of what was about to happen."

All the steps mentioned were chronicled in detail in the AEC's official records. Ramey's charge that Dixy and the staff had "ganged up on him" was without substance.

It is possible Ramey had taken his cue from Schlesinger, who had assured him and others that "nobody was going to expect very much from Dr. Ray." When he saw a large chunk of his once-solid domain begin to crumble, Ramey lost his smile.

Without Ramey's vote the other commissioners made a number of other organizational changes to guarantee openness in operations and accounting and greater responsibility in reactor-safety research and other areas. The day of buddy-buddy, close-to-the-vest dealings was coming to an end. Several other changes revived support for basic research, which had been gradually eroding in the AEC through negligence at the top.

Dixy still had a major hurdle to clear — acceptance by the Joint Committee, where Ramey had some clout. After the commission approved the plan, she wrote a report and sent it to the JCAE on a Friday. As anyone knew who understood Washington, DC, politics, you just don't do that to a congressional committee. You don't send the lawmakers a firecracker on a Friday and make a public announcement the following Monday, giving them no chance to defuse the 'cracker, as it were. But then, Dixy had never been a political animal, she said, so she didn't know better.

She honestly didn't realize at the time how incensed the action would make Congressmen Chet Holifield and Craig Hosmer. Naturally, they thought she had done it that way through stealth and artifice. But they would have disliked anything she did, no matter what day of the week it happened.

That weekend Dixy had to leave the city for a speaking engagement in New Orleans, an absence which added several degrees to the Holifield and Hosmer temperatures. Hosmer was specially hot. No doubt the fact that she had telephoned him earlier in the week to tell him candidly to "get off my back" had something to do with it.

It was late Saturday night that she received word in New Orleans that certain members of Congress had taken it upon themselves to call an executive session for Monday morning. The purpose was to ask the commission to explain the reorganization move. When she informed the committee staff she couldn't get back until Tuesday, the meeting date was changed to that day.

Ramey attended the same meeting in New Orleans at which she spoke. He had decided to play some golf there — no surprise for Ramey — so he was to return on Tuesday, too. In consequence, he was on the same plane going back to Washington, so he sat beside her. Whether it had been done by accident or design she would never know. At any rate, he wasted no time getting to the reorganization issue, but he was very gentle and softspoken about it and never raucous.

"You know, you're making a terrible mistake. This action should be reconsidered . . ." So went his comment.

"Sorry," Dixy said. "It's done. I'm going to stick by it, no matter what happens. We'll have to take our chances . . ."

It was a draw. No tempers were lost. No unkind words were uttered. And nobody's mind was changed. But she could see she was headed for a real donnybrook if Holifield and Hosmer had their way. She had been vilified so often and so mercilessly by the two congressmen that she was ready for a "last stand," if that's what it was to be.

Intuition told her to take no unnecessary chances, so she called every other member of the Joint Committee as soon as she returned to make certain each knew the executive session had been ordered. It may have been the wisest thing she ever did as chairman of the AEC. None knew there was to be such a session until she called! Another stacked deck . . .

That was the beginning of understanding for her on the subject of political "manipulation." Obviously the technique was to call a quick session for some purpose — usually a self-serving reason — and to send written notification to members of the committee involved. It was often the case — congressional mail and messenger service being what it was — that the congressmen receiving the notices got them about the time the hearing was scheduled or afterward. The device was used on hearings involving Dixy at least three more times, but a wiser Dixy made certain every member of the committee knew in plenty of time.

In the beginning the hearing was rough, particularly on Dixy, but she was still very much in the "clenched" state she had assumed the preceding weekend. Illinois' Representative Melvin Price opened the hearing by reading a statement that obviously had been prepared for him. Dixy knew him to be a very kind, gentle, understanding man, so she took with more than a grain of salt the statement's accusatory tone over "the sneaky thing" that had been done by the commission. Then Holifield and Hosmer came on. Chet's usual stormy and blustery attack was no surprise, but Hosmer's calm, controlled approach was.

Holifield ripped off a series of charges loaded with questions that were rhetorical in nature and which drew such expected answers from Dixy as "I thought this was a proper way to handle the question," or "I thought this was a management question that did not seem appropriate to bring to the Joint Committee for resolution . . ."

Of course, the practiced coolness of her replies (behind the facade her fists and jaws were clenched) helped bring Holifield to a boil. He wanted her to lose her temper so she and her staff could be on an equal footing. She refused to play his game, and it paid off.

When Holifield's ranting was at its highest pitch, Senator Stuart Symington broke in:

"I think we have a stupid situation here. We've got a new chairman of the Atomic Energy Commission. She just wants to reorganize one of the offices, and I think it's ridiculous for us to try to tell her what to do."

He had said it firmly and with a look on his face of being disturbed by Holifield's tantrum. Holifield turned in his chair so that his back was to Symington. The gesture was lost on no one.

Much had been made of the 3-to-1 vote in the commission in favor of the reorganization plan. Symington turned from his colleagues to look at the four commissioners before him:

"You, lady," he said looking directly at her, "you stick to your guns, and I'll support you. All I can say to you, Commissioner Ramey, is that you're nothing but a goddamned minority! Your nose is out of joint because you didn't get your way finally and three people voted against you!"

To Dixy it was beautiful! With that Symington got up and walked out. As he passed her, he couldn't resist one parting shot:

"Remember, stick to your guns."

"I will," she replied, and she could feel herself "unclench."

Senator Howard Baker of Tennessee chimed in, indicating great pleasure that reorganization had been ordered and complimenting Dixy on the plan voted. So did Representative Mike McCormack of Washington, the only scientist in Congress. Others then added words of praise and approval.

Finally, Senator John Pastore of Rhode Island, long a power on the Joint Committee and in nuclear affairs, put the clincher on it all with comments he obviously intended to calm the waters:

"I think that what we have here is a management question. We ought to let the chairman decide these things. We shouldn't try to run the agency. We've been running this place too long . . ."

He said much more along that line, then turned to Dixy and put on his peacemaker's cloak:

"Dr. Ray, I understand this. You really were a little bit rough in the way you handled this. Why don't you call Milt Shaw in and talk to him? Will you do that for me?"

"Yes, I will, Senator."

"Milt is a wonderful man," Pastore continued, "and you've hurt his feelings."

That's the kind of thing Pastore was expected to say. But then, almost as if he wanted to be certain everybody knew where he stood on the issue of the day, he added:

"I think we ought to see if this thing works."

Hosmer made a brief comment on the same order and said he thought "we should try."

Now Holifield realized he was virtually alone. Dixy was surprised to hear him call for a vote. He was to learn how much "alone" he was in this case. All except Holifield voted to support her and the commission's reorganization plan. Two thirds of the committee had been present for the vote, and the few who had to leave early had expressed their support before departing.

Holifield got up and walked out brusquely. It was a crushing defeat. Friends on the Hill told Dixy later it was the first time he had ever been repudiated on a strong policy position.

For Dixy the incident served as a declaration of independence. Now that all the cards were on the table, a far healthier relationship was possible with Congress on one hand and the nuclear industry on the other. The ultimate winner was the public — if only the facts could see the light of day. For Dixy the greatest puzzle remained why Congress wasn't curious enough to look into the entire matter . . . .

CHAPTER TWELVE

Advice From an Admiral

A few weeks after she began serving as chairman, Dixy received a phone call from Admiral Lewis L. Strauss, who had been one of the best-known and most controversial of AEC commissioners and chairmen, as well as friend and confidant to Presidents. He had already sent his congratulations in a letter and indicated he would welcome an opportunity to meet and talk with her.

It was some time before they were able to find a mutually satisfactory time. Eventually they met for lunch at a private club in Georgetown. She welcomed the privacy and the sparse luncheon attendance because it would give her a good chance to hear out the almost legendary figure from the most recent nuclear past.

After exchanging the usual pleasantries, Strauss apologized for not finding time earlier for the meeting, but, he explained, he had been released from the hospital only a few days before. He had been confined for some time because of a problem with his larynx that made it difficult for him to speak. It was cancerous and inoperable, and the treatments were difficult. He also said he knew it was terminal and that he didn't have too much time.

Dixy could hardly suppress her feeling of pity when he said he was cheerful nonetheless and was thankful for each day he was given. The malignancy was in remission at the moment. He was recovering, he said, from a severe cold which had aggravated the problem with his voice.

It was painful to Dixy, as well; she felt a constant urge to help him speak. He assured her it wasn't a strain, but she could scarcely believe that. He spoke almost like someone who had had surgery on his vocal chords. The admiral must have been right; he talked half the afternoon, and she absorbed every word.

She lost track of time because his conversation was fascinating, despite the physical stress. It was ironic that the disease that was destroying him and which had also taken the lives of both his parents was responsible for drawing him into the field of nuclear affairs and the work for which he will always be remembered most. Because the disease had taken his mother and father when he was a young man, he became a philanthropist, directing his interests to science generally and nuclear physics specifically. He was convinced a cure for cancer lay within the wonderfully magical sphere of science. And he was at least partly right.

Strauss told her in detail about his early life, how he became interested in nuclear energy, how he eventually joined his interest in the Navy with nuclear power, and many of the details related to his two terms with the AEC. Although she had been chairman only three months at the time of the meeting, Dixy could already appreciate his warnings and the atmosphere that attended his own travails as chairman. It convinced her that the problems may have had different subjects and players, but the conflicts were terribly similar.

Admiral Strauss knew about the scrap over the reorganization proposal. He also knew about Milt Shaw, about Ramey's determination to fight the reorganization and save Shaw, and, perhaps most important, the pipelines Ramey had into Congress in general and the Joint Committee on Atomic Energy in particular. Perhaps that's why the admiral went into such detail on the stormy, bitter sessions he had experienced as chairman. She felt better because of his accounts; suddenly she didn't feel alone . . . and suddenly she was convinced she was right and would stick to her guns, no matter what the outcome.

Strauss knew most of the actors in the nuclear and energy drama, and he was remarkably well informed about Dixy's situation in the AEC and the pesky personality problems she faced. He was clearly sympathetic to her cause, but he seemed more content when he was talking about his personal life. It was he who kept bringing up incidents of his boyhood, as if somehow there were a link between them that went way back, far beyond the Nuclear Age. It was obvious he dearly relished the fact that his life had been a case of a poor boy who made good. He was the epitome of the American dream.

Through his reminiscence came the most important point of all, the reason he had sought out Dixy Lee Ray in the first place. It soon became obvious to her that for most of his life he had wanted desperately to become a physicist. He hadn't made it because of financial restraints or family problems, and as a result he had had to forgo a classical education in physics. Now the message was coming across: Strauss believed his failure to obtain a degree in physics and the proper Ph.D. "union card" was the principal reason he was rejected — or, more correctly, surmised he was rejected — by the scientific elite. Elitists like Oppenheimer, to be specific.

So that was it! Dixy was to be Strauss' apologist. She would carry the message he wanted to tell the world and couldn't because he wouldn't be believed. More than anything else, Strauss wanted the esteem of the scientific community; if he had a reliable messenger, he could face his remaining months with reassurance and grace.

Dixy was willing to accept the assignment, but she hadn't yet heard a clincher. It came soon after Strauss reached his target, an explanation of how the Atomic Energy Commission made its decision to create the hydrogen bomb. Now he spoke excitedly, quickly, almost as if the events had taken place that morning instead of a quarter of a century earlier.

"You remember, Dr. Ray, that the vote to go for the hydrogen bomb was a split decision, 3 to 2. What you may not know or remember is that I was quite alone in the beginning as a supporter of the new weapon. It was a very lonely time for me at first, and then others began to see the light. I have not regretted my role in it. In fact, I'm rather proud on recollection. But I shall not forget the bitterness of the time, that awful business involving Dr. Robert Oppenheimer and other scientists . . ."

When he said "scientists," Dixy noted a mental wince and the briefest of pauses before and after the word.

"I'm sure you know," Strauss continued, "that President Eisenhower and I were very close. We'd been good friends a very long time, but I can say without qualification that I never took advantage of that closeness in government life. When business was being conducted, our friendship marked time. I know many people will not believe that, but it doesn't matter. When we were in session, private or in groups, on government business, both of us maintained the strictest of official behavior. I never permitted myself to forget that he was the President and I his public servant. That is the way it should have been, and that is the way it was . . .

"The Oppenheimer incident was most unfortunate, most unfortunate . . . . That decision caused many heartaches, many cleavages in the nation. Worst of all, it split the scientific community into two distinct camps. It never should have happened. Never . . . . How I wish it could have been averted."

He seemed now to be talking to no one in particular and everyone in general as he stroked his chin and looked out into space over her shoulder. She remembered Dr. J. Robert Oppenheimer and the hydrogen bomb. He had spoken against it from the beginning and Strauss for it from the beginning. Oppenheimer, the organizational genius who had brought so many diverse scientific talents together to usher the world into the Nuclear Age, also had too many friends whose ideological stripe clashed with Red, White, and Blue. He had performed extraordinary service to America, but he hadn't chosen his friends carefully. And who went to his defense when Chairman Strauss and the Atomic Energy Commission declared Oppenheimer a poor security risk and unworthy of handling many of the secrets he had himself discovered or pioneered? Many other scientists.

Strauss had voted to strip Oppenheimer of his security clearance, and, in effect, of his position and reputation. The vote had been 4 to 1, with Commissioner Harry D. Smyth supporting Oppenheimer.

The excitement had gone from Strauss' voice. Now he was deliberate, in mental pain.

"It was wrong. I was not free to act in that situation. The President — and you know what a stickler he was for strong security — ordered the 'blank wall,' as he put it, placed between Oppenheimer and all the secrets he had been working for years to develop. Everybody knows about that. But nobody knows he ordered me to remove Oppenheimer's security clearance forever. Mr. Eisenhower was adamant. He demanded that I take appropriate action. So you see, I was not free to act . . ."

Dixy was shocked. So Eisenhower forced Strauss to take an action he didn't support, and he knew Strauss would follow orders because his President had so ordered. Dixy remembered the severe criticism Strauss had to endure, primarily from scientists, because he was pegged as the chief villain by those who supported Oppenheimer's position. Dixy herself had been critical of the physicist's bad judgment in playing footsie with known Communists, but she wasn't thrilled by the hysteria that attended his case. Now she watched as a man who had been stamped as Oppenheimer's "executioner" nearly came to tears because a President had ordered him to act in opposition to his conscience.

In his book, *Men and Decisions*, written 12 years before his conversation with Dixy, Strauss had defended his decision to vote against Oppenheimer. Now, to Dixy, he was refuting his own words. He reminded her it was he who had been most responsible for bringing Oppenheimer into the nuclear program and that it was he who had voted twice before to set aside objections to the physicist because he had once associated with Communists.

What would have happened, Dixy pondered, if Strauss had defied the President and backed Oppenheimer, despite the damning evidence? More importantly, what would she have done in his place? Despite the fact she was never fond of Oppenheimer and his arrogance, she knew . . .

As a scientist herself, Dixy remembered accounts of the merciless way Oppenheimer ridiculed and belittled Strauss in hearings before congressional committees. And now here was the former chairman, a dying man, who had more reason than anyone to detest Oppenheimer, virtually in tears as he expressed his sorrow for failing to go to the physicist's defense in a crisis. It was significant to Dixy that throughout the long luncheon, Strauss never made a single derogatory remark about Oppenheimer's behavior or character.

A short time after Strauss died the following year, Dixy paid a call on his widow, and Mrs. Strauss corroborated all he had told her. When Dixy considered how long the Strausses had lived with their secret out of respect for the presidency, she was overwhelmed with sympathy.

Dixy never saw Strauss again, but she talked to him by phone. Because he, too, had experienced "great difficulties" with Jim Ramey when Ramey was the Joint Committee's executive director, Strauss told Dixy he'd be happy to intercede on her behalf if she needed a friend at the White House. Two months later she called him to tell him she wanted to take her case against reappointment of Ramey to the AEC for another five-year term directly to the President. He said he would help her, and he did.

She had no doubt her action was one of the principal reasons Ramey was not reappointed. It became evident to her from personal observation and the comments of others in and out of government that the pressure to get Ramey reappointed was stronger than for anyone receiving presidential appointment in recent years. Several senators she had always thought were in her corner called her in to ask her to reconsider her action and back Ramey. So did certain influential executives in other departments of government, including a few from the White House staff — before she went to see the President through the intercession of Admiral Strauss.

Ramey himself finally decided to meet the issue directly. He went to her office to ask her to support his reappointment. It must have been a very difficult thing for him to do, and she appreciated that. But the answer was still an unqualified "No."

"I'm going to do everything in my power to win that reappointment," he told her. "I believe you will probably be sorry you have opposed it."

She was to discover what he meant, but she was never to be sorry.

About three weeks later Ramey tried again. This time he was a bit more conciliatory in his appeal; she had the feeling he was now, for the first time, aware that his ties on the Hill were not so strong as he had imagined and that he was not going to be reappointed. She stood her ground. The answer was still "No."

"If you won't back me," Ramey asked, "whom do you want to take the job?"

"Manson Benedict," she replied without hesitation.

Benedict wasn't anxious to go to Washington, but if the President had asked the distinguished scientist to consider a short term, Dixy believed he might have accepted. And the AEC would have gained a bright new addition. He could have slipped into the Schlesinger term, which had about three years or less to run, instead of being named to the five-year term that would soon be available.

It was all just so much conversation. Things like appointments to major positions were being handled at so low a level at the White House by that time that such an auspicious selection had no chance.

She didn't know how William Anders' name got through that maze, but it did — and she thought it a fine choice. At the time, she had no basis for a judgment on Anders' qualifications, but she was to find the former astronaut a most persevering and dedicated commissioner. She wished she could have said that about some of the others. With his background Anders came to the attention of General Alexander Haig, who was running the White House single-handedly, and Casper Weinberger, the efficient secretary of health, education, and welfare, both of whom became Anders' backers and got him confirmed. Many other names were submitted to the White House, but they were never examined very seriously.

Why had Dixy opposed Ramey's reappointment? For two reasons. The first was that she believed no one, no matter how wise and capable, should have served more than a single five-year term. Even if Ramey had been an exceptional commissioner, she would have opposed his retention; by the time he had served another term he would have been a member of the commission 11 years. The commission form of running the agency or anything else was bad enough in her view; when one person makes a career of it, it's worse. She had studied the legislation Congress passed to create and operate the AEC; it could not be interpreted to mean that Congress intended an AEC commissionership to be a lifetime career.

The second reason, and a bit more important, was the fact that someone had to have enough courage to call a halt to the one-man system Ramey had set up within the AEC and the convenient pipeline he had established to Congress and to the outside world. It didn't take long after she became chairman to realize that Ramey was the "important commissioner" because of his "system" and the arrangement he had made with Schlesinger to run his own ship without interference from the chairman. It was common practice on the staff to "clear it with Ramey." That's all that was needed. If anyone, no matter whom, wished to get support for a project, he'd have rough sailing until and unless he obtained Ramey's approval. What a way to run a railroad, or one of the most important agencies in the world!

Thus, it was quite clear that, if any commissioner could run the agency without being chairman, Ramey was in fact doing so. And, obviously, he had been doing it for some time, not only with Schlesinger's blessing, but apparently with the approval of many influential members of the Joint Committee — and probably with AEC commissioners who had preceded Schlesinger and Dixy. Whether Ramey and Schlesinger ever had a tacit agreement to "slice up" the AEC authority and stay out of each other's way she didn't know, but it was clear that "sliced up" it was.

In many ways Commissioner Ramey operated around the general manager, Bob Hollingsworth, who knew it but could do nothing about it without losing his job.

"It is extremely important," Dixy said, "that I emphasize this point: I believe Ramey was a good public servant. I know of nothing that would indicate he was anything but an honest, hard-working commissioner. Nobody could accuse him of behaving unethically as an AEC official, but I do believe he was unethical in the manner he operated his information system and the way he handled the Joint Committee, ties and all.

"I could not accuse him of flirting with any conflict of interest, but it was clear he had favorites among the big organizations. I'm sure he was not for hire from any of the contractors. He skirted close to that sort of problem by accepting their amenities in the form of expensive dinners, bashes, golf dates, and things of that sort. But I cannot quibble over that.

"Of far greater danger, I believe, was his tie to the Joint Committee. When operational agencies draw too close to congressional committees or key congressmen, proper functioning of the agencies is seriously hampered. Operational arms cannot run properly if they become attachments of congressional chairmen. I learned that lesson bitterly under the aegis of one Chet Holifield."

Dixy drew a corollary that sprouted two fingers. One was that the commission system is undoubtedly the worst method of running anything, in or out of government. It frequently paralyzes action, destroys full responsibility, and encourages anarchy, unless someone strong enough, like a chairman, defies the others and insists on order and progress. Most commissions should be abolished and replaced by a single, ruling, responsible person, she believed.

The other point is that she was convinced such positions in the federal government should not be career jobs.

"America," she said, "is loaded with great talent. We have no indispensable men or women. Why can't many, many more scientists, economists, technological wizards, mathematicians, scholars, artists, management experts, and so on, give a few years to their government, then go home to stay? And why don't we write a prohibition into laws governing such agencies against permitting any such positions to become career jobs? I am certain it would soon discourage the empire-building, conniving, pork-barreling, back-scratching, and even corruption that 'comfortable' bureaucrats often find tempting. Best of all, it might improve the governmental process. No, I'll say it would certainly improve the process."

As she viewed AEC affairs from the chairman's office, it was easy to see a strong, unbent cord running from Holifield to Ramey to Shaw for very important programs, and it stretched throughout the entire agency. It was her conviction that the cozy little network could no longer be tolerated in the best interests of the AEC and the nation itself. That is why Ramey, who was at the operational heart of the system, had to be removed.

Some persons in and out of the AEC tried to represent her clash with Ramey as a "clash of basic ideas." That was nonsense, she said. The fact is she agreed with Ramey most of the time on most issues, and she also agreed with Holifield and Hosmer and other detractors on certain basic positions of the AEC and the nuclear industry. Perhaps the time she did disagree with Ramey most emphatically was with relation to what became known as the "Rasmussen Report."

The AEC, anxious to get an impartial, meaningful study on the true status of nuclear plants and devices in America, commissioned Professor Norman Rasmussen of the Massachusetts Institute of Technology to take on the project. Protests against nuclear development were growing among certain groups in the U.S., and Dixy was anxious to get the truth out, as discovered by Rasmussen, a brilliant scientist and an honest, trustworthy one, as well. Of course, Rasmussen and his staff had to be given a key to any door so the investigation could be complete and impartial. Ramey decided to toss whatever obstacles he could find in Rasmussen's path. Dixy never knew why. He tried hard to prevent the Rasmussen group from considering details of accidents already on the record because he didn't think the details should be rehashed or investigated. He was able to block the probe for two reasons. First, it began while Schlesinger was still chairman, and Schlesinger, for his own reasons, did not slap Ramey down. Second, he drew the backing of Manning Muntzing, then director of regulation, in a move to withhold funds, and they were successful.

That is, the Ramey plan was successful — until Schlesinger left and Dixy became chairman. Then she got the reorganization plan under way, set up the new reactor-safety division, minus Shaw, and transferred funding for the Rasmussen Report into that division. Muntzing and Ramey had been able to withhold funds that had been earmarked for personnel until the new division was created. Now, the Rasmussen crew could get started on its investigation, and it could go on with its work undisturbed. It was now possible to say the probers had free rein and that Rasmussen could poke his nose into any aspect of the AEC, undirected except by himself.

Dixy disagreed with Ramey on a few other subjects, but none was of the importance of the Rasmussen Report. They saw eye to eye, however, on other major issues involving operation of the AEC. Ramey also was one of those persons in the AEC who accepted the fact that she was a woman and that a woman could be an independent professional in her own right. He treated her with reasonable respect and without any pretense as a colleague. At least he was no chauvinist. She could not say the same for some others on the commission, in Congress, and in other departments and agencies of official Washington.

When trying to assess her own experiences and frustrations as chairman of a five-headed monster, she realized that the terrible mistake in the case of the AEC was made in 1954. That was the year Congress amended the Atomic Energy Act in a misguided desire to give each of the five commissioners equal voice and responsibility. It was a foolish, unnecessary move, designed to reduce the authority of the chairman. Congress should have acted in opposite manner. The reason for a commission had already become outdated. A single director was more important than ever to get things done and to make the AEC more responsive to the needs of the nation. Except for the commission itself, the AEC was, in her opinion, the most effective, efficient, productive agency in government and one that was blessed with the greatest number of highly skilled, extraordinarily capable personnel.

Although she was to support a move to split the regulatory and operational functions into two new agencies, she is convinced today in retrospect that the best action Congress could have taken, by far, was simply to remove the regulatory function and leave the AEC intact, merely junking the five-man commission in favor of a single chairman or director.

"Some congressmen who came close to panicking because of overblown criticism of our nuclear effort did the nation irreparable harm in pushing through the ERDA (Energy Research and Development Administration) legislation which submerged nuclear energy to basement or disgraced status," Dixy said. "With an almost whimpering, apologetic leadership that was afraid to look Congress in the eye and speak the hard truth, ERDA heeded the wishes of those few panicking but influential congressmen and all but abandoned the role of spokesman for nuclear power. Since it was obvious to anyone who had studied the nation's energy needs and its energy potential that we must look to nuclear power or forfeit our leadership — and perhaps much more — in the world, that lack of an official spokesman beckoned disaster.

"The strident few who have made so much noise have spread false alarms with their exclamations that nuclear power will eventually destroy this nation. The unvarnished, brutal truth is that if we should listen to these short-sighted Chicken Littles in our midst, we will most certainly destroy our nation if we reject the nuclear power we must have in increasing amounts to run the nation."

Richard G. Hewlett, historian for the AEC and its successor, ERDA, told Dixy he believed that if Gordon Dean had remained as chairman, the AEC would have shed its commission form of control — or lack of control. Dean left the commission at the end of the Truman administration. Being a hard-nosed Democrat, the well qualified and exceedingly capable Dean was not attuned to the political philosophy of the incoming Eisenhower administration. He had been a member of the commission and wanted a rest. But Hewlett thought he was the kind of persuasive man who could have worked with the Joint Committee to change the AEC to one-man direction — or at least very strong, unchallenged chairmanship. There had been talk in Congress of doing just that. But when Strauss, a very powerful, "persuasive" man, came along, few members of the committee were anxious to turn things nuclear over to the admiral.

How frequently major events turn on the whims of a few . . .

CHAPTER THIRTEEN

Recollections of Two Presidents

As chairman of one of the largest and most sensitive operational agencies of federal government, Dixy came to know two Presidents well. Richard Nixon and, later, Gerald Ford, were her immediate superiors, although she answered to Congress, too.

In early encounters, circa 1972 or Before Watergate, she found Nixon to be affable, pleasant, and, on a couple of occasions, even humorous. After she had been sworn in as a member of the Atomic Energy Commission August 8, 1972, Nixon broke the somber tone of the White House ceremony with the comment: "Now you're on the payroll." After the taking of the oath and presentation of a Bible to Dixy, the President was joshingly courteous to all the guests, and particularly to Dixy's sister, Marion. He seemed not to have a care in the world.

The last time Dixy would see him in so jovial a mood was at the White House Christmas Party four months later, the December 18 party at which Nixon revealed "we have something in mind for you . . . yes, yes, indeed we do." It was that evening amidst a ballroom full of Republicans that she reveled most in the frequent subtle comments — always delivered in cloaked phrases — about her being the non-Republican interloper in the administration. On the other hand, she discovered through friends and White House contacts, as well as in hints given her by John Ehrlichman, that she was selected for the AEC — and later would be given the chairmanship — because she could be counted on to be a figurehead, a patsy, and a "good girl" when the White House needed one. Schlesinger had given her that impression, too. All of them had a few surprises coming. Suddenly, she felt a kinship with another "rascal," Pope John 23rd, who was also supposed to be a figurehead and avoid rocking the ship of state.

Although she was to see Nixon in large groups on a few occasions thereafter, Dixy did not get another closeup until late spring, 1973. The whisper that had been Watergate in the fall and winter of 1972 and 1973 became the political holocaust of 1973. Despite what she had read and heard and suspected, she was not prepared for the metamorphosis she was to witness. Because one of the topics at a cabinet meeting was to be nuclear power, she was invited to attend a session at the White House about three months after she was made chairman.

She would be shocked for two reasons: First was the appearance of Nixon, and second was the disorganization and listlessness of the meeting itself. The President walked in — shuffled was more like it — after the cabinet members had assembled. Dixy and other sub-cabinet agency directors sat just beyond the cabinet table in a second circle. No one spoke as Nixon entered. Dixy called it an embarrassed hush. He greeted no one in particular, waved to no one, and seemed to stretch for his chair as he reached it; he fairly sank into it and slumped down. Now, as Dixy saw his face at close range for the first time in several months, she felt a need to look away in embarrassment. The strain of Watergate had already begun to take its toll. He looked haggard, sickly, like a man who had just been told by his doctor that he had only a few months to live. Nixon seemed to have shrunk in stature.

The meeting began, but Dixy could not tell who was in charge. Nixon had very little to say and, in fact, hardly seemed to be listening or caring. The meeting included a review of the budget. Since Dixy was deeply involved in the energy phase of the budget and had been assigned to make recommendations concerning the $10 billion program, she had been asked to prepare sufficient material to answer any questions.

Only a few weeks earlier Nixon had made his major speech on energy — April 18, 1973 — in which he referred to Dixy directly as the person he had asked to produce two comprehensive reports on America's energy sources and resources. He hadn't looked bad on the television screen, but, she thought, the wonders of makeup are many and varied.

As for the cabinet meeting itself, she was astounded by the lack of interest shown by various cabinet members and others in the room. Not all cabinet officers were there; some had sent their deputy secretaries or assistant secretaries. Whether secretary or sub-secretary, an oppressive pall attended the proceedings.

"I was ashamed to hear the questions that were asked in the nation's top executive conclave," Dixy related. "Were these the men who were entrusted with the leadership of our nation? I am not given to praying on impulse, but I have to confess the urge at that moment. From the caliber of questions asked, I wondered if anyone in the room knew anything at all about energy problems or even the budget. Or was it that they saw the signs and simply didn't give a damn? I had attended far better and more intelligent meetings at the Pacific Science Center back in Seattle or at the Zoology Department of the University of Washington. At least those people cared."

Schlesinger was not there. Neither was Kissinger. They were represented by deputies. Secretary of Agriculture Earl Butz was present but not talkative, for a change.

"The person who did the most talking was the one who should have done the least," Dixy said. "He was Claude Brinegar, secretary of transportation at the time, who opened his mouth about everything. What came out had the merit and texture of a thin diarrhea. He said nothing of importance, but he said it often. Equally effective was C. B. Rogers Morton, who seemed to understand as much about the energy and budget predicament as Brinegar. Rogers — or Rajh, as they called him — talked pontifically as if he had done his homework, but it was embarrassing. He was simply repeating what others had said.

"John Sawhill was there and joined in, for better or for worse. So was Fred Malek, the White House 'head hunter,' who talked a lot but also said little. George Shultz, Nixon's financial oracle, was still in the cabinet, and he was there. I remember he spoke once, objecting to something in the budget and disagreeing with the budget office's handling. How dare he! And, speaking of the budget, Roy Ash was present. The director of the budget at that time always reminded me of an elderly Cupid or a Kewpie doll. He had that kind of face, a little bit of his hair standing up in a tuft near the front. Ash was quite glib, as usual.

"A bit of desultory talk took place between Ash and the disinterested Nixon, but no one tried to draw out the President. Of course, in better days protocol had directed that no one speak

unless and until the President addressed him or her and asked
for a report, an answer to a question, or whatever. But, protocol
at that meeting . . .? Since Nixon wasn't much interested in talking himself, nobody else seemed anxious to initiate anything
outside the brief agenda. I was asked only a couple of questions,
and no one seemed interested in the answers. It was dismal, a
terribly deep blow to my vanity as an American, and a warning
that a nation can go to hell when persons like these accede to
power. I had little respect for most of the persons in that room,
and I did not sleep well that night."

The next cabinet session to which Dixy was invited was held
a short time after the October war in the Middle East. Its primary
purpose was to brief the cabinet and others on the ceasefire
Secretary Kissinger had negotiated. Kissinger was on hand, and
Schlesinger also was there this time. If Dixy had been shocked by
Nixon's appearance the first time, it was nothing compared to
her reaction at the second cabinet meeting.

"He looked and spoke like a Zombie, sitting slumped in his
chair as before but this time with his head resting in one hand as
if it were detached from his body, while the other hand gestured
on occasion to signal his intentions. Now, he was plainly a de-
feated man, waiting to be relieved from his suffering. Kissinger
ran the meeting like a general; there was no doubt who was in
charge. Every so often Nixon would interrupt him with a comment like:

"'. . . And, Henry, we did this and we did that, you remember, but, of course, nobody will give us credit for that now.'

"Sometimes it was relevant to what Kissinger was saying and
sometimes it was not. It didn't seem to matter. His interruptions
seemed designed principally to reassure the cabinet that he still
had an important role to play and that he had not yet relinquished the supervision of all foreign policy to the secretary of
state. At best, Kissinger was patient with him.

"Dr. Kissinger did a good job of explaining to the cabinet
what had happened in the October war and how he analyzed the
situation existing between Egypt and Israel, and between Israel
and other Arab nations, as well as the basis for negotiating the
ceasefire and how it would affect the United States. If General
Haig was running the country from the White House, there was
no question that Kissinger was running the nation's foreign
affairs, not Richard M. Nixon.

"But now that I have praised Caesar or Dr. K., let me bury him. Perhaps the next most shocking revelation of all was the recognition at that cabinet meeting that the nation's highest officials were hearing about the entire Middle East situation and America's role in it for the first time!

"In other words, it was painfully evident in the two cabinet meetings I attended that the cabinet did not function as a cabinet at all. It was not a forum for discussion; it was not a time for the different agencies and departments to talk over their problems in a mutually helpful manner and for colleagues and peers to perform as equals. It was simply a Kissinger lecture series. And, most disturbing of all, the President was not in charge."

Schlesinger interrupted a couple of times for comments. It was apparent to everyone that he had developed a total arrogance for the declining President and virtually ignored him, seeming to address his remarks to those who were now in power or who would come out of the national disaster unscathed. But he was not alone. Many of the cabinet officers and agency heads were doing their best to keep their skirts clean, to get as far away from the President as they could. One would have thought they had suddenly discovered a leper in their midst.

Nixon was, to all intents and purposes, isolated, alone, virtually quarantined by the crew he had created or sustained in better days.

As adroit and detailed as the Kissinger explanation was at the second meeting, very little discussion of any significance took place. One of the reasons was that Dr. Kissinger was unmistakably in the saddle and too lofty to be bothered with pesky questions. That stuck in Dixy's craw. It was not her place to ask questions; she was a listener and had been asked to attend for other reasons, so she could not barge in. But she wondered about the cabinet officers there. Wasn't anybody going to ask the obvious questions? How long did Kissinger think the ceasefire would last? What real guarantees did we have of an enduring ceasefire and the beginning of a peace settlement? What was it going to cost the United States? Dixy could think of two dozen other vital questions. But the cabinet officials failed to ask a single one — just as they and others in high places failed to ask them when Dr. Kissinger came in with his deeply controversial plan to bail out both Israel and Egypt at a devastating national cost to America, while our own cities were begging for help to avoid going under.

The last time she was to see Nixon while he was President was on December 3, 1973, the day she went to the White House to hand him the highly controversial report, "The Nation's Energy Future," which he had commissioned her to produce when he addressed the nation April 18 on television. The report was Dixy's greatest accomplishment in Washington, DC. Had the nation followed its recommendations, it would have avoided the disastrous energy crises that were to come. It provided for the development of every form of energy known to man until the most practical, least expensive, and most efficient methods were developed. Engineering was the key. Whether the eventual source of power would be solar, nuclear fission, nuclear fusion, geothermal, coal gasification, giant windmills, waves, or whatever, the test would be which means could be engineered in time and most cheaply. The tragedy was that she delivered the report to a President who didn't care much about anything because he was en route to disgrace.

It is significant that even her attempt to submit the report in person to the President became a cause célèbre. A previous report she had sent to the President in September, 1973, had been distorted so severely by the Office of Management and Budget that she determined it would never happen to her again, regardless of what came of it after the President had it in hand. She tried to keep her appointment at the White House a secret. The exercise was futile. When she arrived for her one-on-one meeting with the President, who should be there waiting for her solemnly in the lobby of the East Wing but John Sawhill of the budget staff. He had been "assigned" to go with her to see the President when she made her report.

"If I were President for a single day," Dixy said angrily, "one of my first actions would be to inform the OMB that it does not have a license to run the United States government, as its officers seem devoutly to believe. The fact is it is damned dangerous for budget-makers to foist themselves on other policy-making agencies and force decisions to be made on the basis of how much money the OMB thinks should be spent.

"The fussbudgets — or is it budget-fussers? — do not have enough expertise to make those decisions. For example, how can a Frank Zarb, or a John Sawhill, or a Bill Simon tell the technical agencies of government how much they may spend for extremely complicated projects or devices? Should it be budget-busybodies or scientists who determine our course in nuclear breeders, solar energy, fusion, or whatever? If we do not curb the rising dictatorial behavior of the OMB clan, we will invite a national calamity."

At any rate, an unsmiling, confident Sawhill, backed by an OMB that had insisted she submit her report through its staff instead of going directly to the President, walked into the Chief Executive's office alongside her. It was 3 o'clock in the afternoon on that December 3rd. An aide said the President was running a bit late. That is, the aide told her, and Sawhill rushed up to make certain he wouldn't miss a thing. So that's how it was to be . . .

Nixon, the aide added, was working over in his executive office. Dixy believed, in recalling the heated nature of the news at that time, that he was listening to tapes. They were taken from the lobby and permitted to wait in the cabinet room. About 20 minutes went by; Sawhill and Dixy barely spoke. The aide returned and said the President was still over in the other office and would probably be along in 10 minutes. Finally, the aide came in to say the President had just arrived and that she could go directly into the Oval Office. The aide opened the door, and she walked in, followed by Sawhill.

As she stepped in, she saw Nixon, bent over his desk in the Oval Office, with a pile of papers before him. He was wearing his glasses and was reading, pen in hand. She waited a few seconds there by the door, and he didn't look up; he was busy. The aide said once again, "Go right in."

She walked across the deep, soft carpet to the edge of the desk before the President looked up, pretending surprise:

"Oh! Oh, Dr. Ray!" He took off his glasses. It was as if he had been sitting there working hard at his desk a very long time. Nixon apparently didn't know that she knew he had come in from the Executive Office Building a minute earlier. The thought uppermost in her mind was:

"Why does he have to pretend to me?" For reasons that were beyond imagination he wanted her to think he had been hard at work at his desk a long time before she arrived. He didn't know an aide had told her the truth.

Once again she was alarmed by the incredible aging process that had affected the once buoyant, energetic man. But she said nothing about his appearance. Nor did he. She sat in a chair beside his desk and Sawhill, who had not left her side an instant, sat in a chair directly across the desk facing the President. Sawhill didn't say a word after exchanging a greeting with Nixon, although he nodded a few times when it seemed politic to do so.

At least the President seemed a bit more attentive than he had in the cabinet sessions. She reminded him the report was the one he had requested in his April speech, told him generally how she had organized and carried it out, then emphasized perhaps the most important point of all:

"Mr. President, we began our work last spring and concerned ourselves with all forms of energy. We did not attack the problem of seeking self-sufficiency, although elements of that problem are answered in part. Some people in the news media are referring to this as a report on how we can achieve self-sufficiency and as our answer to the oil embargo which began just last month. I want to stress that it is not a self-sufficiency report."

She wasn't sure he understood. He had made a November speech calling for self-sufficiency. In fact, he kept referring later to the need for achieving national self-sufficiency in energy by 1980, despite the fact she had told him and repeated to the press many times that self-sufficiency was impossible before 1985, if then — and that she wasn't certain it was a sensible goal. But, then, she couldn't be certain in those hectic days what Nixon had heard in the daze that had enveloped him.

For all that, he had moments of empathy in that December 3rd meeting. She indicated to him that if he wished to pursue the self-sufficiency goal further, it would be wise to entrust such a study to the exceptionally capable group she had assembled at the AEC for the December energy report. He indicated agreement, not with a "Yes, I want you to do this or that," but with a nod and a "good idea" remark. Dixy said she would keep the group intact and start preliminary work on a self-sufficiency report if he wished, and again he nodded agreement. Unfortunately, events of early 1973 wiped out that promising potential. Whatever she said, the President kept returning to the idea of attaining self-sufficiency in a hurry. Since it was obvious she would have to satisfy him on that point or never get her energy report across to him, she began by pointing out there were several ways the U.S. could attack the oil shortage in the future. The one he was interested in most was the mining of oil shale. He was specially impressed when she told him reliable estimates were that the U.S. had 600 billion gallons of oil in its national deposits of shale, and that was probably more than the known petroleum reserve in the entire world. The problem, she said, was to extract the oil from the shale at a reasonable cost, then return the shale with the least damage to the landscape — also an expensive chore. Nixon leaned back in his chair, smiled, and for a few moments his attitude changed from one of resigned depression to one of eagerness and hope. He swung around in his chair and looked out the window into the garden outside the Oval Office. It was a bright day for early December. The President said, as though he were musing aloud with no one in the room:

"Wouldn't it be wonderful if, in fact, the United States could become an energy-exporting country?"

"Mr. President, that is possible," Dixy said, "if we not only developed our oil shale potential but went on to mine our vast coal reserves and perfect a program of synthetic liquefaction and gasification from the coal."

He was astounded to learn the United States possesses more than one third of the entire world's coal reserves.

"If we can do those things with shale and coal," she continued, "then convert everything possible to using electricity and build the urgently needed nuclear-power plants to utilize our uranium, we could not only be self-sufficient but actually export energy."

Excited, the President asked: "Could it be done in 10 years?"

He just couldn't get off that kick. Whatever kind of an answer he needed for his personal or political purposes, she simply could not lie to him for the sake of making points.

"Well, no, Mr. President. That would be terribly difficult, actually impossible. But we could go a long way on the road to that goal in 10 years."

Nixon frowned, then thumbed through the report. At that time he was sold on the idea of promoting the Federal Energy Office, which had been growing from a small embryo. Impulsively, he said:

"I've decided to appoint Bill Simon to be head of the Energy Office and would like John Sawhill here to be his assistant. What do you think of that?"

She was on a spot. Not wishing to prolong the agony, she indicated the two would be good choices, but she wished she could have told him how she really felt about his two choices.

She hadn't been at the White House more than a half hour, but it seemed like a terribly long time, it was so painful.

Far more pleasant a circumstance was her first contact with

the man who was soon to be President. It was a short time after Gerald Ford was sworn in as Vice President, and the handwriting was on the wall. Recognizing that, she sent him a message that the AEC was ready to brief him at any time on the nuclear-weapons program and any other aspect of nuclear energy in which he was interested. He responded almost immediately in the affirmative. In preliminary discussions with Ford's executive assistant, John Marsh, she said she thought the Vice President should learn about the weapons program directly from the AEC, not the National Security Council and the Department of Defense alone. Federal statutes, she reminded him, left no doubt that nuclear weapons were and should remain under control of a civilian agency. One of the reasons she emphasized the point was that she had been deeply concerned about a move under way, particularly since Schlesinger had moved to the Defense Department, to switch authority over nuclear weaponry and research to Defense. If that should happen, she was certain it would be a catastrophe for America. Those who had been harshly critical of all things nuclear, she said, would then discover something truly important to carp about.

(The chairman wasn't whistlin' in Dixie. Later on, antinuclear forces in Congress would succeed in subjugating nuclear research and production to a whimper. When the AEC was split the following year into an operational agency, the Energy Research and Development Administration, and a regulatory agency, the Nuclear Regulatory Commission, the Nuclear Age suddenly had no strong spokesman in the federal government. Robert Seamans, the first director of ERDA, went out of his way to pacify antinuclear sentiment on the Hill and elsewhere by downplaying and almost apologizing for the presence of the nuclear program in ERDA. How could he be counted on to fight to keep the nuclear-weapons program under civilian rule? And, Dixy reflected, would Schlesinger ever give up his desire to keep a hand on the nuclear apparatus? Should a man who had told the world America had not relinquished the right to use nuclear weapons as a "first strike" threat be permitted to exercise total authority over the development of the nation's nuclear arsenal?

(Implicit in a Pentagon takeover would be a switch in control over nuclear laboratories from ERDA to the Department of Defense. Dixy knew from experience that the people in the laboratories didn't want military control and would fight such a possibility with all their strength. The irony was that when Schlesinger was AEC chairman, he resisted with all his power any move by the military to take over any facet of the nuclear program. Once in the Defense saddle, however, he executed an about-face. Schlesinger, Dixy said, was clearly an empire-builder.)

Marsh, Ford's lieutenant, heard Dixy out and relayed the gist of what she told him to the Vice President. As a result, the AEC arranged for several visits by Ford to nuclear installations. On one of them she met with him at Los Alamos, where he was briefed for a day and a half.

She liked him from the start because he was straight-forward, considerate, and an easy man to meet and talk to. He didn't assume airs. Most importantly, he gave her the feeling that he was listening, actually listening and paying attention. Ford also asked intelligent questions that were pertinent to what was being discussed, continuing proof that he heard what was said to him. They visited many departments in the laboratories, then went into a classified chamber, where the secret weapons briefing took place.

It was quite clear the Vice President didn't know a nuclear warhead from a fire hydrant, but that fact actually pleased her very much. It meant that, although Gerald Ford had held a responsible position in the House of Representatives many years and was a leader in his party's caucuses and innermost affairs, information concerning the sophisticated weapons program had never been leaked to him and others in Congress who weren't authorized to get such information. That fact was immensely significant to her. She hoped U.S. secrecy on nuclear weaponry would always be maintained. Information on weapons design and performance, why they perform the way they do, and what their capabilities are should always be guarded closely; it was against the best interests of the U.S. to have such information bandied about, even in the corridors of Congress, because there were too many people who would like to know and who shouldn't.

She was impressed with Ford's courtesy, his consideration for others, the way he asked questions, and with the high level of questions he asked. It was a pleasure primarily because he seemed to be absorbing and learning a great deal in a short time. His education had been in law. He had no background in science or engineering, but she had heard comments and questions from some other congressmen who had such backgrounds but who showed far less perception and understanding of nuclear matters than Ford did his first time out.

She had arranged several other visits for the Vice President, including one to Oak Ridge, the heart of America's nuclear effort, and to the Bendix plant in Kansas City. The Bendix plant didn't get much publicity, which was as it should be; it is under contract to the Bendix Corp. and is the main assembly point for guidance systems for warheads. Not many are permitted to visit the plant, but it was a must for a person who was about to become President of the United States.

It was already the summer of 1974, however, and Ford's time became more and more "scheduled." By July the Watergate tragedy had reached its climax and Nixon's days were obviously numbered. The Vice President was no longer his own man; he had to stay close by. Tours of nuclear installations and of anything else, for that matter, had to be tabled as the countdown began for President Nixon's administration . . . .

The next time she saw Gerald Ford he was President. It was early September, and she had three urgent topics to discuss with him. She asked him to give her authority to open quiet negotiations with the French in an effort to re-establish good relations with Paris and to explore the possibility of forming a multinational organization to control the spread of nuclear weapons. The two other reasons were equally important to her because they concerned the reorganization of the AEC and the effort of the OMB to control everything in sight through its autocratic handling of the budget and, eventually, to control all of government, as well.

But getting to Ford was going to prove to be even harder than breaking through to Nixon. Therein lay the germ of a problem that was to plague Ford more and more as his White House chief, Donald Rumsfeld, built an impregnable wall around him, much like the one Haldeman had erected to shut Nixon off. As soon as Ford was made President in July, 1974, she requested an appointment with him. She talked with General Haig, whom she had come to know reasonably well and for whom she had great respect. When she told him why she wanted to see the new President, Haig said he'd see to it that she was put on Ford's schedule. Thanks to Rumsfeld's interference, Dixy had to wait several weeks to get to the White House. The rivalry between Haig and Rumsfeld became intense, and the general finally appealed to Ford to let him move to another assignment. It was significant to Dixy that the fellow who finally got her in to see President Ford was soon dismissed by Rumsfeld.

The AEC chairman had her appointment, but she didn't have things her own way. She wanted to see the President alone, but Rumsfeld saw to it that didn't happen. Tagging along with Dixy when she arrived at the White House was Michael Duvall, who was acting as a secretarial aide to Ford. He said he had been requested to be there by the Domestic Council. She suspected the worst as he whipped out his yellow pad to take notes at the meeting, and her suspicions were to be justified.

After her conference with the President, Duvall asked her to go into the Roosevelt Room with him for a few minutes, and they went over the things that had been discussed. She thought he expressed himself genuinely in saying he had been impressed with what she had said to the President. He identified himself as the person who would help and see to it that things were followed through. She had to depend on him for that, but subsequently she had to conclude that either her conversation with the President stopped with him or — and this is what she believes actually happened — he notified other people about what she had said to the President, and obstacles were thrown into her path.

In addition to the serious problem regarding the French, detailed in another chapter, she had tried to win the President's attention in other areas:

She reviewed the history of the plan to reorganize the AEC and create from it a research-and-development agency on one hand and a nuclear-regulatory commission on the other. The idea to reorganize the AEC went back well into President Nixon's administration and was initiated by Roy Ash, director of the budget, in his grand plan for reorganization of the federal government as a whole. She told Ford of her opposition to the early plan, which was far too ponderous and which missed the boat on vital needs. At the same time, she told the President she did favor the reorganization act, which was passed by the House earlier in the year but brutalized by certain members of the Senate with a chip on their shoulder against nuclear power.

"Separating the functions of promoting nuclear power on one hand," she told Ford, "while being required to regulate it, license it, and control it on the other is a necessary move. It is also important to eliminate the special tag now pinned to 'atomic fuel' and make nuclear energy just one of many ways in which we can generate electricity. We want to get it into the context of a useful civilian activity and banish once and for all this aura of something terribly special about it — so special that it requires its own exclusive federal agency."

She said it had been in that context that she had supported the ERDA act and so testified in Congress. In addition, she had worked with congressional committee members to help make the act as solid as possible. Had that first bill passed the Senate at about the same time it passed the House, it would have produced an infinitely finer split and two much better halves (ERDA and NRC) than now exist.

"Unfortunately," she told the President, "the bill languished in the Senate through much of 1974, and by summer it was obvious the intent of the bill that came out of the Senate was simply to be an antinuclear, anti-agency bill. This was due primarily to Senator Ribicoff and his staff, who are blinded so completely by their emotional bias against nuclear power that they refuse to hear the other side. This attitude could do great damage to the future of our nation if it persists and spreads.

"If the antinuclear position coming out of the Senate prevails and influences how ERDA is finally created, it will mean the destruction of the AEC, rather than its metamorphosis into a more effective organization. Under those conditions we will lose our momentum in the nuclear-energy field and the nation will be hurt economically. Our posture in the world will suffer, as well, and so will our leadership in the production of energy. In fact, I think the damage has already begun."

In her plea to the President, she said the misguided reorganization was something initiated in the Nixon administration, that it was one of Nixon's acts, and that as the new President, he had every right to reexamine it and make his own proposals.

The President seemed to understand her argument. He told her he would look into the reorganization proposal and reconsider it. That is, he would study it to determine whether the administration could support the act as it then stood in Congress.

In the meantime, she had been talking with many congressmen in both houses, as well as members of the Joint Committee, and it was apparent a large group of them stood ready to oppose the reorganization act that came out of the Senate, at least so that the AEC would not be destroyed. All they needed was a word from the White House and the damage done in the Senate could be repaired.

Dixy made a final point on the reorganization with the President:

"Without question the world is going nuclear. While other nations are adopting nuclear programs at a rate that increases almost daily, the United States could be grinding to a halt if it listens to the dissenters, who have sounded alarms but have no scientific facts to back up their opposition. Most other countries have followed our lead and have an Atomic Energy Commission or similar agency to take responsibility in the civilian field of nuclear power. We must have a similar agency to carry on negotiations and conversations with these countries. If the Senate's antinuclear stance wins out, we won't have a proper organization to meet with other nations for discussions of civilian use of nuclear energy."

The President agreed. It was a strong point. At that, he gave her his definite word. He would ask for a reconsideration of the reorganization act. And he did.

The third issue she explored with President Ford concerned the autocratic, dictatorial nature of the Office of Management and Budget, but her suggestions apparently were buried before they had a chance to breathe. There again she believed she could thank Duvall and his superiors. It must have been he who transmitted the advance information that put Frank Zarb on guard and gave the OMB a chance to quash her ideas before the President gave them any consideration.

Dixy complained to Ford that the OMB was playing God as a result of the leadership vacuum that existed during Nixon's last months in office and the transitional period in which Ford was making adjustments. Realizing that she was probably making more enemies, she said "To hell with it!" under her breath and proceeded to warn the President of the danger inherent in permitting the budget-makers to tell all agencies of government, including the President, how to operate. Being frugal was one thing, she said, and frugality was devoutly to be desired, but putting pressure on agencies to make major policy decisions based only on saving money beckoned disaster.

The danger, she pointed out was particularly great in an

agency like the Atomic Energy Commission, whose personnel included many of the nation's brightest scientific and engineering minds. Their expertise could not be canceled out by a few bookkeepers at the OMB or the politically oriented executives who told them what to do. Ford seemed impressed, and he told her so. But nothing happened. In fact, the OMB's hand actually was strengthened. Now, Dixy's early admiration for Ford began giving away to reservations about his ability to lead. His wish to curb the bureaucracy was understandable and welcome, but his tendency to relinquish so much authority to reckless fussbudgets was a peril the nation could not afford.

At their conference, Ford not only agreed with Dixy's point of view; he asked her to put it into a memorandum to him so he could take appropriate action. She produced the memo immediately and sent it to the White House within four days after the meeting. But she never knew whether he had received it. She did know, however, that several other persons got a copy — because she sent it to them. The memo made huge waves among the hierarchy, and the OMB anger at Dixy Lee Ray grew in intensity and never subsided. She also knew that the AEC was the only agency that stood up and fought against the tyranny of the fussbudgets.

"If the American people, liberal or conservative, could appreciate the dangers in the haughty mien of the budget bureaucrats, they would demand that Congress enact legislation curbing their lust for power. On many occasions I protested the OMB's crass interference with the serious business of the AEC while I was chairman. Because the White House failed to back us up in two administrations, the dictatorship of the OMB goes on, and in fact, increases in awesome power.

"If congressional probers or people with courage in the news media ever recognize the evil, they will find numerous pieces of evidence documented in the AEC files of OMB tampering with the nation's most sensitive policies in the nuclear field. And I would be quite happy to assist them in tracking down the dates, times, and people involved."

CHAPTER FOURTEEN

The French Misconnection

As Dixy soaked in information on nuclear energy in her midnight-oil months as a commissioner, one idea dominated all others in her mind. Somehow, some way the United States had to lead the way in nailing a lid on nuclear weapons, no matter the cost. In time the idea became a personal crusade, but a crusade played behind the scenes.

The International Atomic Energy Agency, which President Eisenhower and the U.S. had created and nurtured, had noble intentions and was supported by Dixy, but she soon realized it would never be more than a debating society — a United Nations of atomic energy. It was significant that one of the nations that remained aloof was France. The French refused to take part and to sign the international Nonproliferation Treaty, which pledged signatories to control the spread of nuclear weapons.

Similarly, Dixy was roiled by the "debating society" approach of Fred C. Ikle and the organization he headed, the Arms Control and Disarmament Agency. She viewed them as busybodies, who were far more interested in holding meetings for the sake of holding meetings than in digging down for basic facts on nuclear weapons and realistic political facts. Dixy was convinced that some large-scale fence-mending had to take place in diplomatic circles before a valid nonproliferation movement could take place.

In 1973 the powers with nuclear weapons in their arsenal and a means of delivering them to targets were the U.S., Great Britain, Russia, France, and China. Dixy believed Israel, India, Brazil, West Germany, and Japan would soon be knocking on the door to gain entry into the World Nuclear Club, but she was convinced there was still time to act on the side of sanity and prevention. When she became AEC chairman, she found inside diplomatic, political, and technical information much easier to come by. Through friends, scientific attachés, and others highly placed in foreign circles, she was able to make a reliable assessment of the "nuclear condition" among the major powers. If the U.S., Russia, Great Britain, France, Canada, West Germany, and Japan could find common interest in halting the spread of nuclear weapons, it could be done. China could then be neutralized, or, perhaps, through a political miracle, might join in a Major-Power ban on the use of the new weaponry.

How could it be done? The solution came to Dixy as soon as she learned the rudiments of "reprocessing" in the nuclear scheme of things. Used or spent fuel from a reactor may be looked upon as "waste" by the uninformed, but it contains highly important materials in the eye of the nuclear scientist. The "waste" includes unused uranium, cesium 137, strontium 90, and, most significant of all, plutonium 239, the stuff of which nuclear weapons are made. These materials cannot be separated except through the use of sophisticated chemicals in a specially designed reprocessing plant. Without reprocessing, the plutonium required for nuclear weapons cannot be obtained. Recognizing that only the major powers had the reprocessing capability, Dixy reasoned that they could organize to insure that only they would retain reprocessing rights and plants. They would no longer sell uranium or other nuclear fuels to other nations; they would lease it!

Under the leasing proposal, then, each nation would have to return the spent fuels to one of the major powers and would thereby have no plutonium stock from which to manufacture nuclear weapons. Only the major powers would make the separations. They would also enforce a worldwide inspection system.

In effect, Dixy was suggesting a nuclear cartel. She detested the word, but this time she detested the alternatives even more. It was a way to freeze the advance of nuclear weaponry, and it just might be the world's last chance to do so. She knew from discussions with the British that they would welcome any positive step in that direction, although she had not whispered the details to anyone. Her eyes and ears in various parts of the world had already informed her that the Soviets also would look favorably on any plan that would keep plutonium from an increasing number of nations; with them it made sense from a political and technological point of view or, more succinctly, a selfish viewpoint. Canada, West Germany, and Japan could be counted on to cooperate. All that remained, then, was to coax the French to cooperate in the world's first "beneficent cartel." The AEC chairman preferred calling it a "peace cartel."

In the beginning, Dixy had been inclined to be critical of the French and their coolness toward the U.S. and Britain, but as she learned the background and history of the dispute among traditional friends, her attitude mellowed. The collapse of France under the Nazi heel in the Second World War set the stage for the British-American policy of keeping France at arm's length. Despite the heroism of DeGaulle and the Free French, American presidents and secretaries of state joined British prime ministers and foreign ministers in refusing to give France an equal role in determining Allied strategy. They ignored the significant French role in international stability. The world may pay dearly one day for that transgression.

British-American suspicions of French intentions and capabilities extended to the realm of nuclear development. From the beginning of the Nuclear Age, the U.S. has shared nuclear secrets with Great Britain, both in the military and civilian fields. But the two nations went on treating the French like untouchables; Dixy couldn't discern at first whether it grew out of greed or distrust, or both, but she knew that the motives had to be driven by stupidity. She discovered that one of the principal reasons General DeGaulle maintained a measure of animosity toward the U.S. and Britain was that both nations turned up their collective nuclear nose at him when he appealed for equal status and exchange of information.

Determined to get to the bottom of it, Dixy went out of her way to make new friends among the French to explore her notions. In the process she made many new and strong relationships abroad, particularly with André Giraud, her French counterpart as chief of the Commissariat a l'Energie Atomique, and

Giraud's right-hand man, Bertrand Goldschmidt, director of international activities for the Commissariat. Giraud was as friendly, helpful, and cooperative as Goldschmidt was puckish, witty, and impish. She was to find Giraud a man of his word and Goldschmidt an entertaining rascal who loved to tweak British and American noses but who also wanted nuclear control as much as Dixy and Giraud did.

Through late 1973 and most of 1974 Dixy wooed the French, preparing the ground for the ultimate design but never popping the question. She met with Giraud and Goldschmidt on several occasions and saw to it that aides met frequently to keep the music playing. By late 1974 it appeared Giraud and Goldschmidt knew what she was about, and they welcomed her many suggestions to bring the two nations closer in the nuclear field. At every turn, Dixy made certain her British counterparts knew of her meetings with the French; that is, she kept them informed of everything except her climactic proposal for a "peace cartel." That could wait for the right moment late in 1974.

It was when she realized the plan had a good chance to succeed that she went to President Ford and obtained his approval to proceed. She was in a race with time. The Senate was emasculating the once-logical bill to split the AEC into a research agency and a regulatory arm, and she didn't know how long she could sustain her position and authority. Whatever happened, she had to go on with her proposal; it was the most important endeavor of her life.

Full of great expectations, Dixy went next to Deputy Secretary of State Robert Ingersoll and explained the proposal to him. He, too, was impressed, and he took her plan to Henry Kissinger, who gave her his approval to open discussions with the French, a surprising action in view of what happened later; apparently Kissinger was not about to counter the word of the President. Not yet. Dixy then tried out the idea on her old friend and the new Vice President, Nelson Rockefeller. He was the most enthusiastic of all and wished her well. Armed with support from the very top, she packed her bags for Vienna, where the International Atomic Energy Agency was meeting in annual session and she would see Giraud again. It was October, 1974. Dixy was specially hopeful of success since it was Kissinger himself who had instructed his office to send word to the French foreign minister that Dixy would be in Vienna and wished to meet alone with

Giraud. To her it meant that the White House and State Department had united in sanctioning her moves leading to what she was now calling "NPEC," or the organization of Nuclear Producing and Exporting Countries, the West's answer to the Arabian oil cartel.

The Giraud-Ray meeting went even better than she had hoped. She spelled out the basics for a new plan of cooperation among the four major nuclear powers, plus Canada, West Germany, and Japan, but minus China for the time being. They spoke of mutual potentials in testing, in the exchange of information, and in the need for pooling talents and even materials where possible for the sake of saving millions lost through duplication. Dixy stopped short only at the point of proposing her NPEC. That she wanted to save for a meeting with all the nuclear powers and for the President himself and the Secretary of State. What a feather it would be in the Uncle Sam top hat!

With a preliminary nod from all participating nations, technical experts from each country could meet to begin deliberation on details. When they had done their work, the political leaders would meet again to shape the final declaration of purpose and the agreement to freeze the production of plutonium and nuclear weapons. It would have been a greater victory than was possible through the long and meagerly productive SALT or Strategic Arms Limitation Talks.

When Dixy returned to Washington late in October, the balloon burst. Fred Ikle and his Arms Control and Disarmament Agency had blundered onstage. She had long believed ACDA to be a totally unnecessary boondoggle, which should have been abolished because of its breast-beating, money-wasting tactics and its passion for publicity. Now she was sure of it. She could never understand why it had not been chopped down to size and placed in the State Department, where it belonged. A report on the success Dixy was having with the French had somehow found its way back to Ikle; he and his staff had seized upon the issue as being within their domain of arms control and, therefore, of legitimate concern to the agency.

ACDA suddenly burped forth "great plans" for a multinational conference of all nations interested in nuclear production and exports, and it would deal with proliferation and control of nuclear fuels and the entire supply-and-production cycle! The State Department apparently had given its blessing to the conference, and so had the National Security Council. All of it would be done in one conference, attended by all and without the most important preparatory function of all — a meeting beforehand of the technical experts to iron out engineering and technological details that were essential for the political decisions that would come later.

Dixy was stunned, disappointed, disgusted.

"My God!" she cried when she first heard of the scheme, "God save us from these imbeciles! They may have just destroyed the last chance we will ever have to stop the nuclear race."

What had happened in less than three weeks? Kissinger certainly could have put a stop to the ACDA and Security Council actions in view of what he knew about Dixy's plan and the President's approval. Worst of all, the call for the conference had been issued by the State Department itself! What in hell was going on!

Kissinger was out of the country . . . again. In a rage Dixy went to the State Department to seek out Ingersoll. After relieving herself of some choice words for Ikle, Kissinger, and a few others, she demanded that something be done about ACDA and that the conference be canceled immediately. The French and the English, she told Ingersoll, would not attend such a conference, and without them any meeting on nuclear controls would be a farce. The innocent Ingersoll, siding with Dixy, said he understood what she was trying to do and that he would try to put a stop to the conference.

Back at her office in Germantown, Dixy called Ambassador John Gaunt of the United Kingdom. She had kept Gaunt and Sir John Hill, head of the British nuclear establishment, apprised of her negotiations with the French. Gaunt was mystified and angry, with much justification for both:

"Dr. Ray, I thought this association with the French on nuclear matters was to be very quiet. But what happens? Our minister was summoned to the State Department to receive some information about proliferation and things of that sort, and he was met by Fred Ikle and was handed this ACDA document, which laid out five points. Then he told our man to return within 24 hours with his government's position on the five points, and his reply was to include a 'yes' or 'no' as to whether Britain would attend a conference of the nuclear-power nations."

She calmed him down, explained to him that it was all the

work of fools and that she was now working to have it squelched so they could return to the quiet deliberations.

Gaunt told her she might inform the State Department that Great Britain had no intentions of answering the document or attending the conference. He was pacified, but she knew it wouldn't be that easy to calm down French tempers. More than a telephone call would be necessary. However, she made a call to Goldschmidt to tell him to disregard State Department invitations to a conference in Washington. When she discovered both Goldschmidt and Giraud were deeply disturbed by the conference plans and believed Dixy had let them down, she knew she had to take much stronger action.

Dixy made arrangements to fly to Paris for an emergency meeting with Giraud. Before leaving, she paid another call on the State Department. Once more, Kissinger was away on another junket. Nobody was minding the store. Ingersoll assured her he had told Ikle and the ACDA to "knock it off" in very clear terms. With that she prepared to leave for Paris. Accompanying her in addition to staff members was Pepper, tiny black French Poodle, who was the latest offspring of her devoted Jacques. Pepper had been promised, as soon as Jacques' amour delivered, to Giraud's daughter, Sophia. Dixy would never find a more auspicious time to present the gift.

Later she said: "I am positive Pepper has been the finest ambassador we have ever sent to France. I also believe that little Poodle had determined long ago that he was going to become a Frenchman some day. He was saucy and proud. The gift did the trick, not only with Sophia but with Papa, too. As a result, our relationship was reestablished and was never better, despite the slapstick going on among the clowns back in Washington."

Dixy invited Giraud and Goldschmidt to visit the United States as her guest, so she could take them on a tour of American nuclear installations and see firsthand how agreements might be effected to the advantage of both nations. Giraud was never more receptive; he was eager also for her to take a tour of French facilities and pleased her particularly with his talk about exchanging information on breeder reactors. France already had one in operation and at that time was building a second one. The United States, which had pioneered breeder-reactor technology and engineering, had still to build its first one. The breeder appealed to her for several reasons. First, it virtually solved the fuel problem because it produced more fuel than it used and therefore helped eliminate the dilemma of diminishing uranium supplies. Second, it was the logical place to get rid of plutonium obtained in reprocessing, since the breeder ran on plutonium fuel. And, third, it worked neatly into her NPEC plan because the plutonium returned with spent fuel from "borrowing nations" would have a place to be utilized, thus solving a storage problem.

Time was running out. Congress had passed the bill reorganizing the AEC out of existence, and Dixy had only a couple months at the most to carry out her last major assignment. Giraud and his troupe arrived early in December, and the AEC staff provided a series of briefings and demonstrations at Albuquerque, Sandia, Los Alamos, the Argonne Laboratory in Chicago, and Oak Ridge. It was an immensely successful visit, and the French were impressed and eager to start cooperative agreements. They did not discuss military weapons because Dixy felt that was out of her jurisdiction, but they touched upon every other nuclear-related issue and laid the groundwork for the "big one," control of nuclear power by the major producing nations, without realizing they had.

The French were specially attentive to Dixy's suggestion that arrangements might be made for all Allied Powers to test weapons using America's most sophisticated instruments and skillful crews at Las Vegas. Test results would be available to all, and each participating nation could save millions in testing costs. Most importantly, tests could be reduced considerably.

When she bid Giraud and his staff good-bye in New York, Dixy was excited, happy, exhilarated. But when she returned to her desk in Washington, DC, her mood was reversed. Ingersoll had failed to get ACDA to "knock it off." The ACDA plan had not been turned off, and her immediate inquiries brought her the heartbreaking news that Kissinger apparently had changed his mind and had become resentful over her invasion of his field of diplomacy. He had not only given his support to the ACDA scheme, which was certain to fail, but had also persuaded the President to turn his back on her NPEC proposal.

As the Christmas holiday approached, Dixy's morale was at its lowest in her career as a federal employee. On one hand the AEC, which she considered the finest operational agency the federal government had ever created, was about to be dismantled. She had a good chance to become chairman of the new Energy Research and Development Administration, despite the bad-mouthing Chet Holifield was directing her way; however, her spirits were so low she didn't have the will to fight for a job for which she was remarkably well qualified. And now, thanks to the shortsightedness of a few persons in leadership roles, the most idealistic and ambitious plan of her life was disintegrating before her eyes. Suddenly Dixy was tired and weary, but most of all she was worried — worried about what was in store for her country and for the world.

Without some kind of mechanism like her NPEC, Dixy ruminated, the worst can happen.

"If the nuclear powers continue to behave as they have without trying to reach a mutual agreement to control plutonium production, we face the awesome prospect that within a very few years we will see an international black market operating in plutonium and highly enriched uranium. Worse still, we will witness helplessly the rapid growth in the number of nations that have the capability of producing nuclear weapons that can be delivered. Some may become black-market producers or suppliers; some may simply rely on the production of weapons. And some may do both . . . ."

Dixy Lee Ray had never felt more like crying. But the tears wouldn't come.

"Where are the clowns, Mr. Sondheim? Never mind; they're here."

CHAPTER FIFTEEN

Playing Out the String

It was ironic that Dixy Lee Ray, one of the first and strongest backers of a move to reorganize the Atomic Energy Commission, would see the move used by her enemies to destroy her power and influence in the capital. Upon joining the AEC, she recognized almost immediately that no agency should be called on to promote energy production on one hand and regulate and license it on the other. The two functions were clearly in conflict. She actively sought to divorce the energy-producing agency from the nuclear-regulating arm.

Dixy's determination to accomplish the split intelligently began with her appointment as AEC chairman in February, 1973. Her enthusiasm was to wane early in 1974, when Congress began tacking on amendments that first distorted, then virtually reversed the intentions she had in mind for the two new agencies. Worst of all from Dixy's point of view was the fact that the antinuclear voices in Congress, led by Senator Abraham Ribicoff of Connecticut, were succeeding in subjugating the role of the federal government in the development of nuclear power.

Dixy was less inclined to blame the congressmen than the staffs they hired.

"Government by GS-15," she repeated. "Most government workers are trying to do a good job in the federal system, even though only half of them would be needed if we chopped government down to adequate size. But the people who are elected or have to answer to those who are elected have turned over too much responsibility to staff members who don't have to face the music. And many of these administrative aides reside in congressional offices and wield remarkable power because they have the ear of congressmen who are too busy or too disinterested to question the work of the staff on difficult questions.

"If Americans were aware of how much influence the GS-15's possess through influencing the votes of congressmen, they'd be shouting for a change in the system. There's nothing wrong with the system. It's the congressmen who should be called to account for their actions."

(At the time Dr. Ray served in Washington the pay of the GS-15 hovered just over the $30,000-a-year mark.)

Headache No. 1 to the AEC chairman was not Ribicoff, however, but the chief administrative aide to his Senate Government Affairs Committee, Nader-like Paul Levinthal. Levinthal made a career of fighting nuclear power and persuaded his boss to take what Dr. Ray considered "ludicrous, uninformed, panic-button" positions on atomic energy. Although a large majority of senators favored continuing use of nuclear energy for military and civilian purposes, staffers like Levinthal exercised enough influence over their employers to cause them to insist on de-emphasizing the role of nuclear power in the projected Energy and Research Development Administration, one of the new agencies. The other was the Nuclear Regulatory Commission. Over on the House side Holifield & Co. were so intent upon getting rid of the chairman that they sat by and watched the "fear" camp emasculate the nuclear wing of the new agency. She had broken up their little ball game so they decided to take away her bat and ball.

Nevertheless, friends of Dr. Ray believed she could have won the day, as well as the new chairmanship, if she had not listened to bad advice, or what they considered to be bad advice.

David Jenkins, her chief aide, was most succinct: "She got good advice too late. The early bad advice came from the 'yes' men around her in and out of the AEC. They told her that opposition had congealed in both houses and that she wouldn't have a chance to be confirmed as the new chairman of ERDA. They also told her the growing opposition marshaled by Holifield and Hosmer probably would make it impossible for

President Ford to appoint her in the first place. I think they were dead wrong. Dixy didn't realize until too late that she had tremendous support in both houses because of the hard-nosed, honest job she had turned in as AEC chairman. If she had fought for the appointment and then the confirmation, she would have made it. But by the time she realized she had a chance and could have put on the gloves to get into the ring, the sports fans and judges had already gone and the main event was over."

Jenkins and others whose advice had not been heeded in time knew that Dr. Ray could rely on a powerful ally, Nelson Rockefeller, the Vice President, to exert influence on President Ford to keep Dr. Ray in Washington. They knew Ribicoff was in the minority in the Senate and that Dixy could command enough support to overcome any challenge from the antinuclear forces, including Ribicoff's committee chief. It was also apparent she had overestimated Holifield's power and the force of his anger toward her. How could a congressman whose monumental support of the nuclear capability had won him, deservedly, a generous slice of history in the Nuclear Age now turn against the edifice he had helped build — just as he was preparing to retire from Congress?

But the "panic" crew had already done its damage. Convinced it was time to leave federal service, the AEC chairman began talking about "how nice" it would be to return to her beloved Pacific Northwest and "the real Washington." The prospect of spending more time on her hillside farm on Fox Island in Puget Sound waters brought a smile back to her face. She began to accept the inevitable.

Thus, when she received a request from the White House to consider taking a position as assistant secretary of state under Dr. Henry Kissinger, she quickly said, "No, thanks," and continued to pack late in 1974. She had reckoned without Nelson Rockefeller — and, again ironically, Kissinger himself. Rockefeller had enormous influence over Kissinger (and vice versa), and both men could exert great influence over President Ford.

Rockefeller had always admired brainy, courageous persons. He liked to be around them and he liked to help them and have them working for him, wherever possible. It was natural for him to cultivate the friendship of Dr. Henry Kissinger and Dr. Dixy Lee Ray. He had first come into close contact with Dixy through his brainchild, Critical Choices for America, headquartered in New York. Because of the organization's deep interest in the energy future of the U.S., Dr. Ray and members of her staff had been invited to New York for a conference. Among the Ray contingent were Dr. Hans Bethe, internationally noted nuclear physicist, and other scientists, along with Jenkins, Dr. Ray's aide. She impressed all of them with her knowledge of nuclear energy. Although her discipline was marine biology, she had become an authority on nuclear power through a characteristic ability to throw herself into a subject around the clock till she grasped it. She was now a physicist without portfolio.

"When Congress approved the AEC split and Dixy prepared to return to the Northwest," Jenkins said, "Rockefeller wouldn't hear of it. He asked her to stay on in some other capacity. She was deeply pleased and flattered, but she told Rockefeller it was too late. Undaunted, Rockefeller cabled Kissinger, who was on one of his shuttle trips to the Middle East. I believe he was in Egypt at the time he received Rocky's communication. Kissinger called her to press the Rockefeller suit, and she was moved by such an appeal, particularly in view of what he had done to her 'peace cartel' plan. Henry followed up his call with a detailed cable, asking her to take the job and promising her that he would support her in anything she felt it necessary to do to make the new position productive for the U.S. With that example of support, plus the entreaties of many scientists in and out of Washington, DC, Dixy telephoned, then wrote her acceptance to the White House."

However, it was indicative of Dr. Ray's mood that she attached a significant provision to her acceptance. In a "love me, love my dogs" stand she informed both the White House and Kissinger:

"I will take the job on one condition: I come with two dogs. They come with me, or I will not be there."

Both men agreed, but then they had a precedent. When Dr. Ray accepted President Nixon's request that she join the Atomic Energy Commission back in the summer of 1972, she had laid down one condition: she wanted big Ghillie and little Jacques with her. In the AEC case, no real problems existed. Dr. Ray's offices as a commissioner and later as chairman were spacious, and the grounds of the massive AEC headquarters out in Germantown, Maryland, were made to order for canine comfort and strolling. In fact, most employees at the AEC befriended the dogs and enjoyed watching the little old chairman in liederhosen marching the powerful Scottish Deerhound and the tiny but majestic French Poodle as they made the rounds of the many trees and shrubs on the vast acreage.

But down at Foggy Bottom in Northwest Washington, the State Department building had no such advantages. Ghillie and Jacques had to be satisfied with marble corridors and treeless avenues. In the building a few timid souls took exception to coming face to face with the two dogs on elevators, in corridors, and in the assistant secretary's office, as well. But most persons took the dogs in stride, many of them actually pleased to have a "true character" roaming the halls of the usually sedate and unexciting "stately" department.

Two Presidents and a secretary of state had now given her a privilege seldom provided in official Washington. Strangely enough, the problems that arose had nothing to do with her unusual privilege. They came from the preoccupation of the news media with the fact that anyone in public life would have two dogs as constant companions and live in a motor home. Perhaps the press reaction infuriated her more than anything else.

"I think I have been more generous with my time for the press than most other public officials," she said. "But what often happens? The reporter comes in, along with a photographer usually. I am sitting atop many crucial issues here — agreements or disagreements over ocean-exploration issues, international questions on the distribution of scientific and technological information and devices, environmental compacts . . . I want to talk about the great issues in which this bureau is involved and the promise of its future. And what do the reporters want to talk about? My dogs. My motor home. My private life. They don't seem interested nor concerned in the vital issues of our time. Is this the way they are trained? Is this what their editors and publishers and station managers expect from them?"

It was a repeat of her experience at the AEC with a handful of reporters who cared little for the problems of the Nuclear Age but a great deal about canine pedigrees and homes on four rubber tires. Dixy couldn't understand what was happening. She had always had the most pleasant relations with the press; in fact, her years of contacts with reporters, radio, and television personnel had contributed greatly to her immense popularity in the

Pacific Northwest and with national audiences who watched her on her frequent science shows for public broadcasting.

What had soured some of the press members? Undoubtedly it was her new relationship with nuclear power, never palatable with a certain element in the press — usually those who refused to do a little homework but preferred to follow the emotional responses of the Nader adherents and let them do the thinking for them.

Dr. Ray would leave the AEC on its last day of existence, January 19, 1975, and assume her new position as assistant secretary of state January 20. At the State Department she would be the first director of the Bureau of Oceans, International Environmental and Scientific Affairs, the creation of Senator Claiborne Pell, Rhode Island Democrat, who got the bill through Congress with the help of Senator Howard Baker of Tennessee from the other side of the aisle.

The incident of birth of the new bureaucratic baby was a tipoff on the troubles that lay ahead, both for Dixy and the bureau. When Pell pushed the measure through Congress in 1973, he had done so despite the opposition and enmity of the State Department. It was to be the only bureau imposed upon the department by Congress, and its statutory nature called for its director and assistant secretary of state to report to Congress directly and make its budgetary and organizational needs known to Congress. How could the diplomatic clan be expected to swallow such nonsense? All other bureaus were part of the State Department structure, and their directors reported to the undersecretary and secretary alone. They were accorded no such prima-donna status, with Congress as the perennial watchdog.

For the nation's press, in the meantime, the new assistant secretary of state was saying such things as:

"This will be something like coming home to me. I'm going to enjoy getting back to affairs of the sea. I will also be back in the business of energy, this time on an international scale. The President was specially interested in my continuing my involvement in this field. It is a new area for the State Department, and I hope to be able to pull together the various scientific efforts and have an effective voice for the role of science and technology in the modern world."

What a disappointment she faced in that regard! What frustration she would meet at the hands of the secretary of state who had cabled her from halfway around the world to pledge his "support in anything she felt it necessary to do . . ."

Lost in many of the reports of her acceptance was a comment from Dr. Ray to the effect that "I would have been quite happy to serve either in the nuclear regulatory post or as administrator of energy research and development." The latter, yes; there was heartbreak there. The former? Definitely not.

Dixy took the State Department post, but her heart was never in it, despite the fact she gave it — in characteristic fashion — every hour of the day, weekends, holidays, whatever. She had her bureau going at hours seldom worked by other divisions and bureaus within the department. Her staffers soon became acquainted with the "hamburger hour" on Saturdays and often on Sundays. Nobody worked harder, longer hours than the new assistant secretary. She went to work on organization of the bureau as soon as she first walked through the door. A veteran of State Department operations, who was not exactly an admirer of the new assistant secretary, acknowledged the department had never seen a quicker, more efficient "takeoff" of a fledgling within the diplomatic framework. Dixy had job descriptions, a table of organization, operating procedures, and a new budget ready for congressional scrutiny within the first two months. She had the help of a budgetary and organizational genius named John Abbadessa, once the administrative brain of the AEC. She acknowledged she had "stolen" him from other agencies when she departed the AEC headquarters at Germantown, Maryland.

Unfortunately, she was to lose Abbadessa to the International Atomic Energy Agency in Vienna — and was unable to grab him back later when she sought his services as budget director for Washington State when she became governor. Abbadessa was considered close to "genius" stature as a budget officer in federal government circles, and he probably could have written his own ticket in private industry. But he had a special feel and preference for government work, and, strangely enough considering the American psyche and the penchant for a buck, he preferred to do the kind of work he liked, rather than slave to pad his bank account. Little wonder he was a favorite of Dixy Lee Ray's. They were very much alike in that respect.

In the early months at the State Department the excitement of creating a new and important bureau took Dixy's mind off the fact she wasn't thrilled over life among the diplomats. She was so busy with the organizational effort and the promise of the bureau that she overlooked the incongruity of her predicament — a straight-talking, outspoken maverick among hundreds of disciplined, double-talking diplomats trained to say very little of substance.

Some time later, when she found she could bear it no longer and resigned in protest, she characterized the State Department as an "overblown, overstaffed, and overpaid cadre of lily-livered striped-suiters whose main purpose in life was to make certain that nothing ever happened."

She should have expected such frustrations from a department that had fought creation of the new bureau and would continue to fight its existence as an intrusive, crude, congressional ploy to take foreign policy out of the hands of the Executive in a crass "violation" of the Constitution. Once, when advised of the mental attitude among many of the State Department old-timers, Dixy reminded those present that if anybody was violating the presidential right to shape foreign policy, it was the department's own "egocentric and arrogant" boss, Dr. Kissinger.

In the early weeks of 1975, Assistant Secretary Ray entertained the notion that she could overcome the snobbery of the elite in the department and even break through to help Kissinger frame U.S. policy on the oceans, in energy, in technology, in the sciences, and in environmental questions. She had a short, cursory meeting with Kissinger, the undersecretary, and the deputy secretary in the first days of her tenure, but she never dreamed it was to be her last conference with the earth-shuttling secretary, who was too busy packing and unpacking to attend meetings with anybody except the President.

It is probable that Dixy was the only person in the big C Street emporium who didn't laugh at the many gags about Kissinger's travels. Although she always liked a good joke, she was not amused when a wag on the staff reported tongue-in-cheek that Henry Kissinger had been "sighted" in Washington, DC and had been turned away by the State Department doorman.

Of all the problems she encountered in her lonely post in the midst of a fuming elitist bureaucracy that detested interlopers like Dixy and Henry Kissinger, the greatest and most vexing was her inability to get to Kissinger to determine his policy, her policy, and that of the State Department and the new bureau.

Perhaps the most frustrating and most telling incident came

in mid-March, 1975, after Dixy had sought in vain to arrange a policy session with Kissinger on the serious issues of international energy, undersea mineral-exploration rights, and technology transfer — all subjects Congress intended be handled in the new bureau. Because of Kissinger's yo-yo existence, projected meetings were scheduled, canceled, and rescheduled. Finally, in desperation, Dixy approached an equally befuddled Deputy Secretary Robert S. Ingersoll to ask him, in effect, "howinhell am I supposed to carry out U.S. and State Department policy and take action if I can't determine whathehell that policy is?"

"Why," the answer came back as if it had been given many times before, "if you want to know what our policy is, just read Dr. Kissinger's speeches."

The new assistant secretary was dumfounded, and she discovered a few expletives she didn't know she had. She left no doubt about what she thought of the arrogance and callousness of the traveling genius. Dixy had never thought much of Richard Nixon, but she thought it dangerous that a secretary of state who wouldn't speak even to the Cabots had taken over direction of American foreign affairs, and more. Things were to get worse.

She had not been in her new office more than six weeks when she read newspaper and department reports of a speech by Thomas O. Enders, assistant secretary for economic and business affairs. The subject of the speech was energy. It wasn't so much that Enders had goofed badly on specifics of nuclear and other energy sources with which Dixy was so familiar. It was that he hadn't bothered to touch base with her on an area of concern that had been assigned to her by law and Congress. She complained bitterly to the deputy secretary and Undersecretary Charles Robinson, who served frequently as peacemaker and pacifier in the explosive department. But Enders went on preaching "energy policy" as if he had been given that charge by Kissinger himself. Perhaps he had. It apparently occurred to no one in the department hierarchy that State policy on international energy matters was being spouted by one who knew virtually nothing about it in specific terms, while sitting ignored in the maverick bureau was one of the nation's most practiced authorities on energy issues — and on an international scale, too, for she had conducted many conferences and had numerous experiences with the energy leaders and industries of foreign nations while with AEC.

The twin obstacles of an arrogant, messianic secretary of state, who acted as if the State Department that had preceded him didn't exist, and the career cadre of foreign officers who felt the same way about Henry, made Dixy's life increasingly miserable. Even though she hadn't really wanted the position in the first place, she bit the bullet seven days and nights a week and went on hoping that some light might shine through eventually. Once again she noted that the GS-15's, like vultures over Death Valley, were simply biding their time and waiting for the carcass to fall. Some of the pin-stripers were brazen about it, like the one who openly displayed a sign on his desk that implied "I outlasted the last one, and I'll outlast you, too." It wasn't directed specially at Dixy; it was meant for any short-stay non-elite executives foisted on the department by the crap game called politics. The fact that the snobs cared less for Henry Kissinger than they did for Dixy herself was no consolation to her. It is little wonder, then, that an incident for which Dixy should have been acclaimed something of a heroine was permitted to go unnoticed by a department that was selfishly involved only in its own prejudices.

Had it not been for Dixy Lee Ray, it is probable the North Vietnamese Communist forces would have "inherited" an operating nuclear-energy plant intact.

When Dixy, an avid reader of the news, discovered the North Viet army, which had all but destroyed the South Viet ground forces early in 1975, was about a five-day march away from a nuclear plant the U.S. had helped install for the South Vietnamese, she called Robert Seamans, who succeeded her when the AEC was split into two agencies. He headed what was to be the short-lived Energy and Research Development Administration, soon to give way to the Department of Energy.

Seamans was nowhere to be found. Worse, he was off on a skiing vacation in Colorado and had left no telephone number or address at the ERDA office. Dixy, then assistant secretary of state, said to herself, "To hell with protocol."

She called her staff together, particularly those who had had experience with nuclear energy, and called the Defense Department within an hour.

What she told the military, in effect, was "get off your butts and get some planes in there pronto to bring out the nuclear fuel rods. Then gut the plant so the Reds can't use it."

The Defense Department took her advice. Two planes were flown in, barely in time. Crews removed the rods, bombed and gutted the plant, and flew their precious cargo back to Guam and eventually to the United States.

Some observers thought the action unnecessary because they believed the North Vietnamese didn't have the ability to utilize the plutonium waste from the plant to produce nuclear weapons. Maybe not, reasoned Dixy, but they have important friends who can do it for them or show them how. And "we shouldn't be sitting around here in Washington thinking up reasons for not acting. The debate society can meet afterward."

The Air Force and the Army merited applause for the daring escapade, in which no lives were lost. But it was Dixy Lee Ray who should have taken the bows.

Dixy worked hard at reorganizing the bureau's representatives abroad, particularly the corps of scientific attachés who were supposed to keep the bureau and the department informed regularly of any negotiations, discussions, or relationships with foreign governments in the scientific field. She was appalled by the flippant, lackadaisical attitude assumed by so many of the attachés, and she began to clean house. Had no one ever demanded discipline from them? Hadn't anyone tried to train them to serve American interests and put in at least an eight-hour day, instead of treating the assignments like three-year vacations?

Day by day Dixy's reaction to department practices abroad and at home turned from bewilderment to alarm and to anger. If the taxpayer knew how much insignificant work he was subsidizing, he would certainly rebel. When she tried reorganizing the work of department employees abroad who were also expected to report to the bureau, she encountered an impossible mass of red tape in personnel handling and, worst of all, an insidious loyalty among foreign service officers to protect each other at all costs. They stuck together more closely than a class of graduates from West Point or Annapolis, and they were far better disguised. She was able to make several changes and replace some of the worst of the clan, but she soon gave up, recognizing that she wouldn't be in government long enough to make a dent and that she had much more important issues at hand.

Sometimes a career officer would cause her to wonder aloud: "Whose side is he on?" One of the stories she liked had been told by a comic-strip artist:

"An American tourist in Washington, DC, for the first time,

became lost as he approached the Potomac. Finding a guard, he asked:

"'Could you tell me, please, on which side is the Pentagon?'

"'Ours, I hope,' said the guard with snap and relish."

But her favorite anecdote was a true incident that occurred within the State Department itself while she was working there. An old friend, Tom Foley, a congressman from her own state and a man who had achieved considerable stature as a statesman in the lower house, had been invited to a conference at the department on many issues concerning American relations abroad. On hand for the conference were State Department officials who ran the various desks — the Canadian Desk, the French Desk, the Indian Desk, etc. For nearly an hour they took turns at asking questions which indicated the needs of foreign countries and the shortcomings at home in providing help and funds to people abroad.

Finally, with a grimace and a show of weariness, Foley said in loud tones so none would miss it:

"Perhaps what we need most in the State Department these days is an American desk."

The laughter was immediate. But it was apparent the remark had struck a bull's-eye. After that, the questions were phrased more judiciously. Dixy has reported the Foley anecdote many times and in many places. Her affection for the congressman's remark points up her own exasperation with the ugly Americans in or out of pin-stripe suits who downgrade whatever action the U.S. takes or doesn't take in foreign affairs. Most of all, she was distressed over the perilous American practice of giving away its technological supremacy.

"This nation," she once told a university audience, "insists upon giving away its most important advantages in the scientific and technological field without getting anything of value in return. Now, I am for tradeoffs, particularly when they benefit both factions in the trade. But we are so naive in our giveaways that we are making it possible for enemies as well as friends to challenge us in the market places abroad that we ourselves have created — with products we have originated and engineered.

"I think the American government should level with the people and detail the sophisticated, sensitive secrets that are being handed out under the guise of a 'a helping hand' to other nations. The situation is this: American science, technology, and industry pay out millions annually to create new devices, new machinery, new electronic marvels, new industrial processes. Some of these developments have taken years, decades to perfect. Most of them should remain in the proprietary category. But what do we do as a nation? We give them away as if they were insignificant and as if those who receive them have an absolute right to have them.

"But that is not the most frustrating aspect on the giveaway. The tragedy is that we refuse to utilize our largesse to obtain some very worthy, practical end. We have been fools not to make our technological, agricultural, and economic gifts count for something. Just once I would like to have America say to a nation that has caused grave problems and threatened world peace:

"'Certainly, we will be happy to renew our agreement to send you food, tools, chemicals, electronic devices, and all the rest, provided you enter into immediate negotiations with your neighbor and end the border wars and raids. And if you fail to seek a peaceful solution, we will withdraw our assistance.'

"The faint-of-heart in our society might call that carrot-stick diplomacy or, even worse, blackmail. But their kind of thinking got us into the miserable bind we're in in the first place."

Dixy was specially critical of compacts engineered by Kissinger's crew and his predecessors with regard to backward nations.

"These so-called trade agreements involve setting up committees to arrange exchanges of properties or ideas of relatively equal value between the U.S. and the not-so-fortunate countries. Good idea? Maybe. But how on earth do you implement such exchanges?

"Let us say we will arrange through one of these committees the exchange of our latest developments in cybernetics or nuclear medicine or metallurgy. These are some of those very sophisticated engineering wonders fresh out of research laboratories or the multimillion-dollar factory. Our State Department and its beneficent commissions arrange an exchange with, say, Tunisia. That nation takes our technological jewels, and what can it give in return that could be considered of equal value? Anyone can see the nonsense in that supposition — unless he or she works for the State Department, I suppose.

"Now, please understand, I have no quarrel with Tunisia. I think it has been the mark of America's greatness that we have gone to the aid of people everywhere in the world. No other nation in the world's history has been so unselfish and philan-thropic. We should continue to help. But why can't we do it on sensible, realistic, practical grounds?

"If a nation has no usable materials, resources, or ideas to trade, why can't it offer something even more precious — friend-ship, loyalty, and a visible demonstration of its willingness to keep the peace and live in a true family of nations? That is where we missed the boat after the Second World War. The Marshall Plan could have been the greatest idea of man if we had insisted on a 'matching' program from receiving nations — a 'match' that would have guaranteed good will and an international spirit of compromise. If we had played our cards right, we could have solved the problem of nuclear-weapon proliferation with that philosophy."

In the meantime, the cold shoulders at the State Depart-ment grew even colder, and the career diplomats didn't bother to disguise their disdain for the little old marine biologist from the Pacific Northwest. Just wait 'er out, and she'll soon be gone, like the rest of them. How right they were!

The fact that Dixy and her staff worked diligently days, nights and weekends on the reorganization and new budget and then were treated coolly and curtly by the very Congress that had created the incipient bureau didn't help Dixy's morale either. Perhaps that was the time she first saw the handwriting on the wall. The personnel she needed to do the job were not provided, and the funds she would have to have to improve the U.S position abroad in the areas of energy, environmental considera-tions, and scientific and technological exchange were not forth-coming. Despite the magnificent efforts of Abbadessa and others on Dixy's staff to show congressmen what their own creation could accomplish in the otherwise stagnant State Department, the dream was banished by the yawns in the hearing rooms.

Was it true, Dixy asked herself, that the bureau was simply window-dressing, a place to get answers to irate constituent letters to congressmen and not much else? Were Senator Pell, the creator, and Senator Baker, the well-wisher, the only ones who really cared about turning the State Department into an active, positive function, instead of the recalcitrant wallflower it has always been? Always been, that is, except for the presence of a Henry Kissinger, who couldn't have cared less about the depart-ment because he had his own foreign office going.

"It is a deep disappointment to me," she confided to close

friends, "that I have had the misfortune to move in my brief federal government career from the best-managed department to the worst. I am convinced that the old Atomic Energy Commission and the State Department must be considered the two extremes in government management. The AEC was blessed with the best brains in government and the best administrative minds. We had our problems, but the daily operation of that gigantic complex (more than 90,000 employees, direct and indirect) was tuned like a Swiss watch. When a briefing, a special study, an investigation of some problem in physics or chemistry or engineering was ordered, the pieces came together like a high-precision watch. Everybody seemed to know his assignment, and it was a delight to work there.

"The remarkably successful energy report we submitted to the White House in December, 1973, at the request of the President was a case in point. It is still the basis for reports on energy production, sufficiency, and conservation in this country, and it dealt realistically and statistically with every form of energy, including that produced from coal, gas, nuclear fission, fusion, solar power, windmills, ocean devices, geothermal—everything.

"I don't think any department of federal government could have produced so thorough, so technically accurate and revealing a report in so short a time — less than six months. The disturbing element was that I had to submit it to a President who was already half out of his mind over the indiscretions of Watergate.

"On the other hand, I don't think the State Department could have produced a teamwork report of that magnitude in 50 years. Or, maybe I should say it would take at least 50 years to get one from the State Department. Without question the State Department is the most unmanaged department in federal government. When Henry Kissinger came in, he brought in his own troops, imposed his 'club' over the department like an umbrella, and went about things as if he were running his own country. When he left, his coterie went with him, for the most part, thank God. But the department, once again forlorn and unmanaged, just continues sitting there until the next secretary of state comes along to perch atop the structure like a new hat waiting to be blown off with the next political breeze.

"What a helluva way to run a railroad."

An uncomfortable Dixy Lee Ray went about her bureau

business with as much diligence as she could manage. Without direction from above or from the White House, she was like a pianist without a piano. In this case she didn't have any music, either, so she had to play by ear.

Although the die was cast and Dixy knew what was coming, she hung on in the State Department, looking for the miracle that never came. In early spring, 1975, a glimmer of hope appeared with the possibility that Congress and the White House might approve a measure restoring the position of science adviser to the President. When that potential became known, messages of support for Dr. Dixy Lee Ray to assume the position came from science colleagues and friends in the laboratories, the universities, and the coal, nuclear, gas, and virtually every other energy-related industry.

Dr. Dixy Lee Ray in the White House advising the President? What a battle that would have signaled between the scientists of America and the pseudo-scientific Nader fringe! Perhaps it would have cleared the air and shown for the first time the fact that the vast majority of scientific minds in America and in the world were in direct opposition to the small handful of pro-Nader scientists.

The hope for a brilliant, fearless scientific mind in the White House at the President's side was never fulfilled, despite the fact Congress eventually made provision for the important scientific consultant at the request of President Ford. Nixon had eliminated the position many years earlier — in the interest of economy, he said. By the time Congress acted on the matter, the nation had another President. A Democratic President. And Dixy would be packing her bags again. The political irony is that she returned to her native state to run for governor as a Democrat and became Washington's first woman to be elected chief executive.

Two events combined to spur the Ray mind into a decision to chuck it all and return to Fox Island, Washington, her goal six months earlier. Both came in early May, one back at Fox Island and the other in the department.

One day, while weeding a bank on a steep hillside at the island farm, Dixy's sister Marion grabbed a large number of weeds and pulled hard. They gave away easily, too easily, and a surprised Marion Reid fell backward and down the hill about 15 to 17 feet. It was a catastrophic fall for Marion, who was in excellent physical condition but was no longer a youngster. She hurt her back, head, and legs severely. At the hospital it was first feared she might have suffered permanent injury and could lose the use of her legs. Her speech also was seriously affected.

Back in Washington, Dixy stayed close to the telephone to await reports several times daily. She could not leave the capital and visit Marion for at least two weeks because of important travels and conferences involving foreign delegations.

"It's all my fault," Dixy confided to a staffer the day she first heard of Marion's fall. "If I hadn't badgered her into coming up to Fox Island to share the place with me, this wouldn't have happened to her. And I have to take some of the blame for Gordy, too . . . "

It was strange talk for the usually hard-headed, realistic scientific mind from the Evergreen State. But close friends could understand her feelings. She and Marion had never been very sympatico in childhood years, and they hadn't been very communicative through the years, mostly because their interests were as diverse as one could imagine. But in recent years, perhaps because of the humorous, gutty, and earthy quality Gordon Reid brought to Fox Island, the sisters rediscovered each other. After nearly 40 years Marion and Dixy were to find a warm friendship they had never enjoyed — thanks in great measure to Gordon, whose irreverent speech and backwoods wit melted the ice for the sister act. When Gordon died in December, 1974, Dixy was as deeply affected as Marion. Perhaps the tragic loss was actually the final, irrevocable bond.

It was clear that Dixy blamed herself for Marion's fall, and she told her closest friends:

"That does it. I must leave this place for good and go home to take care of Marion. She needs me, and I'm not accomplishing anything here anyway."

Staffers and friends prevailed upon her to stay on. In addition, the news from the hospital back in Washington State was a bit more optimistic the second week. Marion was still having severe head pains, but it was quite certain now that she would not lose her ability to walk and talk.

That was a great relief to Dixy and everyone else, but the shock was never to wear off completely. At that point, it was obvious Dixy was merely awaiting the right time. Conditions at the State Department had worsened, and the careerists were already licking their chops at the prospect of another victory for the vultures. Indirectly, it was Kissinger who gave Dr. Ray the final nudge to go along with the countless other nudges he had provided the previous four months. And he did it through his press secretary, Robert Anderson.

The hassle evolved over the agreement West Germany made with Brazil to supply the South American nation materials, equipment, and technological know-how for its growing nuclear industry. In almost characteristic fashion Dixy got into hot water because of her strong belief in supporting the free-enterprise system and giving it a chance to work. She had often been extremely critical of some of the giant American power firms because of their close relationship with the congressional faction she had accused of fashioning a cozy nuclear cartel by-passing the AEC — or at least working through a "friendly clique" within the AEC. At one time she had suggested the possibility of mounting a congressional investigation — by those not involved, of course — into the arrangments that seemed to exist between the firms and certain members of Congress. Had the AEC never been split, she might have made good her wish.

In the Brazilian instance, however, she was strongly on the side of one of the firms because the company plainly was getting the sharp end of the stick — sometimes called the shaft — thanks to the ridiculous nature of U.S. policy and statutes governing the sale of nuclear materials and equipment, as well as technical skills, to foreign nations.

"The United States," Dixy explained, "had already determined through Eisenhower's 'Atoms for Peace' program that its policy would thereafter be to make the advantages of nuclear power available to all countries that demonstrated the need, the ability, the integrity, and the honest desire to utilize such power for the economic benefit of their people. I think it was a good policy and a sensible one in view of the fact that other nations already had nuclear capability and would start supplying such materials and equipment if we didn't.

"Nevertheless, the Luddites and the fear faction among us made such a fuss that Congress amended the Atomic Energy Act to prevent private companies from making any agreements with foreign nations to supply reprocessing and uranium-enrichment facilities. This is plain head-in-the-sand policy. To understand that, you need to know that other nations make no pretenses about the division of government and so-called private industry within their borders.

"The American firm tried but it was refused permission to supply the reprocessing plant Brazil wanted and needed to keep its new power industry going. It was also ruled out of the game in its attempt to provide the enrichment facility Brazil had ordered. The most unpleasant fact is that the Brazilians went so far as to use the U.S. company's format when they went shopping for what they needed in Bonn!"

The State Department got into the act when Kissinger & Co., heeding the strident demands of the antinuclear minority, declared the U.S. would stand fast and not permit its nuclear materials and equipment, plus know-how, to be sold to Brazil. It didn't matter that the U.S. would thereby lose more than $1 billion in sales at a time when its balance-of-payments posture was in serious deficit. It didn't matter that our willingness to sell our products to Brazil would not keep that nation from getting them anyway from one of the other nuclear powers.

"We behaved like a bunch of goddam fools," Dixy said in private. "We made it possible in the first place for all these countries to have an expanded power industry. But now we automatically forfeit the entire foreign market because of our political stupidity. It simply doesn't make sense for us to create a market for any product abroad, then eliminate ourselves from the competitive race because of the damned idiocy of the Ralph Naders among us who seemed determined to destroy our country — and who apparently are succeeding. Will we awaken too late? Will Mr. Nader and his disciples be able to save us when we become a third-rate power in the world and must take orders from Moscow, Peking, or even Sao Paolo?"

When Dr. Ray arrived in New York for a major address, she was interviewed by a *New York Times* reporter, who asked her what she thought of the German-Brazilian billion-dollar deal and the fact that American industrialists were prevented from doing what their counterparts in other leading nations were encouraged to do in partnership with their governments.

She said what she thought, as she always did, and the *Times* reporter wrote it as she said it.

In her hotel room at mid-day the next day, Dixy received a call from Robert Anderson, Kissinger's apologist, as she called him.

"'I'm afraid I must inform you,'" Dixy quoted the press secretary as telling her, "'Dr. Kissinger is not very happy over your remarks to the *New York Times* in this morning's edition. Neither he nor other department executives think it is a very good idea for policymakers to disagree openly in the public prints.'

"He went on and on that way. With each of his words my temperature rose another degree. By the time he was through, I was ready to commit an act of violence. It is fortunate for Dr. Kissinger and Mr. Anderson that neither was in my room at the time. But I had already made up my mind that I would not open up on Mr. Anderson. I would save my ammunition for a more meaningful approach.

"If I couldn't say what I thought on the basis of experience in the nuclear area, the sciences, and energy matters in general, I didn't want the damned job. I knew that now, for sure. While other countries are free to sell their nuclear and other equipment and fuels to whomever they wish, we can't shove our head in the sand and expect the problem to go away if we refuse to sell."

It was no longer a time to brood. Dixy returned to Washington, DC to plan her resignation and her departure from the capital. And she would not do it with the whimper others had offered on resigning.

But before taking her case to Congress and the public, she decided she must submit her resignation to the two men who had asked her to take the position — after coaxing from Nelson Rockefeller. If only Rocky had been in the White House, she thought . . .

Because he had been such a good friend, Dixy informed Rockefeller of her intention. He made an attempt to talk her out of it or at least to wait, but even he understood the impossibility of the situation and the hopelessness of any move that would force the two opposite poles, Kissinger and Ray, to work together.

In early June the news from Fox Island was good. Marion had improved considerably and was now able to walk without assistance. Only a headache now and then and plenty of adhesive tape around the middle hampered her existence. But Dixy had made up her mind. Now she called her closest staff members into conference to arrange for her resignation and departure.

As she intended, Dixy sauntered over to Dr. Kissinger's office, also on the 7th floor, and asked to have an appointment with the secretary of state as soon as possible. The reason?

"The reason!" she exploded. "It's a personal problem and I want to tell him about it first!"

She could not believe what she heard next from Kissinger's secretary:

"You'll have to prepare a briefing paper outlining the purpose of the conference you request and giving details of the subject and enough information for the secretary to determine whether a conference should be scheduled."

Dixy would never repeat what she told the administrative aide, but it had something to do with where she might insert the briefing paper. Later she complained:

"I'll be damned! Imagine that! I was told I'd have to prepare a bloody briefing paper to tell his highness that he could take his job and file it. That incident exemplifies what I was up against throughout my brief tenure as assistant secretary of state running a bureau established by Congress for special purposes; I must prepare a briefing paper just to see the prince! What arrogance! What a monumental ego! How do others in executive positions manage to put up with it? Many of them have told me their problems have been similar to mine. With a palace guard protecting a secretary who isn't even there most of the time, how can the important business of the State Department be handled properly? Well, however they handle it, they're going to do it without me."

As if to pour salt into the wound, Kissinger added a final insult just at the time she was trying to get in to see him to resign. She told reporters:

"On Wednesday Dr. Kissinger addressed the prestigious Japan Society and told its members, 'It is the intention of the United States to enter into agreements with the Japanese on research and development on scientific projects.' Nobody said anything to me or any members of my staff about such a proposal, and certainly no one in the bureau has been consulted or even has the preliminary studies that would be essential to such a proposal. Dr. Kissinger seems to think it will make people happy to suggest a transfer of United States technology to other nations and that somehow the U.S. will benefit from the agreements. As far as my division is concerned, there have been inadequate studies, if any studies, as to what these exchanges and transfers will mean from a standpoint of cost, patent rights, and royalties.

Once again we are confronted with an American giveaway and nothing of significance promised in return. When will we learn?"

Dr. Ray went further in a daring attack on the Kissinger action. She strongly suggested Kissinger's policies went far beyond the authority Congress had provided. In effect, he was proposing to give to a foreign nation what Congress had already indicated was not his or anybody else's to give.

"These exchange committees of his are formed with words and great expectations, and no appropriations. He and his cohorts apparently have never learned that you can't do something with nothing. You have to finance it or generate a program to get private industry to see the value of financing it."

To crown it all, Dr. Ray told the press: "The people of this country would be fearful if they knew the way Secretary of State Kissinger and his top advisers are making decisions on foreign policy."

Since she couldn't get in to see Dr. Kissinger in person, she said "To hell with it!" to the secretary's aide and returned to her office to write her resignation and simultaneously send a detailed letter to President Ford explaining why she had to take the action. Her letter to the President should have caught the eye of every concerned news reporter or commentator in America and most certainly those in the national capital. But only a few understood and tried to break through Dr. K's inner sanctum to discover how enormously mismanaged — or "unmanaged," as Dixy put it — the State Department was. Someone on Dixy's staff commented the dispute had no sex, so the press soon let the entire incident slip into history little mourned.

In her letter to the President, Dr. Ray said:

In my letter of resignation to Secretary Kissinger, I made brief reference to the circumstances within the Department of State that thwart those of us who are responsible for information and advice on the policies that guide United States international programs in science and technology from exercising our proper role.

Public Law 93-126, passed by Congress in October, 1973, mandates a policy role for the Bureau of Oceans and International Environmental and Scientific Affairs. Under present departmental procedures, the Bureau can do little but acquiesce in the policies set by others, and attempt to implement its broad responsibilities with little authority and few resources.

Similar kinds of problems plague our nation's domestic science policy.

Although steps may be under way to improve the present situation — e.g., the establishment of a Science Advisory Office in the White House, as you have proposed — I am deeply concerned that the imperative to use existing knowledge and proven technology for vigorous attack on today's problems is not fully recognized nor appreciated at the highest levels of government.

Of course, technology must be used wisely and with proper regard for both economic and environmental consequences. An energetic research and developmental program on problems that are not yet solved must be pursued both by government directly and by government providing the climate — financial, intellectual and practical — to marshal the great talent and human resources of this land. That pitifully little is being done is nowhere so clearly evident as in the area of energy resources and technology.

On January 16 of this year, 32 of our nation's most outstanding scientists, including 11 Nobel Laureates, made a public statement on energy policy. It is a significant and disturbing document — significant because is is a thoughtful and sober expression of concern for the future of our country made by a group of our most knowledgeable citizens and disturbing because it has been virtually ignored by the leaders of government. The scientists' statement, a copy of which is attached, says, in part:

"We . . . believe that the Republic is in the most serious situation since World War II. Today's energy crisis is not a matter of just a few years but decades. It is the new predominant fact of life in industrialized societies. The high price of oil which we must now import in order to keep Americans at their jobs threatens our economic structure . . ."

The importance of secure supplies of economically priced energy (fuels and electricity) cannot be overemphasized. Although energy provides the power for all manufacturing, business, commerce, transportation, and distribution of essential goods (all this means jobs and whether there is employment or unemployment), the great energy debate focuses, ironically, on gasoline for the family automobile.

Although we are, correctly, dedicated to a clean and healthy environment, the means to accomplish this laudable purpose requires more, not less, energy. Our alternatives are severely limited. We have no choice other than to practice conservation on a scale not yet imagined. This will take dedication and will require that the leaders of government set an example in energy saving measures.

But conservation alone cannot recover or maintain the strength of our economy. Our need for reliance on solid fuels — coal and uranium — is real and must be recognized.

It is now 18 months since my report to President Nixon, 'The Nation's Energy Future,' was submitted. Many of the recommendations, especially the long-term research and development proposals that are painless and noncontroversial, are being implemented at glacial speed. But other programs, aimed at carefully planned, step-by-step conversion to heavier reliance on solid fuels, languish or are submitted to stultifying and interminable feasibility studies. The innovative Pioneer Synthetic Fuels Program, proposed in cooperation with private enterprise, has yet to receive serious consideration.

Our country is drifting. We seem neither to have the will to conserve energy nor the courage to map out a national program that will free us from the bondage of too great a reliance on imported energy whose price and security of supply we are powerless to influence. Painful decisions are needed for there are no easy solutions that will please everyone.

In the three years I have served in the Federal Government, I have done my best to face up to whatever problems have emerged and to resolve them in an open and honest manner. Thank you for your appointment and the opportunity to serve. I leave with no regrets.

Sincerely,

DIXY LEE RAY

If President Ford wrote a reply, he never sent it. None was ever received by Dr. Ray. Similarly, Dr. Kissinger kept his silence — at least in answering her directly. But he did make comments. To a reporter he would say only that he was sorry Dr. Ray had decided to resign. It was left to Philip Handler, president of the National Academy of Sciences, to draw reaction from Kissinger, albeit rather an oblique reply.

In a letter co-signed by George S. Hammond, the Academy's foreign secretary, Handler spelled out "our very grave concern" over the "unsettled state of our international relations" with regard particularly to science and technology. Establishment of the new bureau within the State Department gave everyone hope that "serious deterioration" of U.S. relationships in the area of science, environment, and technology would come to an end. Then Handler added:

"The resignation of Dr. Ray is symbolic of continuing failure to establish coherent policy for the utilization of science and technology in U.S. foreign policy and to reexamine current programs in the light of that policy."

The letter went on to reiterate many of the charges Dr. Ray had made herself in protest to State Department policy or lack of policy, most strongly in the area of technology transfer and the shortcomings of the exchange agreements Kissinger had embraced with less developed nations.

In summary, Handler pleaded for immediate "review and reformulation" of America's international programs in science and technology because of the clear failures of the past. Perhaps the charge that stung most in the Kissinger hide was the assertion by Handler that the U.S. State Department should create "a carefully planned and integrated strategy, rather than a melange of ad hoc, uncorrelated actions." It was an unmistakable reference to the hodgepodge of conflicting policies emanating from the many-headed State Department, as well as Kissinger's apparent indifference to what others thought or said, including Dr. Dixy Lee Ray.

Handler's letter was dated June 24, a day after Dr. Ray made a public announcement of her resignation. Nearly a month later, July 17, Kissinger replied to Handler.

The first two paragraphs were devoted to the secretary's comments on issues in which he and Handler obviously agreed. Then, the secretary of state declared:

"Therefore, I was surprised that the National Academy of Sciences would jump to hasty conclusions about Dr. Ray's resignation; that it is symbolic of a major policy difference or of downgrading of science and technology. The resignation was largely the result of differences between the various personalities involved. That the National Academy of Sciences should draw such sweeping conclusions on the basis of unsupported press stories is perhaps symbolic of the difficulty in establishing a productive dialogue between the academic community and its government.

"We in the government certainly have an obligation to take into account the concerns and counsel of intellectuals as we formulate policy. But intellectuals have a reciprocal responsibility to judge policy-makers objectively, and not to read dark motives into every event which may often be caused by extraneous cir-

cumstances. We are willing to do our part to establish a more
confident relationship and hope that you are, too.

"I would welcome the opportunity to discuss these issues
with you soon."

Arrogant to the last! Kissinger's letter could go down as a
prize example of a non-answer. Was the Ray resignation the
result of "differences between the various personalities involved"? How could Dr. Kissinger ascribe the difficulties to a
clash of personalities when the two leading personalities never
met anywhere to clash after Dr. Ray joined the department?

Mr. Handler had not jumped to any hasty conclusions. For
years he had watched and complained about the failures in and
out of the State Department in the realm of international policy
in science and technology. Dr. Ray's charges of being ignored on
policy throughout her presence at the State Department are
easily and clearly chronicled. Where was the personality conflict
there?

Obviously Dr. Kissinger was caught short-handed without a
good excuse. He had simply chosen to conduct his affairs as if Dr.
Ray and her bureau did not exist. Why not acknowledge it? But
then, to acknowledge it would have been embarrassing to a
prima donna who didn't hesitate to enunciate the arrogant principle, as he did in his answer to Handler, that this was a matter for
"intellectuals."

Little doubt existed that neither Dr. Kissinger nor President
Ford wanted to tangle with the feisty Dixy Lee Ray. Why the
silent treatment from the department and the White House?
Could it have been recognition that they were now in opposition
to a newly born Democrat, and a gubernatorial candidate, at
that? And that they couldn't win a national debate with her
because she was a woman and a spectacular speech-maker — and
that she was right?

CHAPTER SIXTEEN

The Dixyland Roadshow

When Dr. Ray made her final, definite decision to quit the State Department, she called me into her office.

It was on that occasion that she acknowledged her worry and guilty conscience over Marion's accident and her belief that she owed it to her sister to go home and share the duties of running the island farm. I was not surprised to hear of her decision; I had been with her in New York when she received the call from Robert Anderson informing her that the secretary of state was not happy with her comments over the German-Brazilian nuclear deal and that she was "in the diplomatic doghouse." When she abruptly changed the subject, I was surprised to hear her ask:

"What would you say if I told you I am thinking seriously of returning to Washington to run for governor?"

I said nothing at first, but my half-open mouth and instant goggle-eyes gave me away.

"Mind if I sit down?"

She grinned that big, tomato-red Dixy grin and was obviously enjoying my momentary speechlessness.

When I recovered and got used to the notion of thinking of this truth-telling, no-holds-barred scientist as a politician, I looked her straight in the eye and put on a grin myself:

"What the hell! Why not? Anybody propose it to you from back home?"

"Oh, a couple, maybe three friends. Why?"

"Let me do some canvassing across the state with a couple dozen key people and see what tbe reaction is. O.K.?"

"Sure, go ahead."

"Oh, by the way, what kind of political animal are you, Republican, Democrat, Independent, or Tory?"

I thought she would laugh at that. She didn't. Instead, she looked puzzled, then said:

"Hell, I don't know. You tell me. What am I?"

"Let's see. Let's think this one over. What do you feel like?"

"Well," said Dr. Ray, stroking her chin and looking up at the ceiling. "Most of my influential friends back in Seattle are Republican, I think, and I suppose most people in politics and public life regard me as Republican because I went to work for a Republican administration."

"Let's look at the facts of life," I said. "Back home the state is waiting for Dan Evans to make up his mind whether he wants to run for a fourth term. I know that his wife Nancy is pressuring him strongly to get the hell out of politics so they can enjoy some life out of the fishbowl. On the other hand, the Republican Party is split. It isn't really terribly fond of Dan because he is too liberal for most of them. The party pros want Dan because they think he can win. But the businessmen and industrialists who supply most of the cash would much rather have John Spellman (King County Executive)."

"Well," said Dixy, "Why not run as an Independent?"

"Because you will be clobbered by strong party organizations at each end. You'd be caught between Wes Uhlman, the Democrat, at one end and either Dan Evans or John Spellman at the other. What you would do is trim the size of their votes but not get enough to beat either one."

"You think I should run as a Republican, then?" Dixy asked.

"Now, wait a minute. Let's figure this out. If Dan Evans runs, you could beat him in the final election but not in the primary. The history of the voting booth shows that only the stalwart Republicans show up to vote in primaries. but they do show up in large numbers. They would undoubtedly favor Dan over you. If you could get Dan in the finals, however, you can whip him because that's when the big Democratic vote shows, particularly in an election year.

"At the same time, I figure you can beat Wes Uhlman any time and in any election. He is probably the slickest, smartest politician in Washington State, and he will give you one helluva race, but you will beat him in King County because he is disliked there by thousands."

"O.K., so what does all that mean?"

"Let's think some more." It was my turn to stroke my chin and check the ceiling.

"Dixy, whoever told you you were a Republican?"

"I'm not. I've never been a member of any political party. You remember yourself I told you I was the only one Nixon ever appointed who refused to profess membership in the GOP. It didn't make him and his staffers happy that I insisted on carrying no party label."

"You know," I said, "it seems to me that in many ways you are better suited to the Democratic philosophy anyway. You could be a Democrat very easily, you know. You get along well with labor. You showed that at the AEC. You were never one of the rich kids on your block. You had to work your butt off to get where you are today. Do you know what you are?"

"No, what?"

"You are a conservative Democrat."

Her eyes beamed. Then they took on that foxy twinkle I had seen so many times when she had outfoxed an opponent in a debate or a conversation.

"All right. I'm a Democrat. Funny. I don't feel any different."

"Well, you will. Analyze your feelings and philosophies about government. I really believe you are more at home under the label of a conservative Democrat."

"By golly, I think you're right. Most members of my family were Democrats, and I do believe in most of the principles of the Jeffersonian Democrats, at that. O.K., start your canvass and report back to me. But be discreet, please. I haven't made up my mind exactly what I will do, and besides, the people back home may decide I'm not for real."

Dr. Ray asked a second question. Should she contemplate a lecture tour? After all, she would soon be out of a job, and she didn't want to go back to teaching zoology — at least not right away. The thought of trying to manage a freshman class in beginning zoology, she said, ran shivers down her back — especially since her classes ranged up to 1,000 students at times.

I immediately began a check of all the major lecture managements in New York — about a dozen of them — to see what kind of a contract she might draw. At first, Dixy had contemplated having me or her sister manage her lecture tours, but I talked her out of that. It would be worth paying a New York agent 25 percent of her fee because managing lecture appearances was a tedious job that required thousands of contacts only an experienced agency could amass.

It didn't take long to learn from the eagerness of the agencies that Dixy was a hot property on the lecture circuit. They all wanted her. I made my report to her and she picked the most advantageous offer.

At first, Dixy commanded a lecture fee of $1,500 to $2,000, depending upon the size of the organization and the audience expected. However, she reserved the right to cut her fee or charge nothing at all if the requesting group was of a charitable nature or one close to her in her earlier life. In addition, she eliminated all fees for lectures within Washington State when she decided the chance was good she might make the race for governor.

From the time she returned home in June, 1975, to the time she made her announcement to run for governor nearly a year later, Dr. Ray was on the lecture trail. She was in such great demand that her lecture manager tried to talk her out of entering politics. He wanted to raise her fee to a minimum of $3,000 a lecture and up. Had she not decided to enter politics and quit the lecture circuit, she would have been worth at least a quarter of a million dollars a year making speeches.

At the same time, she kept turning down offers from universities and colleges to serve as president. I counted at least 14 of them, and she told me she had dissuaded others before they wrote the letters I answered for her. At least half of them were from schools of national and international reputation. One offered her $110,000 a year and asked her to write her own contract.

What did Dixy talk about in the Year of the Lecture? Except for a few instances in which specially appropriate messages were required, the marine biologist and former nuclear administrator and assistant secretary of state rang an alarm bell. When she left the State Department, she was not only bitter over the treatment she had received but deeply worried over the future of the nation in the hands of so many incompetents in the capital. When I told her she should be telling her story in a book, she said, "Yes, certainly, and we should title it 'Good-bye, America.'"

Why?

"If we stay on our present course of giving away all our hard-earned technological advances," she said, "and if we refuse to give our private business and industrial firms a chance to be competitive in foreign markets, and if we continue to build up our friends and enemies so that they can shut us out of world markets, we will be doomed. But most alarming of all is our unwillingness to see the greatest threat of all — our increasing reliance upon foreign oil and energy. If we fail to put everything we have into promoting and encouraging every possible source of energy at our command — like coal gasification, nuclear power, geothermal, fusion, solar power, any potential that offers a future — we will forfeit leadership to other nations. Who will save us when we become a third-class power? Ralph Nader?"

That was to be the Dixy Lee Ray theme, and how she hammered it out! Across the country, from coast to coast, in any town and city that would listen to her, Dr. Ray said things like:

"The Luddites are alive and well and living in America, and they will do for the Russians and Krushchev what he threatened to do and could never do alone — bury us. You know about the Luddites. They were a band of English raiders who protested the use of any new machinery or any sign of progress in England in the early 19th Century. Well, they were gone at the first sign of prosperity, but our new brand won't disappear that easily. They are the Ralph Naders and Barry Commoners of our time, and all their blind followers, who believe that technology and progress are the enemy of mankind and must be stopped. They want to turn the clock back. If they succeed, and, unfortunately, a lot of misguided individuals are helping them in their effort, we can truly kiss America good-bye. A lot of countries in this world appear eager to take our place as a leading nation — and we seem to be helping them in their ambition."

Wherever she went, Dixy was asked the inevitable questions about nuclear power and the environment. She never hesitated to speak her piece with plenty of gusto and often with considerable humor. Perhaps the word mentioned most was "radioactivity." Because of the emotional fear applied to the word by two atomic bombs that ended the world's worst war and because the antinuclear fanatics had made it a veritable bogey-man, it came up in every appearance she made. Although she was usually deeply serious in her explanation, she could joke about the scare stories of the "Luddites," too. For example:

"Did you know the sun itself, that wonderful, soothing round yellow ball up there, is a gigantic nuclear reactor that keeps sending us radioactivity 24 hours a day? Did you know you were radioactive? So is everything on earth, even the marble that forms the walls of this building we're in. What's so horrible about radioactivity, then?

"So you see, radioactivity is a part of our natural environment, and the question shouldn't be: Is it radioactive? It should be: How radioactive is it? We have failed in our educational system and in our news media to teach people the relative nature of radioactivity. As a result, the public has no sense of perspective on the issue. We say something may be radioactive to the point of one part per billion. We hear that often — one part per billion. To someone who isn't quickly aware of the meaning of that description, it might sound awesome.

"But how much is that, really — one part per billion? What kind of mental picture do you get when I say billion? If I said, and it is true, that Jesus Christ was alive a billion minutes ago, you would immediately get the sense of a billion. It's a big number, a very big number.

"Suppose you could detect it with some sense of your own. As a matter of fact, you can. The olfactory sense is capable of detecting certain molecules in a concentration of one part per billion. Mercaptan, for example. The mercaptan is that stinky smell from a pulp mill. We know it well in my part of the world, and you can detect it in one part per billion. How much is that? Is it enough to be dangerous? It smells bad. But that's all.

"Well, let me try to put it in a context that will provide you with a mental picture. If your tongue, your sense of taste, were sufficiently sensitive for you to detect one part per billion in tasting, you would be able to detect one drop of vermouth in five carloads of gin! Now, there's a dry martini.

"So, the next time somebody throws that one-part-per-billion ploy at you in an effort to scare you half to death, tell him to go cry on his local bartender's shoulder."

As a scientist, Dr. Ray preached two principal themes. The first is that we must not be afraid of technology; we must master it and use it in solving the grave problems of a world that needs food, better health, and more than lip-service brotherhood. The second is that the earth is full of resources, but we must not hide them; we must learn to use them wisely, but use them we must.

Because she was an environmentalist long before most of her critics knew what the word meant, Dr. Ray could be critical herself of the new breed that preached environmentalism at any cost. Those who attacked her while she was at the AEC obviously didn't know of her accomplishments as an environmentalist. She had played a major role in saving the beautiful Hood Canal in western Washington from the incursion of resort builders, who would have driven piers far out into the canal and permanently damaged sea life and navigation there. Washingtonians owe it to her that the Canal remains as nature created it.

Similarly, Dr. Ray joined a fellow biologist, Dr. Gordon Alcorn of the University of Puget Sound, in 1973 in compiling research and a report to the Washington State Legislature that saved the Nisqually River Delta, also in western Washington, from a massive industrial complex. The complex, she and Alcorn informed legislators, would deface the only major river in Washington State still unsullied by ports, dams, or the battlements of man. Although they were only two against powerful commercial odds, they won the fight and convinced the Legislature to thwart the project.

In scores of other ways, Dr. Ray, who "lived" in the waters of Puget Sound as a marine biologist and an endurance swimmer and snorkeler, protected the ocean waters from many attempts at offshore drilling and the construction of shoreline edifices that would have seriously hampered sea research, fishing, and ocean farming. She was like a cop on the beat in whistling down interlopers harming clam and oyster beds up and down the coast.

It was typical of Dr. Ray that she could be on what some considered "the other side," too, in such issues. A few years later she gave her support to an industrial project near the Nisqually Delta because it was safely out of range and would have no effect on the delta's ecology. To her it was a matter of being logical and sensible; move a project a few miles away from an environmentally sensitive area, and you solve the problem. But, then, it was that very sense of logic and common sense she said was most lacking, and most needed, in America today.

No greater charge was ever leveled against her than the irresponsible accusation that she was insensitive to nature. It was made when she proclaimed many years later that large oil tankers, well constructed and properly policed and controlled by the Coast Guard, could bring oil into Upper Puget Sound in safety. The issue was to haunt her in her campaign for governor and as governor, but to this day she believes she was right. Her stand on the oil-tanker dispute and her adamant views on the safety of nuclear power cost her the support and the votes of the environmental camp. It was a hard blow to absorb, but she grinned, said "So be it," and won anyway.

In her correspondence, her conversations, and her speeches Dr. Ray and later Governor Ray stuck by her belief that America had to find a middle ground, a balance between environmental and practical considerations, or it was headed for deep trouble. In fact, she forecast the nation's commerce would come to a halt in a few years if the "irresponsible, radical environmentalists" gained the upper hand.

On May 29, 1975, just a month before her resignation from the State Department, Assistant Secretary Ray made one of the most important speeches of her career. It was subdued in tone in deference to the University of Maryland graduation exercises and the presence of all those young people who undoubtedly had been over-exposed to the kind of environmentalists she was concerned about. But it crystallized the "new" Dixy Lee Ray, the marine biologist who was still an environmentalist but who had found through years of experience and experiment that we had to learn to use the earth's resources intelligently, not abuse them or leave them buried.

Dr. Ray told the Maryland graduates that as "we approach our 200th year as a nation, we're given to reflecting quite a bit about what our society is all about, what our country means, and what modern civilization has brought." It was a more serious, more concerned Dixy Lee Ray than I had heard or seen in some time. For a graduation audience, it was unusually quiet, as if something truly important was being said. It was.

"Two hundred years . . . We think the U.S. is pretty old. We have a lot of problems and many doubts about our sciences, about our technology, about the way we use our knowledge . . . How old are we anyway? Human society, we say, has been around a long time, Has it, really? The earth's been around about four and a half billion years, maybe five, and every generation of human beings that lives on it thinks its problems are the worst and that humankind has never faced such difficulties before. Each believes that if we don't find all the answers right away, all will be lost.

"How long is five billion years and how do homo sapiens fit into the picture? Let's imagine we can compress the history of the earth into a single, hypothetical year. Imagine the earth is born on the first day of January. Then, in geological terms, nothing happens the first four months, except enormous cataclysms as the continents are built and the mountains and the atmosphere form. It rains, water appears, the continents move around and come more or less to occupy their present position.

"Along about the middle of May the first tiny, pulsating bit of living thing gets its start in some warm tropical sea. It is in the early fall that the great forests rise from the lowlands. About the first of November dinosaurs begin roaming the earth. Mammals appear the day after Thanksgiving. At 10:30 the evening of December 31st our first recognizable ancestor stands up and looks around him. Probably looking for a woman. At 11:44 the Pyramids are built; 57 seconds later Columbus reaches North America. We enter the Industrial Revolution one second before the new year!

"And you think your generation must do and solve everything or we are doomed on this earth?"

Dr. Ray used the hypothetical word picture with great effect. The audience was with her, apparently having checked its opinions in the cloak rooms for the time being, at least. Building her case gradually, Dr. Ray pointed to lack of communications between the scientific-engineering community and the public, and she put much of the blame on the scientists and engineers for remaining cloistered. However, she said, that lack of communications must never be interpreted as meaning science and technology could not be trusted.

Because of that failure in communication, she said, "we face a constant diet of accusation and defense. To a large extent the discussion about modern society, its difficulties and its problems becomes one of polarization in which the public at large is left to guess who is speaking with the greatest expertise, who has the best facts, and who is the most eloquent. Our spokesmen are very often self-elected."

The names of Nader, Commoner, and a half dozen more of

the "professional dissenters" were on her lips, but she did not use them this time before so young an audience as she repeated a proposal for which she had been seeking support three years:

"We are a nation of laws, and we should take a leaf from the book of law. I am suggesting that we consider creation at the national and state levels of what might be called a 'Supreme Court of Science and Technology,' a device that would apply the rules of evidence and fair play to the major scientific and technological questions of our time. It might function like our Supreme Court, but it would make no decisions. It would simply develop evidence from all sides of an issue to help congressmen, legislators, local officials and councils, the private sector, and the public make decisions.

"If any person called upon to state a case could not justify his or her contention with facts, such evidence would either be ruled out or labeled 'unproven.' Cross-examination might be permitted, but it would be conducted within the rules of American court procedure, not like some of the kangaroo courts I've witnessed in so-called environmental debates.

"The record produced by such a tribunal, then, would be made available to all, and the tribunal itself would take no sides, other than to point out which arguments were not substantiated by evidence or fact. Such a tribunal, I believe, would have a most beneficial effect on our society. It would help us resolve many of our most volatile controversies and help us get on with the job of making decisions. Without such guidance, I'm afraid we're headed for a complete stalemate in our economy, stagnancy as a world power, and a diminishing star among nations. Can we or the world afford that?"

Dr. Ray first made her proposal for a fact-finding science court in the spring of 1974. It was well received thereafter on the many occasions she repeated it while with the AEC and the State Department and later as a national lecturer and governor. But it didn't receive much significant backing in public quarters until a physicist with impressive credentials supported the idea in a speech before the august American Physical Society two years later. He was Dr. Arthur Kantrowitz, chairman of the Avco Everett Research Laboratory in Everett, Massachusetts.

Dr. Kantrowitz's proposal was virtually a carbon copy of Dixy's. He perceived such a court as having no decision-making powers, too, and, like her, he insisted that information produced by such a tribunal would be of value to the public and the politicians equally.

In her associations with audiences and the usual questions after a speech, Dixy discovered overwhelming acceptance of the idea and the need. Similarly, she found most of her scientific and engineering colleagues supportive, as well.

Although opposition was never vociferous, it was pronounced, and as expected, came primarily from legal minds and newspaper editorialists. The editorialists said in the main, however, that the idea was good; they doubted that such information would find its way to the public — which amounted, as far as Dixy was concerned, to a condemnation of the press itself. She believed the idea should have appealed more to the press than to any other segment of American society. After all, wasn't its primary purpose to seek the truth and convey it to the people?

Why has the gutsy marine biologist from Puget Sound continued to hammer the idea? This is the way she once explained it:

"The nation should be fed up with arbitrary, usually unsubstantiated 'scientific' judgments of bureaucrats. Pity us. The GS-15's are at it again, mostly in the Food and Drug Administration. Wouldn't everyone much rather trust the fact-finding of large numbers of accredited, reputable scientists through a tribunal using the rules of evidence than the snap decisions of phantom 'experts' hiding behind the facade of a federal bureau?

"Saccharin, a scientific discovery that has been a godsend to millions of diabetics and others throughout the world, was suddenly declared out of bounds because some rats died from an overdose in a laboratory experiment. Because it affected the lives of so many in the U.S., it was later reinstated. But the bureaucratic wizards haven't given up yet.

"Cyclamates, another remarkable creation of scientific minds, were similarly declared unfit for human consumption, again on the basis of laboratory experiments whose deductions must be challenged.

"DDT, probably the greatest fighter against destructive insects ever produced by science, was also ruled too destructive to use. Like many other chemical products, it can be dangerous if not used properly or if overused. But when controlled with ordinary good sense, it is a fantastic aid to mankind. Thanks to DDT around the world, we finally brought the incidence of malaria under control. What has happened since we got cold feet and permitted the panic gang to get a ban on DDT? Malaria has made a comeback in several parts of the world. Who is to blame?

"For many, many years women used lipstick with no concern for their safety because it had never caused any problems. However, the same fear-crowd took over and 'discovered' that the Red Dye 2 also produced cancer under conditions that could not possibly be duplicated by women wearing lipstick. So what happened? The Red Dye 2 that had passed women's tests for a century or more was verboten overnight. The mini-minded bureaucrats had struck again. And what did they do? They substituted Red Dye 40, which is a problem and is much more dangerous than Red Dye 2 could ever be. Where is our reason?

"They tried to do the same thing with caffeine, caffeine substitutes, nitrites, and a flock of food additives. It's quite true that things absorbed into the body can damage or even kill a human — *if taken to enormous excess*. That's the element missing in our bureaucratic deliberations. Tolerance levels must be observed. Even water can kill you if you drink too much of it. But who does?

"We once had a prosperous and important swordfish industry — until some of our panicky friends reported the noble fish had absorbed mercury from pollutants newly released into ocean waters by industry. Once again the GS-15 brigade and fellow bureaucrats rushed into the breach and announced that swordfish were dangerous to health. They were believed. The fishe men and the fish industry never had a chance. Their business was dead overnight. Rebuttal? Impossible. Then, a painstaking researcher discovered the pollutants had virtually nothing to do with the issue. Swordfish that had been dressed and mounted by proud fishermen many, many years earlier were found to have a certain amount of mercury in their bodies. It was there naturally and it was infinitesmal in amount; it could not have had any effect on anyone eating it. But how do you revive a dead industry after the first headlines have pronounced it a 'monstrous peril'?"

Dixy's counter-attack against the "Luddites" was not relegated to food products alone. In her demand for balance, reason, and responsible environmentalism, she also took off after the "so-called guardians of endangered species."

As a career biologist and environmentalist, she said, "I love ducks, and fish, and everything that flies, runs, or swims. But I am more interested in making certain that human beings don't become endangered species in our zeal to protect everything else with unreasonable demands. For example, starlings, ducks, and other birds are great dangers to airline flights and have caused many disastrous accidents, but I don't hear the 'endangered species' people calling for their elimination. It's not a matter of choosing between birds and people. It's a matter of common sense. But whenever there is a standoff and the lives of human beings are concerned, the decision for action should be in the interests of people, not ducks or starlings."

The U.S. may not be at war, Dixy asserted, "but this is the most critical time in our history. Oil producing nations are bankrupting us, charging us grossly excessive prices because we can't do anything about it. Instead of scratching to obtain energy from every source available to us, we have let the radical environmentalists talk us into a stupor. They have paralyzed attempts to increase coal production, to permit strip-mining where it would actually improve the land. They have been hysterical in opposing nuclear-plant construction and operation. They have delayed new energy plants for years, then complained that they were now too expensive to build; their delays were the reason for the increased costs. What arrogance! What hypocrisy! What dangerous meddling!"

How much longer could the U.S. go on relying upon foreign nations for nearly half its oil needs? Dixy asked the question wherever and whenever she could. She pressed for American efforts to concentrate on research to produce energy from coal in-situ, or where it actually lies underground. With the largest coal reserves of any nation on earth, she reasoned, we should make use of the resource.

"Billions of gallons of oil exist untouched in the shale of our Western states. It is expensive to extract it and to restore the land. But that would be better than selling our souls to the Mideast and South American oil nations.

"We must try everything — geothermal sources wherever they may be, energy farms to grow plants that can produce methanol to increase our gasoline supply, windmill and wave power, solar power, and fusion."

Dixy could quote most responsible scientific organizations as verifying that the two most promising sources of energy in the future — solar power and fusion — were decades away from development.

"Some of the advocates of solar power are simply not being realistic. It's coming along. We can use it to heat water — where the sun shines quite a bit. And we can do a few other things with it. But the engineering required to turn solar energy into a mass producer of electricity for our factories and homes is 20 to 40 years away, at least. So is nuclear fusion, which is my choice as the energy of the future.

"But until then — and this is the most important point — we cannot sit by and wait for the oil-producing nations to devour us financially. We absolutely must develop what we have, coal and nuclear power, until other forms are feasible from engineering and financial viewpoints."

It was the basic rationale for her support of nuclear energy. Nobody in America has been a more fervent and effective defender of the Nuclear Age. When she left the State Department, Dixy was wooed by the energy industry and at least two national organizations supporting nuclear power. Once again, she could have written her salary ticket. But she turned them down. Why was she in demand? It was her persuasiveness. And her unparalleled ability among scientists to simplify the most difficult issues so anyone could understand them. To wit:

"I have never said, and no responsible scientist would ever say, that the production of nuclear power is without risk. Any form of energy production has its hazards, whether it's coal, steam, oil, geothermal power, hydroelectric dam construction, or even the simple act of burning wood or other materials. The indisputable fact is that the nuclear industry is the safest in the world. Not a single death or serious injury has resulted from radioactivity in a nuclear plant in the past quarter century. There were some accidents that resulted in a few deaths during weapons production many years ago, but they were in wartime or military operations and the persons involved were responsible because they ignored simple precautions. The civilian use of nuclear power is unblemished. Can any industry of any other kind match that record?

"Three Mile Island, the most serious accident, killed no one and injured no one. What we have discovered there is this: We can improve the safety systems in nuclear plants, but we know the ones we have do work! The panic condition at Three Mile Island was not brought on by the accident itself but by a combination of the hysteria of the press and the mishandling of the entire incident by the federal government's own Nuclear Regulatory

Commission. Three Mile Island will solidify safety procedures and make nuclear power even safer, if we could just cool off the noisy fringe that makes a lot of clatter but little sense.

"We kill thousands annually on the nation's roads and highways, but nobody is heard calling for the abolition of the automobile. We lose hundreds more each year in air, ship, and train travel, but I don't hear any demands for elimination of airliners, passenger ships, or trains. Hundreds lose their lives in surgery because something goes wrong in the application of anesthetics or the body seems to be intolerant of them, but no sane person would think of suing to halt the use of anesthetics in hospitals.

"Yet, because of the aura of nuclear energy, nurtured by the specter of the bombs at Hiroshima and Nagasaki, the mere mention of this new and wonderful kind of power brings horror to minds poisoned by the emotional alarms of the Nader types who play to fears, rather than to logic and common sense.

"The Nuclear Age has brought us spectacular gains in health, medicine, industrial development, space travel, and the prospect of even more remarkable achievements in the treatment of sewage and the protection of food supplies. Are the opponents of nuclear energy trying to rob us of such monumental advances? Do they want to turn the clock back again? It's bitter irony to me that while they talk of cancer risks that don't actually exist or which they can't prove, nuclear implements and radioactive processes are saving or prolonging life in hospitals throughout the world. Many of those helped are cancer patients.

"The most strident antinuclear forces have targeted in on waste products from nuclear plants. They don't care about facts and realities. They scream that there is absolutely no way to store nuclear wastes safely. The fact is that technologies, several of them, have existed for some time for the safe storage of wastes. It is simply a matter for the federal government to make a decision on which method to use. Perhaps it may use more than one. At any rate, it will not have to make that decision until the mid-1980's or later because the problem in civilian wastes will not become critical until then.

"Furthermore, there is a strong probability that we may have a better use for most wastes than burying them forever. Science has on many occasions discovered that today's garbage is tomorrow's useful product. Radioactive waste contains an isotope, cesium 137, which is similar to radioactive cobalt. It is now possible to separate it from other wastes and package it relatively inexpensively. Experiments have already shown it could be placed in the stream of municipal sewage to sterilize it. Imagine what a bonanza that could be for cities like New York, which continues to foul its waters with untreated sewage. Those millions of tons of sewage from the cities and towns of America could not only be made safe with the instant destruction of the parasites and disease organisms they contain; the sewage could be utilized as precious fertilizers or soil conditioners, and it could also be converted into liquid or gaseous fuel. Why aren't the environmentalists following up on it? Is the radical fringe interested only in arguments that support its prejudices?

"Anyone who follows news developments knows that millions of tons of foodstuffs, primarily wheat and other grains, are lost annually to bacteria and fungus. I think particularly of the enormous stores of wheat this country has shipped to needy nations only to have much of it rot on docks for lack of storage or quick use. Considerable success has already been reported in experiments which will make it possible to treat such foodstuffs and kill all the insects, bacteria, and fungus without damaging the food — and leaving it harmless for human consumption.

"Research is very promising in the use of other wastes, notably strontium 90. Many reputable scientists agree with me that we may have to find permanent storage for a relatively small amount of nuclear waste products. The problem is not really method any more but expense. It costs a great deal to process most of the radioactive substances. But even the cost factor may eventually be diminished by the extraordinary gains to be made if we keep an open mind and refuse to panic."

But Dixy Lee Ray was not optimistic.

"It will take a miracle to reverse the madness cultivated by those who have no faith in the future nor in Man's ability to use the resources of the earth wisely. Of course, a crisis could do it, too. Another energy debacle, like the 1973 oil shortage, might wake up Americans. I would rather have the awakening come about through natural, intelligent means. Science and technology have given us the most advanced society history has known. A little more trust and a lot less hand-wringing and phony tears would help."

CHAPTER SEVENTEEN

The Road
to the
Mansion

Sampling opinion back home for Dixy's newfound wish to taste political life was as entertaining as it was revealing.

"Dixy run for governor? You're kidding, of course . . . (pause.) Aren't you?"

One fourth of those queried offered the "you're kidding" response, not because they didn't believe it but because they didn't want to. They were the ones who were afraid she was serious because her candidacy for governor would affect their own fortunes. If she ran, they would be knocked out of the box or someone they preferred for their own interests would be.

Celebrities who suddenly decide they want to seek public office create gigantic waves, or, to put it more appropriately, create vast changes in the arrangement of political chairs. The John and Jane Does who are the party faithful and move up in orderly fashion from one party position or level to another expect to be rewarded on schedule with promotions from chair to chair, whether it means public office or political prestige. Insert an interloper at any high point and the entire line of chair movements is disrupted or stalled — in both parties, because a victory for a "nonpolitical animal" brings a severe added impact to the losers, as well. Thus, it happens that the new face from the nonpolitical world is actually unwanted by both camps.

It was not surprising, then, that the Dixy feelers generated a monumental ripple through political ranks in both parties. The fact that she had announced herself as a Democrat was surprising to every one of those interviewed, but they were much more disturbed by her presence than her politics.

Another fourth of those called were disappointed she had chosen the Democratic standard. For the most part, they were VIP's in private business and industry who were not specially fond of the rather liberal tendencies of Governor Dan Evans and who were afraid the pipe-smoking, obedient John Spellman, King County Executive, who wanted to succeed Evans, didn't have enough charisma to make the grade. They proved to be right on the latter score.

The majority of the VIP's called were genuinely pleased and offered no reservations. Most of them voiced what was to become the theme of Dixy's successful campaign for governor:

"It would be nice to have a nonpolitican in high office for a change."

Simple sentiment. But Dixy was the right person for the right job at the right time, the formula for winning in star-conscious America.

The count was 15 "for" and enthusiastically so, 6 "sorry she had chosen the Democratic banner," 5 guardedly disgruntled because a maverick had upset their ambitions, and 4 noncommittal. Among the four was a doctor who begged me to talk her out of it because "it was criminal to toss such a fine woman into the miserable abyss of politics." That's just the way he said it. He may have been the wisest of them all.

It didn't take long for the "rumor" to travel. And when it did, the immediate press comment from columnists, radio and television commentators, editorialists, and others matched the results of the preliminary nose-count. Dixy had been extremely popular with the press as a teacher at the University of Washington and as director of the Pacific Science Center ten years. Her television series of weekly science programs had made her face and voice familiar to millions in Washington State and across the nation. Despite a few sour reports from the national capital in her AEC days, Dixy's reputation and character were intact, unsullied. After all, everybody was already acquainted with her stand on nuclear energy, and her passion for liederhosen, dogs, mobile homes, hamburgers, and fried chicken undoubtedly won her more friends than enemies. Her character was not only intact; it had been given additional dashes of color, good for painting political futures.

Like a scientist, however, Dixy adopted an "I'll believe it when I see it" attitude on her political chances. Even polls and off-the-cuff commentaries reporting her "way in the lead" in the summer of 1975 failed to persuade her to throw her bonnet into the ring prematurely. She was cautious for several reasons. First, she distrusted unscientific political polls, although a few of them were to give her a boost at the beginning of the campaign. Second, she was a realist; first-blush reaction to the name of Dixy Lee Ray in the gubernatorial derby was promising, but she wasn't taking any bets until she heard from people throughout a state she had traveled many, many times before. Third, Dixy had always liked three-time Governor Evans, and she wasn't fond of the idea of running against him, despite my insistence that she could beat him if they were to meet in the November final. Fourth, she was yet to learn how the Democratic Party felt about her and her candidacy. Some of the old party hacks had already indicated they were unhappy over the upstart who had not consulted them beforehand. Finally, Dixy was sensitive to her financial condition; she had virtually no cash in the bank, and the Fox Island property was the last thing in the world she would mortgage or break up for the sake of a political career. Dixy didn't realize it at the time, but lack of cash was to become one of her most attractive assets as a budding politician. But it produced a giant headache, too.

Each of her "cautions" would be resolved to her distinct advantage. The early private telephone polls and the first published polls showed Dixy so far out in front she was suspicious. They were too good to believe, so she didn't believe them. Nevertheless, I am convinced they had a tremendous influence on her, perhaps decisive. I believe that if those early polls had shown the reverse situation — with Dixy trailing all the other candidates instead of leading the pack — she might have been encouraged to chuck politics and concentrate on the extremely lucrative lecture trail.

I can remember several instances, particularly in late 1975 and early 1976, in which Dixy was so disappointed by the lack of standup support and fiscal promises from the state's more substantial citizens that I feared she would say "To hell with it" and leave the gubernatorial race to the familiar names. After all, she could be certain of a lecture career that promised a quarter of a million a year when she warmed up; how could anyone prefer a thankless, mud-slinging, constantly hectic political taffy-pull at less than $55,000 a year — and with an end to a private life?

If Dixy needed a clincher, she found it soon after traveling the state on roads she knew well. She had informed her New York lecture manager to leave her plenty of time for speaking engagements within Washington State. She knew she would be losing many large fees — and so did her manager — but she had to find out for herself what public reaction might be to her possible candidacy.

It was one of the wisest decisions she ever made. Thousands of farmland and small-town people who had never seen, heard, nor touched a gubernatorial candidate "in the flesh," as they said, immediately took a liking to this easy-smiling, assured, gutsy woman who could have been Aunt Madge or Sister Sue. She refused to acquire a svelte or stylish wardrobe, preferring the simplest and most comfortable skirts, moccasins, and even slacks and sweaters.

If I differed with others in her camp on any single major point, it was the matter of Dixy's dress. I am convinced her casual, down-on-the-farm dress and her disdain for dandy trappings — a point she never hesitated to make in public — were primarily responsible for her popularity, particularly in the rural areas of the state.

A few persons, most of them women in the large cities, were severely critical of Dixy's penchant for rummage-sale wearing apparel, and they usually sought me out to complain "because you are close to her and maybe she'll listen to you." But I had absolutely no intentions of relaying the complaints to her. She probably hears them anyway by indirect means. In fact, I encouraged her whenever the subject came up to dress as she liked. Part of the charm of the brand-new politician was her "Mother Earth" look, and I didn't want the Dior or Pucci-Gucci fringe tampering with a sociological masterpiece. Perhaps most importantly, Dixy felt more at ease in her folksy digs and could make a better impression if she didn't have to worry about jazzy hairdos, a couturier's obsession with cleavage, and Emily Post's admonitions on how to cross your legs gracefully in public.

How Dixy detested pantyhose, makeup of any kind, and formal gowns! She also had a horror of corsages, a fact we never

made known during the campaign because of the many instances in which hurt feelings would have resulted. ("Whythehell
do people have to cut flowers and pin 'em under their noses?
They're so beautiful! The Lord meant them to be in dirt, and
that's where they belong.")

However, I don't believe she was allergic to them. It was her
opposition to flower-cutting that produced a semblance of a
sneezing allergy, not the pollen.

The time came when Dixy had to pay some attention to a
new wardrobe, particularly when she won her way to the Governor's Mansion, but it took a heroic effort on the part of her sister
Marion to effect a wardrobe change. Dixy disliked shopping, so
Marion had to do the chores for her, frequently taking home
several choices with the hope of talking Dixy into at least a few
new garments. Because of her size and shape, Dixy was hard to
fit. She liked to wear jackets with her skirts, but she was difficult
to accommodate. Her size was hard to find. Frustrated and tired
of looking during her years in Seattle, she had said "The hell with
it" and bought her jackets at a men's store, the only place she
could find her jacket size. It was "nobody's damned business."

Dixy insisted nobody would have known the difference,
except for those pesky buttons and buttonholes, which are on
opposite sides on jackets for men and women. As a scientist, she
wanted to know what damfool in sartorial history made the
decision to put buttons on one side for women and on the other
for men!

It was a battle Marion eventually won, as only she could
have.

Throughout a battle of the bulges, I often had to steel
myself to withhold a chuckle or even a smile. If anyone had
emerged who could talk Dixy into wearing the latest Paris (or
even Sears Roebuck) creations, I would have rebelled and
thrown a tantrum. But I could rely on Dixy's obstinacy. Nobody
was going to make a Marie Antoinette out of Molly Pitcher. And
it was Molly Pitcher Washington State wanted in the governor's
chair. So did I.

The third "caution" — the possibility of having to run
against the incumbent, Dan Evans — was taken care of by Evans
himself, no doubt with a large assist from Nancy Evans, who had
had her fill of politics and wanted a chance to enjoy life outside
the fishbowl. In a tearful, touching farewell, Evans said he would

not run for a fourth term. As it happened, that was tantamount to giving the election to Dixy, because her popularity far surpassed that of her two principal challengers, Mayor Uhlman of Seattle, Democrat, and King County Executive Spellman, Republican and heir-apparent to the Evans crown.

The fourth "caution" was one she would never surmount — the objections of the party hacks and hoary leadership. They saw her as an instant threat to their empire and a maverick who didn't know anything about politics and the need for keeping the troops happy at all costs. It didn't matter to them that the Democratic Party in Washington State has virtually never existed as a single entity supporting objectives and policies mutually agreed upon. The Democratic Party in Washington has been Senator Warren G. Magnuson and his own followers and treasury, Senator Henry M. Jackson and his own followers and treasury, and so on down the line. The two senators learned long ago that they had better establish and sustain their own political organizations. They couldn't rely on the state party to get elected.

Dixy had no such ready-made political platoons and cash-to-match. Outspoken from the start, she antagonized the party workers of both extremes and never managed to win them over — even when she won in November, 1976. However, it was the quality of nonpolitical frankness that cut through the political fog and got through to the people who would go to the polls. The big-city newspapers and radio and television stations weren't terribly impressed, but the people who shook her hand out on the trail saw and heard something they liked.

The classroom teacher was now telling it like it was to a lot of willing pupils who were tired of hearing about but never seeing those clone-like models of politicians out of Seattle. Their faces might be different, but the words, the handshakes, even the dress were repeats of hundreds of slick urban dandies who had come before. Now, the little old round lady in liederhosen, who liked dogs, hamburgers, and fried chicken, gave it to them straight, just like Cousin Gert next door. And, boy, could she spill out them words! This li'l ole teacher was gonna wax their ears and tan their hides!

The combination teacher-and-homespun-neighbor approach bowled them over. None of it was improvised or contrived. I couldn't have written the script for Dixy's campaign tactics if I had tried. And no one else could have either.

From July, 1975, through March, 1976, Dixy accepted no money for her appearances anywhere within Washington State, and she carefully skirted political issues. She had to because of the new Washington State statute on public disclosure. That didn't stop Uhlman and Spellman, who had put their organizations together more than two years before the election; because they were still in office, they could speak on virtually any political issue they chose without penalty. It is one of the weaknesses of an otherwise inspired state law.

Dixy refrained from political talk until she filed for the governorship on the Democratic ticket in March, 1976, just two weeks before I had obtained an important spot for her on the Johnny Carson "Tonight Show" on the NBC-TV network. Dixy jumped the gun because the State Public Disclosure Commission had indicated she had to file and declare income, holdings, et al, since she was "beginning to sound like a candidate." Uhlman and Spellman had "sounded like candidates" from birth but they didn't have to file because they "had a right" to discuss political issues that were part of their job. Little wonder that one of Dixy's first demands was that any person filing for a new public office should resign the old one before starting a campaign.

Because he feared the consequences of the federal equal-time rule, Carson had to cancel Dixy's appearance. He gave her a raincheck, and she appeared three weeks after her election.

The ten months preceding her decision to file as a candidate were alternately very happy and very frustrating. They were happy because she was once more in "Paradise," the Fox Island hillside hideaway Dixy and Marion had decided to label Fox Trot Farm — certainly for no scientific reason (or logic, for that matter). It was a small farm, but the name meant nothing. It pleased them, and that, they said, was all that mattered. Dixy lived out of a suitcase much of the time, but she didn't mind that because she knew she would return on each occasion to the island and the "old socks" living she adored. Her good humor came back, and the big, broad smile reasserted itself on a relaxed face.

So much for the happy moments. The fiscal frustration, which was the fifth "caution," grew from the fact that she had very little in the bank and was never able, from the beginning, to generate the financial support she was certain she needed to make the race for governor. Her decision to devote a great deal of time to touring her own state cost her thousands of dollars in the out-of-state lecture engagements she turned down. Those she accepted gave her just enough money to pay her bills.

Until Dixy filed, she rationalized the lack of financial support as "natural," because the big bucks would never come to a candidate who boasted of being a maverick to be controlled by no one. But once she threw her bonnet into the ring, we guessed, the support would pour in from the "little people" willing to put $5 to $50 into the treasury of an honest nonpolitician. It didn't work. Tragically for the American political system, it never does. The only time a campaign of poverty funding — "We want a buck from the little guy and no money from the rich" — is successful is when a high-powered organization takes on the job and uses old-time arm-bending techniques on "the little guy." Americans in the middle and lower income brackets have always nurtured distrust for anyone seeking political office; while they may tolerate chicanery, they are not about to subsidize it unless pressured by a steam-roller campaign organization.

Wherever she went, Dixy wowed 'em, as even the press was acknowledging in those days. Her popularity grew by the hour, and her speeches were usually accorded ovations — not simply loud applause, but standup, cheering, shouting responses. In retrospect, I think we should have adopted the old revival-meetin' strategy and passed the hat. It would have been a stroke of genius, but nobody thought of it at the time.

Why was she wowing 'em out in the hustings? Dixy was a voice who came at the right time. She was a true conservative — not a reactionary — and she preached an unsophisticated patriotism the public sorely needed in the wake of a Vietnam war that had given most Americans a guilty conscience and some doubts about the "greatness and the mission" of the United States in a miserable world. On one hand she bolstered her listeners' confidence in the vast engineering, scientific, technological genius of America, and on the other she pledged a continuing scrap against big government and its excesses and taxes. In effect, Dixy was in the vanguard of the new conservatism that swept the nation in the late 1970's and triggered the revolution highlighted by California's Proposition 13. Dixy didn't like Proposition 13's meat-axe approach to spending cuts, but she knew action had to be drastic in the beginning.

Under Washington State's election and disclosure laws, the candidate cannot accept funds unless he or she has filed intent to

run. Dixy could not accept contributions until March, 1976 —
but it made no difference. None of any substance was being
offered. Unfortunately, that condition prevailed after she filed,
too.

I blame myself in part. As managing editor and executive
editor of *The Seattle Post-Intelligencer* ten years, I had pounded the
importance of investigation and kept a staff of sleuths working
constantly, despite friction with the publisher and the budget
office on expenditures. In that ten years, we stepped on many
toes, Democratic and Republican, banker and labor leader, in-
dustrialist and government chiseler. From welfare cheats to six-
figure embezzlers, we hounded them all.

In the process, we destroyed a payoff system that touched
the lives of scores from the cop on the beat to the city council, the
county sheriff's office, the police department, and the county
prosecutor. We retired from politics the most powerful Republican in the state. Almost at the same time, we prevented the return
to the governor's chair of a Democrat who had held a comfortable lead in the campaign until we published an exposé of his
continued association with the state's major racketeer. Our inves-
tigative reporters had blown the whistle on several unsavory
leaders in the state legislature, as well. In all those instances,
powerful political figures were crunched by the publicity and
either forced to retire from the limelight or surrender much of
their power.

With that reputation, I wasn't surprised that many doors
closed to Dixy Lee Ray. In the early stages of our telephone work
and doorbelling, I visited her at Fox Island one day and
suggested:

"I'm a thorn in your side. I know the facts of life, and so do
you. You can't run a political campaign without money, and you
can't get money with my kind of basket unless you're an
evangelist. It would be better if I left the campaign and you took
on a real pro."

Dixy's answer was typical — and she repeated it many times
in the future when I felt the political pros were avoiding her
because of me:

"We've come a long way together. People are going to take
me as I am, with my friends. The day you leave will be the day I
throw in the towel. I don't give a damn what these people may be

saying about you. If they don't want you around me, I don't want them. Now, shut up and eat your hamburger."

After the March filing we began our fund-raising in earnest. What a cruel surprise awaited us! Armed with press clippings and the notion that everyone would cheer our appearance and pledge thousands of dollars to the leading candidate, we started our fiscal odyssey in Seattle on a Tuesday following the filing. I remember it well, and Dixy will never forget it either. We had five days a week full of Black Tuesdays for many weeks after that.

The cruelest of weeks came at the very beginning. I had arranged, among other meetings, a two-week series of personal visits by Dixy to the "wheels" of Seattle and the Pacific Northwest, most of them bankers and retail-store executives. They were the same persons she had known so well as her rooting section when she went calling on behalf of the Pacific Science Center. But that was for science, and now she was proselyting for a scientist turned politician. We made it a walking trip, up and down the streets of downtown Seattle.

In every case, the greeting was warm, sincere, and congratulatory. But in every case, the response to our request for financial support was cool, polite, and almost embarrassed. I wish those men — and they were all men — had leveled with Dixy and told her what we discovered later. They had pledged their support to the Republican, John Spellman. at least a year earlier and would stick with him. That kind of an honest reaction would have cleared the air and eliminated the hypocrisy so prevalent in American society. Business, industry, and labor often try to play both sides, although they put most of their greenbacks on one and token cash on the other.

Adding to Dixy's woes was her problem with the Democratic Party. The regulars disliked and distrusted her because of her conservative philosophy. As a result, she couldn't find an experienced campaign manager who was also a whiz at fund-raising. A bit of skullduggery was employed, as well.

For example, I had tried for six weeks early in 1976 to interest a man named Frank Keller in running her campaign. He was by no means her first choice, but he had a reputation for being able to raise political funds, and, besides, we were now desperate after at least a dozen turndowns. Keller at first said he was flattered at the request and would think it over, but he really intended quitting politics and spending all his time lobbying. He was bitter because of the way he had been treated by the party, he said, and he wanted more to do with political campaigns.

I called Keller several times in the next six weeks, trying to get him to change his mind. He remained reluctant, but he gave me the distinct impression he might yield. Finally, on a morning in early February, 1976, I called him and said:

"Frank, we're in a real bind. Dixy wants to file in a month or so, but we have nobody hired yet to put the campaign together. Please, take the job."

"I'm sorry, Lou," he said. "I have just made up my mind. I'm through with politics. and I'm going to open up my own shop in the capital. Good luck."

Two days later the Seattle newspapers reported Keller had accepted Mayor Uhlman's offer to be his campaign manager:

Why didn't Keller level? It wasn't the last time we would encounter questionable tactics from the Uhlman camp. I am still convinced the former Seattle mayor had much to do with the financial cold-shoulder Dixy received from downtown merchants; I can only conjecture how he did it because those who felt the pressure of City Hall would not spell out the details.

Four years later Keller realized he had made a boner, and he joined Dixy's re-election campaign.

Another factor was important. Despite the fact Dixy's popularity was at a peak and she was enjoying good press in the early months, it was obvious on many occasions that her candidacy was not taken seriously.

"You mean it? Does she really intend to run for governor? Why would such a smart lady want to get mixed up with politics? Shouldn't she be running one of the universities or colleges? Isn't that where she belongs? She's a teacher, isn't she? She's a scientist, isn't she?" They were the same questions I'd heard a year earlier in calls from Washington, DC, to VIP's.

Some of the professional Democrats actually tried to talk her into holding back and running for the United States Senate. With Magnuson and Jackson stationed there for an eternity? They had to be joking, but they weren't.

The strangest part of the "run-for-the-Senate" routine is that some professional Republicans once wanted her to run for the Senate because they couldn't find anybody to challenge

Magnuson and Jackson! Of course, that was before she announced she was a Democrat. Both parties apparently were more interested in throwing mavericks to the lions of the Senate than in recruiting new talent.

In the meantime, Spellman and Uhlman were polishing up their machines — machines they had oiled and lubricated at least a year and a half to two years earlier. When the time came for them to comply with state law and file "officially" for the governorship, they had the cash all but delivered. Both had more than $300,000 collected for the primary in the space of a month or two. Dixy scraped and pleaded and put at least $10,000 of her own money into the campaign and came up with less than $90,000. She would have put more of her funds into the campaign if she had had any, but politicking cut her lecture career short and she had no means of support.

Dixy had no choice. That was all she was going to get, so she had to make the most of it. Fortunately, she had a clever promotion man on her side, an advertising and public-relations whiz with plenty of experience. He was Bob Root, whose principal claim to fame was a brilliant political-advertising campaign that had permitted former Governor Albert Rosellini to knock off heavily favored Senator Martin Durkan in the Democratic primary of 1972. He did it with newspaper advertising, but Rosellini came up with the bucks to make the expensive campaign possible. Since Dixy's cupboard was bare, Root had to use his wits overtime. And he succeeded.

With Root leading the way, Dixy's campaign profited from lack of profit. Like it or not, here was, at last, the truly penniless candidate, who was determined to run regardless of the odds and the plush bankrolls her opponents were bragging about. We were about to find out if a candidate with no bank account but unlimited popularity and name familiarity could beat a couple of experienced professionals.

Dixy's campaign sputtered and coughed and made blunder after blunder. But all the sputtering and coughing and blundering apparently added conviction to the public's belief that here was a proven amateur who had to be honest and dedicated. Having run out of names for a campaign manager, Dixy decided to give David Sternoff, a likeable young man, a trial. The only experience he had had was as state chairman of the Young

Democrats; it proved not to be enough. At that, he might have made it work if he hadn't insisted on continuing to run his commercial business at the same time.

When Dixy finally decided to make a change because the campaign was floundering, she turned to Blair Butterworth, a tall, bespectacled, brainy young man with plenty of political savvy but an Ivy League cuteness that invited trouble — and it came often. Butterworth worked hard for Dixy and managed to keep the campaign intact through the final, but he brought an element into Dixy's coterie that spelled instant poison with the news media and much of the public. Butterworth brought with him the influence and some of the friends of Leonard Sawyer, deposed as speaker of the House and a wheeler-dealer in Democratic politics. I didn't want the Sawyer influence, and I never hesitated telling Dixy what a danger it was to her candidacy. But Butterworth prevailed; he had me where he wanted me for the time being. An open quarrel between him and me could cost Dixy the primary election. As it was, Dixy barely beat the moneyed Wes Uhlman by 7,000 votes, and we had to wait until 4 o'clock the morning after the election to be sure she had won.

The election should never have been that close, even with the Uhlman bankroll asserting itself the last two weeks. While Butterworth was flaunting his past and his friends, I was reassuring the news media and anyone else who would listen that Dixy was no captive of the Sawyer crowd. Had I walked out of the campaign when Butterworth brought in his crew, there might have been a swing of more than 7,000 votes in King County, where I was identified as a crusader against corruption.

Dixy was aware of the situation, too, and she was deeply worried about the Sawyer presence, but she, like me, didn't dare rock the boat at the 11th hour.

With such witches' brews fogging up the background, it was truly a miracle that Dixy barely pulled out a victory in the primary, then shellacked Spellman in the final by nearly 150,000 votes. In a state with a million voters going to the polls in a good year, that is a resounding, belly-whacking trouncing.

Dixy had been far more worried about Spellman than Uhlman. After all, Uhlman, who had survived a recall vote in Seattle only a year earlier, was unpopular in his home city and not very well known in the rest of the state. If it hadn't been for his large treasure chest, he probably would have been far down the list in the primary balloting. But the untouchable Spellman was a darling in the press and the Seattle and Washington State establishment. He had been a reasonably good, if unimaginative, administrator of King County as its first executive under a newly structured charter. It wasn't that he had accomplished a great deal; it was that he stayed out of trouble and avoided the kind of fracas that destroys politicians. One exception had to be noted. Spellman was credited with being the person who got the domed stadium built in King County.

Of course, the stadium was built in the wrong place, is woefully short of such important amenities as public toilets, food facilities, elevators, corridor space, meeting rooms; has a scoreboard that cost nothing because Spellman's troops preferred the advertiser's constant flickerings at captive audiences; has too-narrow staircases that invite accidents; creates a traffic jam whenever a crowd appears because the facility is in one of the worst sites in town; has poor lighting in the corridors and over the playing surface. But the stadium is there, and Spellman's backers and friends want everybody to know he built it. Newspaper editorialists have parroted the same refrain ever since.

It was considered sacrilege to criticize John Spellman over the Kingdome — until Dixy came along. Dixy agreed it was necessary to attack him where he was strongest, and since I had been in the forefront of the campaign to build a stadium in Seattle more than 20 years, I drew the research assignment. Spellman was deeply vulnerable on the stadium issue, but the public was weary of the hassle and was ready to accept construction of the building in the heart of the industrial site or anywhere else. Just build the damned thing, and get it over with. That was the common reaction.

How do you fight that kind of resignation? You don't, and fortunately Dixy discovered it in time. Complaints that a $40 million stadium now had a price tag of more than $70 million seemed to have little effect on voters. When she pointed out that taxpayers were going to get the bill later for "Spellman's Basilica," which he put up too fast but just in time for the gubernatorial campaign, they yawned collectively. When she charged that items like public toilets, lounges, elevators, safe stairs, and adequate corridors were sacrificed so Spellman could build a monument to himself, the comments were buried in political roundups or ignored. If only she could talk to voters directly.

Dixy tried attacking Spellman for his administrative lapses. She didn't have a chance on that score. The newspapers, radio, and television had built up such a goodie-goodie caricature of the man that the truth could never touch him.

Spellman now began topping Dixy in the polls, and he did so throughout the final campaign. The pollsters involved have yet to explain how they could have been so embarrassingly wrong on the final count. Dixy didn't believe the polls, but that was almost incidental; the point was the public was being told Spellman was in the lead and appeared to be the eventual winner.

At the time, I had no way of measuring the pollsters' accuracy, so I was worried. Spellman had the bank account and the press on his side, and now he had phony polls no one could at that time prove phony.

It was ironic that Spellman himself provided the means for insuring his own defeat. He and his campaign staff were convinced he could bury his Democratic opponent with a series of debates. After all, the wavy-haired, pipe-smoking, soft-talking political leader with the father image was certain to destroy the little round lady in the field socks, plaid skirt, and blousy tops. Dixy would just as soon have canceled the debates, but she decided she had no choice but to go through with them.

Four major debates were scheduled. Now Dixy's work was cut out for her. The staff went to work on research. What could I do to help Dixy?

Study your enemy, the general said. He will defeat himself, with your help, if you know him well. The idea came out of the blue. I had seen Spellman deeply irritated on one unguarded occasion, and he seemed to come apart — lost his cool, as the contemporary jargon had it. I had also heard of another occasion in which the same thing happened, apparently worse, at that. A few phone calls to mutual friends who had known him many years confirmed my suspicion. John Spellman didn't like the heat; he rattled when criticized.

That's how the "Dixy Zingers" were born—tactical poison arrows I believe put her in office and kept him out. When Dixy heard the details, she was sold immediately, particularly when assured Spellman would crack and go into a rage under fire. She played her role perfectly.

The strategy went this way: In the first debate, Dixy would

keep calm, answer all questions, and refuse to taunt Spellman. Then, just before the end, she would Zing him with a powerful charge that would show he wasn't the administrator he was cracked up to be, and that pun must be forgiven. In the second debate, she would apply a Zinger at the beginning. In the third, she would let it fly whenever she sensed it would serve best, and that proved to be about half way through. In the fourth, she would repeat the first three and add one early in the program.

Since all four debates were widely televised, Washington State residents got an eyeful. They saw a smiling, cool, confident woman answering questions firmly and without excessive verbiage. They also saw a smiling, cool, confident man doing the same thing — until the first Zinger hit. Then they saw a father image turn beet-red and become unglued in his anger.

Dixy accused him of failing to tell the people the truth about the cost of the domed stadium. They'd get the bill after he was safely in the Governor's Mansion — according to his plans, that is. A $40 million stadium was going to cost twice that much, and there wasn't a thing they could do about it.

Spellman rose to the bait. He thought it was a dastardly thing for a candidate to make such an accusation, just as the debate was coming to an end so he didn't have time to make an adequate reply. How could she suggest such things when it was plainly evident to anyone that King County wouldn't have a stadium if it hadn't been for John Spellman? What he didn't realize was that for the first time in public — with more than a million people watching — John Spellman was losing his cool!

The reaction of some of the reporters covering the debate was predictable. They were as angry as Spellman, and they sided with him in his condemnation of Dixy's attack. But there was nothing new in that. They had been stacking the deck in Spellman's favor anyway. What they didn't realize was that the public got a good look at a public official blowing his stack over a rather ordinary issue. If he could do that so easily on a subject he once crowed about, what would he do in the governor's chair when a really tough one came up?

Spellman didn't realize what he was doing, and Dixy, who did, enjoyed the debates immensely. He went off with each Zinger right on cue, like the old geyser in Yellowstone.

It can never be proved that the Zingers provided the margin

of difference in the November tally, but I get a chill thinking of what might have happened if we had tried to do without them.

On November 2, 1976, Washington State voters elected their first woman governor, and that evening Dixy Lee Ray took the first step in her promise to dance across the state. When it was clear she was the winner, she told the throng at her Tacoma victory party election night:

"Come January, I want to see you all. We're not going to have just a governor's ball. We're going to have a series of them across the state and they're going to be the best parties ever held."

A few moments later, when I was able to get to her to congratulate her, she finally said, whispering:

"I promised 'em we're going to have inauguration balls all across the state. What am I gonna do? I don't know how to dance! In fact, I hate to dance!"

She learned fast.

But the most important sidelight of the victory evening was Dixy's long-restrained comment, restrained from way back in early summer of 1976, when it was obvious the political writers of the urban press were going to make it tough for her. In her victory flush, she kicked caution in the seat of the pants, and said on network television:

"I find it necessary to comment that our success tonight reflects the failure of the newspapers to elect the people they wanted elected. They backed the wrong horse."

It was one of the loudest shots in a Dixy-news media war that has never abated, although many of those who were once influenced against her have changed their minds.

CHAPTER EIGHTEEN

The State Has a Governess

Despite her one-sided, popular victory at the polls in November, 1976, the state's first woman governor found the dice loaded against her as she took office in January, 1977. Some of the roadblocks Dixy Lee Ray met were there because of archaic, unrealistic provisions of the state constitution, but the more serious obstacles bore political, ideological, and even chauvinistic stamps.

First, she had to live with her predecessor's budget when she faced the legislature because a new governor had neither the time nor the staff to prepare one. Second, reliance upon another's budget seriously hampered the new governor's ability to propose a program of progress to legislators. Third, the constitutional requirement that a new governor take office at the same time the legislature begins a regular session gave Governor Ray no chance to learn the rudiments of office; that factor favored politicians who had experience as legislators and militated against mavericks like Dixy who dared win the governorship. And fourth, the new governor was expected to come up with more than 2,000 appointments to some 350 boards, commissions, and councils while making all the other decisions required of the chief executive.

It was an impossible task, and every legislator knew it. So did every experienced observer in the news media and elsewhere.

Yet, when Governor Ray delayed appointments past statutory deadlines because she was not satisfied with the caliber of applicants, she was chastised as if she had been in office a dozen years. A high rate of turnovers among appointees was a foregone conclusion because a vast number of them had to be named hurriedly to insure continuation of state services. It was, as the sage once observed, a helluva way to run a railroad, and the state constitution itself was directly responsible. A measure that would have given a new governor at least two months to form an administration and make the bulk of the most important appointments and related decisions before the legislature convened drew little support and was shelved.

The greatest problem of all, however, was political. Most members of the legislature on both sides of the aisle seemed sincerely interested in cooperating with the new governor to make things work. The majority and minority leaders of both houses, however, were themselves interested most in running for governor and were not about to enhance the image of the Mansion's new tenant. It was a disgraceful exhibition of political selfishness. The most disturbing element to me, a lifelong newspaperman, was that the news media let them get away with it. Opposition from the Republican side could be rationalized as everyday politics in the American scheme of things, but the failure of the two Democratic leaders to help their own governor get through those miserable early months could never be forgotten by Dixy.

Without strong cooperation from her own party's leaders, Dixy had to shift for herself. Characteristically, she found other ways to get support for her own ideas. Important Democratic legislators who were themselves irritated by the leadership's failures carried the ball for Dixy; they not only brought many other Democrats along with them but succeeded in winning considerable Republican backing on many key issues. As a result, Dixy and her quiet new coalition achieved some miraculous results. The accent in state government was now on conservative measures — spending cuts, elimination of red tape, reduction in taxes, better management of services, and a crackdown on chiselers looking for public handouts — and such things didn't appeal to a few highly influential ultraliberal members of the capital press corps. Thus, the Dixy Lee Ray victories were ignored or played down in the urban press, but her clashes with political rivals always found their way to Page 1 and the evening news telecasts regularly.

Her Republican predecessor had been unable through 12 years in office to find answers to a half dozen crucial state dilemmas, but Dixy and her new friends in the legislature solved them in her first session, despite remarkable odds. For years a proposal to establish a new Department of Transportaion languished in committee rooms; the new-style "Dixycrats" put it over on their first try. They did the same thing with one of the most critical issues in many years, reform of the state pension system for policemen and firefighters; if it had remained unsolved, it would have bankrupted the state. Also bouncing around for several years were proposals for revising the state's archaic juvenile code of justice; Dixy & Co. brought them out on the floor and hammered out a new code that sailed into law. Still another measure that had been banished "to committee" time and again — the one-stop licensing system — finally saw the light of day and was adopted by the legislature at the urging of the new governor. The one-stop system made it possible for persons seeking business licenses to get one with a minimum of red tape and paperwork. Through Dixy's influence, a bill requiring annual audits of nursing homes finally made it through the political booby traps in both houses. Everybody complained about the cheating in the nursing-home field, but nobody did much about it until Dixy put her foot down.

In the 1976 campaign Candidate Ray had taken considerable abuse from political reporters in Seattle because she refused to promise pie in the sky to teachers and the professional education associations, who insisted the state had to solve the financial crisis in the public schools. She was the only candidate who offered no easy answers, yet it was Dixy Lee Ray who was primarily responsible for solving the dilemma. In her first year she demanded a proper definition of "basic education" and got it. And in the next legislative session she demanded full funding for the schools to supplant the runaway levy method and got it. It was no surprise that she received little or no credit for the enormous accomplishments — not even from the teachers. Obviously the "What have you done for me lately" syndrome was alive and well and residing principally in the realm of education.

Perhaps Dixy's most significant contribution to state government was to insist upon and obtain, at last, a new approach to budgeting. Daring to do what others had simply talked about, she ordered a freeze on all expenditures, an immediate curtailment of spending for travel, publications, and state contracts, and a revamping of the accounting system. At the same time, she ordered a start on planning for zero-based budgeting in the state's Office of Financial Management. The grousing throughout the bureaucracy was instantly audible, but she stuck to her position. However, the complaints were mild compared to the general wailing that prevailed when Dixy ordered a 10 percent chop across the board in every department's budget when she produced her own budget for the 1979 legislature.

There were disappointments and failures, too. In her determination to slash the size of government and remove the burden from the taxpayer's back, as she had promised in the 1976 campaign, Dixy had put together a "laundry list" for her first year in office. Close to the top were two major bills. One would have given her authority to revitalize the entire state executive branch, just as Congress had granted President Carter for the federal government. If the legislature did not veto her changes, they would stand. The other, urgently needed in a state cracking under the strain of excesses and duplication in the school system, would have given Dixy Lee authority to appoint a blue-ribbon commission that would reorganize the entire educational system from kindergarten through graduate schools and clean out the duplication and frills in the curricula. Both revolutionary measures barely missed approval in the legislature; they would have succeeded if they had had the earnest support of her two Democratic competitors in the Senate and House.

From the time she took office Dixy was in almost constant conflict with certain members of the press, most notably from the large urban areas. She was sometimes to blame in the continuation of the feud because of a short fuse, but more than 40 years of experience in newspapering convinced me the few self-anointed reporters were far more responsible for the unfair treatment she received. Some of them had attacked her savagely in the 1976 campaign, and they were merciless with her; it was obvious they had to prove they had been right all along. I had kept a file on press handling of major events, and I compared reports in the Seattle, Tacoma, and Spokane press with the transcripts of her news conferences. The nature and amount of distortions were a shock and robbed me of any chance I had to defend the press successfully before Governor Ray.

The tactics used by those reporters who clearly disliked her included ploys that were apparent only to those persons who were offended or experienced newsmen themselves. For example, the anti-Dixy coterie was antinuclear, as well, and its members weren't smart enough to hide their prejudice. If Dixy made a speech and spent 28 of her 30 minutes on a variety of social issues and only two minutes on nuclear energy — usually because someone in the audience asked her a question about it — the news report that evening or the next day was based primarily on her nuclear comments. Another tactic of the Dixy opposition was to utilize the "second day" device on a first-day news report. If she made a statement on a controversial issue, the reporter immediately sought a countering statement from a legislator or other opponent of the governor's and featured the opposing view in his lead and early paragraphs. As a result, the reader, listener, or viewer was given the criticism before he knew what had prompted it.

I frequently tried to explain to Dixy that reporters who operated that way were decidedly in the minority and that their editors would set things right if they knew how readers were being taken. But she had been abused so severely by the small group of Dixy-haters that she became bitter toward them. When the distortions became ludicrous in the spring of 1977, she banned news conferences and did not reinstate them for a year. Nevertheless, she continued to grant interviews to any reporters who requested them — except the three or four who wore their prejudice on their typewriter keys.

Outside the urban areas Dixy welcomed the news media and they welcomed her. As she moved into the second half of her term, a noticeable change occurred. Many members of the press, particularly among radio, television, and newspaper staffs in the big cities, began speaking openly of their resentment toward what they called the "prima donnas" in the press corps who believed their opinions were far more significant than the news itself. The swing was marked by improved treatment and even defense of a governor they didn't always consider right but a governor who "had the courage to speak her mind, no matter what it might cost her in public sentiment or votes."

It was a swing I had predicted in the darker days of 1977. I had admired Dixy Lee Ray most for her uncompromising honesty and candor, and although I sometimes disagreed with her philosophy or political ideas, I could never fault her courage. If only all politicians had even a fraction of what she possessed . . . In time I knew the sincere men and women in the news media — which means the great majority of them — would discover Dixy and admire her as I did. They need not see eye to eye with her, but they would always know where she stood on any issue. What more should a reporter ask?

Male chauvinism was a factor in Dixy's problems with the press. A few reporters simply could not acknowledge that a woman could do a good job as a governor. After all, hadn't they demonstrated in the 1976 campaign that she was unworthy of the position — and haughty, and caustic, and unwilling to answer personal questions? Some reporters were supremely egotistical and oversensitive. When a gutsy individual like Dixy Lee Ray countered a stupid question with "Your premise is wrong and your facts are twisted, but I'll answer you if you rephrase it," the prima donna's feelings were hurt. He should have been overjoyed to meet a feisty, courageous person who was worth interviewing.

When Dixy finally resumed press conferences in 1978, it was a far different governor the reporters met. In the early months of 1977 she had known relatively little about state government and its detailed operation. As a result, she had to duck answers or plead lack of knowledge. Now, thanks to her ability to burn midnight oil and cram till she learned a new subject thoroughly, she emerged as an authority on state government. The capital press corps, whose members had once known more about governmental operations than she did, was surprised by her grasp of the most intricate facet of the budget, all departments, and the entire administration. The teacher was back in charge. Those who wished to badger her could do it no longer with embarrassing in-house queries.

In the sometimes bitter confrontations with political opponents and her continued jousting with some reporters in the urban press, what happened to the inner Dixy Lee Ray? She liked being governor; she often said so. But how did the fishbowl existence and the daily scars affect her character?

Some deep changes were evident. From the standpoint of

political ideology, a few of the changes were drastic. For example, Dixy had once been interested in reducing the size of the legislature to its constitutional minimum and experimenting with a unicameral body in time. The possibility of making it a professional legislature also appealed to her at one time. After watching the system work — or, rather, fail to work on numerous occasions — she told staffers:

"A professional year-round legislature? Not on your life! How wrong I was! Now I am of a mind to do everything I can to insure the retention of what is called a citizen or part-time legislature. The less time they spend in Olympia the better, and I'm going to do everything in my power to keep them home. We need fewer laws, not more. We also need a helluvalot less government, not more. I didn't like the meat-axe approach of Proposition 13 in California, but I can see its justice and reason. The lawmakers of California simply were not listening, so the voters had to spell it out for them. Sometimes I think public officials are the last to hear what the public is saying. And I think the taxpayer revolt hasn't really begun yet in this nation, but it's just around the corner. As inflation continues and people on fixed or retirement incomes find it increasingly harder to make ends meet, we're going to wake up one day and find a genuine revolution on our hands. Government is the major culprit. It is the greatest of all tyrannies. It's way too big. Soon half the people will be working their butts off to support the other half, most of it governmental. If we don't cage the monster, the people will do it for us, as they did in California. And more power to them!"

What is the true measure of Dixy Lee Ray? Where does the truth lie? Both the pro and the con camps have been asking, like the old song, "Is It True What They Say About Dixy?" Those who professed a dislike for her have called her cruel, callous, inconsiderate, selfish, dictatorial. And they could cite instances to sustain each point. Those who swear by her have called her extremely generous, compassionate, kind, polite, warmhearted, and, above all, astonishingly brilliant and capable in everything she has ever attempted to do. They, too, could cite many examples to support each point. Who is right — or closest to being right?

I confess a prejudice reflecting a 20-year acquaintance and can list an impressive number of persons who have known Dixy for many years and would agree with my prejudices. But I can also acknowledge the faults that attend a woman who must be accepted as one of the great minds and personalities of the 20th Century. Her shortcomings in public and private life are not unusual in a character of such exceptional brain power and self-discipline. She could be brusque, impatient, and rude to her closest friends or relatives and not remember having been so. On matters of principle she would defy anyone opposing her, no matter what the consequences. Within the first two years of her administration as governor, she found it necessary to fire several persons who had once been good friends or campaign workers. They made the mistake of misjudging her loyalty to principle. Some of her critics called her actions barbaric and insensitive; they didn't know how difficult those actions were for her; she agonized over the loss of a friend, but she had the gumption to right things, bite her lip, and move on. I think the firings were the most conspicuous examples of her courage. She placed principle above all other considerations and never could accept the term "crony" as a cover for incompetence or chicanery. How many politicians have the moral courage to fire a friend who has "screwed up"?

Some of Dixy's problems derived from her fierce pride and desire to excel. From childhood on, she demonstrated a dogged insistence on "being first." As her sisters and friends testified, she had to be No. 1 in everything she tried — or she would pass it by altogether. My observations convince me Dixy has always been petrified by the notion of failure. For that reason she hated to be placed in a predicament of not having ready answers to any inquiry. It was one of the principal reasons she detested press conferences in her first months as Governor. The few reporters who had never liked the idea of having a woman in the state's highest office in the first place rushed in for the "I told you so" kill. When she read their reports and saw firsthand the results of her own inexperience in government, she boiled over and eventually canceled the conferences. I agreed with her that distortion of what she said seemed to be the order of the day, but I disagreed with her decision to shelve news conferences; she was actually playing into the hands of her critics.

When Dixy had been governor four or five months, a writer dragged out the ridiculous political-and-journalistic cliché and suggested "the honeymoon was now over and it was time to challenge Governor Ray." Dixy's response couldn't have been more typical:

"Honeymoon? Hell, I don't even remember the wedding!"

Typewriters and cameras aside, I don't believe Dixy was afraid of anybody or anything. When I was with her in Washington, DC, she would ride, fly, or sail anything that would move and never show the least sign of fright or worry. Once she and I flew from the national capital to Morgantown, West Virginia, in a two-seater that must have been borrowed from the Smithsonian. The weather was miserable, and the otherwise timid mountains were invisible behind a curtain of hard rain and winds near gale force. Immediate retirement from federal service seemed to me to be the best idea; the only thing worse would have been to confess that thought to the boss. As if the weather weren't enough of a problem, Dixy brought along her little sidekick, Jacques, the French Poodle, and big Ghillie, the Irish Deerhound, who was tall enough to be saddled. I don't know why Noah and the Old Testament came to mind for a brief instant.

The four of us crowded into that tiny plane, and I could see Ghillie didn't like it a bit. Can dogs retire? Jacques couldn't have cared less; as long as he could nuzzle his beloved Dixy, he would have enjoyed the last moments of the *Titanic's* disintegration.

As the plane moved down the runway, Ghillie panicked and began to howl and jerk his head from side to side. When the plane left the ground and sneezed its way into the cloud mass, Ghillie made a move for the exit, which was a leather flap buttoned on rather precariously. Dixy had her right hand on Jacques, who had already closed his eyes in ecstatic slumber, and her left arm around the massive neck of the yelping Ghillie. She tightened her arm and went on talking to me without the slightest change in tone or speed. I myself was frightened to death and didn't hear a word she was saying, because I was waiting for big Ghillie to plunge through the exit, taking me with him. However, I watched her left arm strain, the muscles taut, and gradually pull Ghillie back to his seat. He sensed her calmness and settled down, despite the fact that the turbulence continued until we rose above the clouds. I forced a smile and pretended no concern, but I could have used a change of shorts.

Wis (Alvista), the Governor's youngest sister, swears Dixy is

the bravest person she has known, but she remembers a time—
only one—in which her big sister showed some fright but never
lost her self-control. They had been out on a camping and
boating trip and were due home one afternoon at the tail end of
summer. Dixy decided they had time before dark to row the small
boat back to Fox Island, where the family had been staying. They
tried hard not to notice the thunderheads moving in fast over
Puget Sound. Before they were half way home, all hell broke
loose and the wind and rain pummeled them. The little boat
danced on the waves. Dixy told Wis to grab a bucket and bail
water to keep them afloat. She rowed like a Roman slave. The
current was pulling them hard away from the home shore, but
Dixy never let up. If she had, the boat could have been carried
out to the open channel and the two girls would have cashed in
their chips.

"For the first and last time in my life," Wis recounted, "I saw
Dixy worried. But she never panicked. For my sake she pretended it wasn't such a big deal, but I knew better. She brought us
in, and I know she was as happy to set foot on shore as I was. Mom
was there waiting for us, and she cried with thanks. We were
about four or five hours overdue."

Dixy always disdained formality and high fashion, and she
took criticism of her rustic wardrobe in stride. They were right
and she was right; fine, let's go from here. That was her attitude.
The marine biographer, a bonafide sea dog who would have
made Marie (Steamboat Annie) Dressler look like a landlubber,
preferred shorts, slacks, sweatshirts, jogging pants, and loafers to
elegant clothes. One afternoon at the Pacific Science Center,
Claire Jones, her personal secretary, reminded her she had a
dinner meeting downtown in half an hour and should get ready.
A frowning Dixy rushed to her closet, changed into her "dinner
meeting" dress, and said "Good-bye" to Claire.

"Oh, just a minute, Dixy," said Claire. "Your slip is showing."

"Jeez," said Dixy. "Gimme your scissors."

Snip, snip.

"There," she said, handing Claire a four-inch-wide strip of
silk. "That's one slip that will never be too long again. Good-bye."

Because she drove herself without letup, Dixy drove those
who worked with her similarly. Most could cope with it, but the
few who couldn't dropped out, sometimes with rancor. She
grasps truths and information so quickly that she is often impa-

tient with those who don't. This quickness is another of the reasons she has problems with some reporters at news conferences. That was a paradox because as a teacher she had been noted particularly for her ability to simplify the most difficult subjects so any student could understand them.

Dixy has no patience for stupidity. She also has a pet peeve: Small talk. How she hates trivia! It was one of two reasons she stayed miles away from any cocktail parties. The second reason was her one-woman campaign against smoking.

A cigarette smoker once herself ("but less than a pack a day"), she had to quit because of severe irritation of her throat. To protect herself, she became a crusader. Wherever she set up shop, the "No Smoking" signs appeared overnight. It didn't matter who the offender was — from office clerk to admiral, general, or the highest federal executive — Dixy quietly but firmly announced she wanted the cigarette, cigar, or pipe doused in her presence.

Once a highly placed diplomat who had arrived in her State Department office for a conference braced himself, lit a cigarette, and announced that "If I have to put up with your dogs, you're going to have to put up with my smoking!" Both laughed, and the conference went on. By God, she liked a fighter!

If one "problem" characteristic stands out above all others, it is Dixy's penchant for saying exactly what she thinks in public, regardless of the impact. Many consider it a defect; I have always believed it to be her most significant asset. Partner to that characteristic is her quickness to show anger or displeasure. It is a costly habit.

I remember that David Jenkins, her onetime administrative aide at the AEC and the State Department, used to play a game with me. There were no prizes, no rules, no deadlines. It was a guessing game. Each tried to be the first to guess which question or silly statement would bring out the Dixy tongue-lashing. She was a dead giveaway to us. When Dixy's temper rose, a redness showed itself first at the jawline and crept up the side of the face; when it reached the cheekbone, the face broke out into a ruddy grin just as the lips formed to deliver the broadside. The Ray-gun and its shrapnel seldom missed their mark.

Her faults have been insignificant alongside her exceptional plus-marks. Dixy's innate honesty is incomparable; I've never known but one Dixy. She is the same in public view as in private. Dixy is something of a Victorian in many instances; while she cares nothing about the behavior and habits of people within their private domain, she demands and gets nothing but the most proper behavior from persons who work for or with her. Hanky-panky is out of bounds on the premises, and the punishment is often severe.

No one I know loves the United States more. She's not a flag-waver, but she defends America furiously against criticism at home or abroad. At the same time, she is a relentless critic of those public officials who think nothing of giving America's industrial and technological riches away to the rest of the world without getting something in return — not even a promise to keep the peace.

If Dixy has one worry over any other, in fact, it is her consuming concern for the future of America. Danger from abroad has always disturbed her, but she has always been far more alarmed by the danger from within. "No tyranny from afar," she repeats, "can ever match the growing tyranny of expanding government."

With each passing week Dixy finds more and more solace at her unspoiled Fox Island farm, "where I can breathe and think and regain my perspective." She has always been aware of the humiliating caricatures, the cruel wisecracks, the whispered innuendos about her administration and herself, but with time she built up a resistance against them. She has never learned to ignore them, but she no longer permits them to put her into a full day's anger. Her time would come . . .

What might be her greatest regret?

"The absence of Jacques and Ghillie," she once said. "They were dogs, but they never complained, unless I was gone too long, that is. They were always loyal, always glad to see me, and they never said an unkind or false thing about me. How many people can you say that about?"

Curriculum Vitae

Born: Tacoma, Washington, September 3, 1914

Degrees: Mills College, B.A., 1937
Mills College, M.A., 1938
Stanford University, Ph.D., 1945

Positions Held:

1977-	Governor, State of Washington
1945-1976	Assoc. Prof. of Zoology, Univ. of Washington
1975	Jan.-June, Asst. Secretary of State, Bureau of Oceans, International Environmental & Scientific Affairs, U.S. Goverment
1972-1975	Atomic Energy Commission; Chairman, 1973-1975
1963-1972	Director, Pacific Science Center, Seattle
1964	Visiting Professor, Stanford Univ.; Chief Scientist, *Te Vega* Expedition, International Indian Ocean Expedition
1960-1963	Special Consultant in Biological Oceanography, National Science Foundation
1939-1942	Teacher, Oakland Public Schools & Pacific Grove Public Schools, California

Honorary Degrees:

1978	Rensselaer Polytechnic Inst., D.Sc.	1974	Union College, D.C.L.
		1974	Ripon College, D.Sc.
1976	Univ. of Missouri, D.Sc.	1974	Michigan State College, Ll.D.
1976	Kenyon College, D.Sc.		
1976	Russell Sage Univ., D.Sc.	1974	Univ. of Puget Sound, D.Sc.
1975	Univ. of Maryland, Ll.D.	1974	North Michigan Univ., D.Sc.
1975	Univ. of Long Island, D.Sc.	1973	Hood College, D.Sc.
1975	Smith College, D.Sc.	1973	Simmons College, Ll.D.
1975	Stonehill College, D.A.	1972	Seattle University, D.Sc.
1975	Univ. of Alaska, D.Sc.	1971	St. Martin's College, Ll.D.
1974	St. Mary's College, D.Sc	1967	Mills College, Ll.D.

Honors:
Phi Beta Kappa, 1937
Sigma Xi, 1940

Honors (Cont.)

John Switzler Fellow, 1942-1943
Van Sicklen Fellow, 1943-1945
Guggenheim Fellow, 1952-53
William Clapp Award, American Society of Corrosion Engineers, 1958
Danish Royal Society of Natural History, 1965
Maritime Man of the Year, Seattle, 1967
Woman of the Year, *Ladies Home Journal*, 1973
First Citizen Award of Seattle, 1973
Frances Hutchinson Gold Medal for Conservation, Garden Clubs of America, 1973
Axel-Axelson Johnson Award, Royal Academy of Science and Engineers, Stockholm, Sweden, 1974
Women of Science Award, ARCS, Hollywood, 1974
YWCA Gold Medal, Philadelphia, 1974
Molly Pitcher Award, Women's Forum on National Securtiy, 1975
Thomas Wildey Award for Distinguished Service, IOOF, 1975
Woman of the Year, National Campfire Girls, 1975
Proctor Prize, Sigma Xi, 1975
San Francisco Women's Round Table Honors, 1975
Abram Sacher Award, Brandeis University, 1976
Top Ten Most Influential Women in the Nation, *Harper's Bazaar*, 1977
Man of the Year, State of Israel Bond Organization, 1977
Walter H. Zinn Award, American Nuclear Society, 1977
1978 National Honoree Award, Beta Gamma Sigma
Washington Award, Western Society of Engineers, 1978
Freedom Foundation Award, 1978
American Academy of Achievement Gold Plate Award, 1979

Organizations:

Executive Committee, Friday Harbor Laboratories, Univ. of Washington
Special Consultant in Biological Oceanography, National Science Foundation
Presidential Task Force on Oceanography
Special Marine Life Research, Marine Laboratory, Naples, Italy
Board of Directors, Brookhaven National Laboratories
Science Research Advisory Committee, U.S. Coast Guard
Defense Science Board, U.S. Department of Defense
Visiting Committee for Nuclear Engineering, Mass. Inst. of Technology
Board of Directors, Americans for Energy Independence
Board of Directors, Associated Universities, Inc., N.Y.
Member, Washington State Federation of Business and Prof. Women's Clubs
National Chairman, Education Commission of the States
Executive Committee, National Governors' Association
Transportation, Commerce, and Technology Committee, National Governors' Association
Executive Committee, Council of State Governments
Executive Committee, Education Commission of the States

Index